Praise and Acclaim

T0268274

A *New Yorker* "Best
A *New York Times* "Ec
A *Town & Country* "Must-Read Book of Summer"
A *BuzzFeed* "Best Book of June"
A *Washington Post* "Book to Read This Summer"
An *Advocate* "Best LGBTQ+ BOOK OF 2022"
A *USA TODAY* "Book to Celebrate Pride Month"
A *Kirkus Reviews* "Hottest Book of Summer"

"[A] concise, meticulously researched, century-spanning chronicle of queer life on Fire Island captures, with a plain-spoken yet lyric touch, the locale's power to stun and shame, to give pleasure and symbolize evanescence."

—*New York Times Book Review*

"A fascinating, throbbing history that asks the most urgent of contemporary questions: what does paradise look like, and who does it exclude?"

—**Olivia Laing**

"Jack Parlett's *Fire Island* is that rare book: a compelling social history of a time and place that, through carefully assembled detail and astute analysis, brilliantly illuminates American culture as well as its topic."

—**Michael Bronski, author of *A Queer History of the United States***

"The zingy tale of one magnetic place—as well as a sprawling rumination on the intertwined urges to get away and get together. Clued-up but insatiably thirsty, poignant, packed with literary intrigue, *Fire Island* is a beaming beach read."

—**Jeremy Atherton Lin, author of *Gay Bar***

"Vibrant...uniquely insightful and colorful cultural history... An illuminating, well-written history of a unique place."

—*Kirkus Reviews*

"Poetic and moving...beautifully written... Readers of all stripes will appreciate this fast-paced general interest title."

—*Library Journal*

"A fine account of an important place in gay cultural history."

—*Booklist*

"Delightfully chronicled...the history of a queer landmark, its beginnings, its influence, and its seemingly constant evolution."

—*The Advocate*

"A must-read. [Parlett's] prose illuminates and educates as well as lovingly shimmers across chapters... A memorable tribute to an unforgettable queer vacation destination."

—*Bay Area Reporter*

"A riveting social history of Fire Island... Supremely engaging and highly informative."

—*BuzzFeed*

"[An] engrossing history... This is essential reading for the ferry from Sayville or wherever you happen to be."

—*Town & Country*

"[Parlett's] book breezes by with beach-read ease but is packed with enough facts, theories, and anecdotes to inspire weeks' worth of dinner conversations.... Wonderful...detailed, inclusive, and compassionate."

—*Jezebel*

"[*Fire Island*] takes a 30,000-foot view, helmed by one of the island's greatest gifts: literature."

—*Esquire*

"With its stunning beaches, legendary parties and rich cultural history, Fire Island is celebrated in Parlett's deeply researched book."

—*New York Daily News*

"[A] richly textured history."

—*The New Yorker*

Also by Jack Parlett

The Poetics of Cruising: Queer Visual Culture from Whitman to Grindr

Same Blue, Different You (poetry)

FIRE ISLAND

A CENTURY IN THE LIFE OF
AN AMERICAN PARADISE

JACK PARLETT

HANOVER
SQUARE
PRESS

If you purchased this book without a cover you should be aware
that this book is stolen property. It was reported as "unsold and
destroyed" to the publisher, and neither the author nor the
publisher has received any payment for this "stripped book."

HANOVER
SQUARE
PRESS™

Recycling programs
for this product may
not exist in your area.

ISBN-13: 978-1-335-45497-3

Fire Island

First published in 2022. This edition published in 2023.
Copyright © 2022 by Jack Parlett

All rights reserved. No part of this book may be used or reproduced in any manner whatsoever
without written permission except in the case of brief quotations embodied in critical articles and
reviews.

This publication contains opinions and ideas of the author. It is intended for informational and
educational purposes only. The reader should seek the services of a competent professional for
expert assistance or professional advice. Reference to any organization, publication or website does
not constitute or imply an endorsement by the author or the publisher. The author and the publisher
specifically disclaim any and all liability arising directly or indirectly from the use or the application of
any information contained in this publication.

Hanover Square Press
22 Adelaide St. West, 41st Floor
Toronto, Ontario M5H 4E3, Canada
HanoverSqPress.com
BookClubbish.com

Printed in U.S.A.

To Frank

CONTENTS

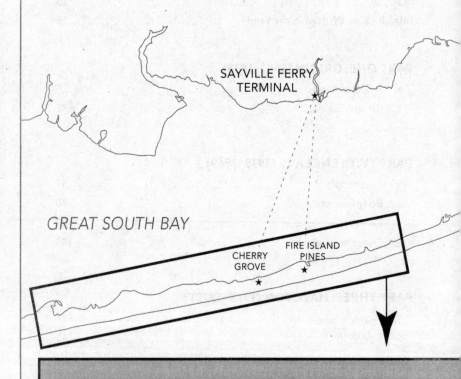

LONG ISLAND

SAYVILLE FERRY
TERMINAL

GREAT SOUTH BAY

CHERRY
GROVE

FIRE ISLAND
PINES

FIRE ISLAND

SALTAIRE

FAIR
HARBOR

OCEAN
BEACH

SEAVIEW

POINT
O'WOODS

SUNKEN
FOREST

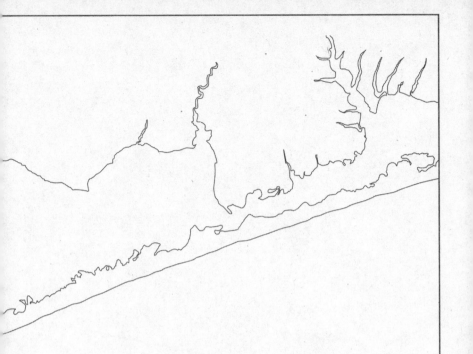

ATLANTIC OCEAN

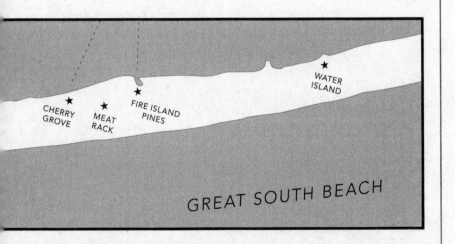

CHERRY GROVE ★

MEAT RACK ★

FIRE ISLAND PINES ★

WATER ISLAND ★

GREAT SOUTH BEACH

INTRODUCTION

Written in the Sand

ONCE UPON A TIME, A NAME BECOMES A PLACE. MY JOURNEY to Fire Island from New York City was a familiar one to many: two train rides on the Long Island Railroad, a bus to the ferry port, and a boat across the Great South Bay. I was an eager traveler that July day in 2017, costumed in my new denim shorts, hailing from the UK but living in the city, and anticipating what I'd read of hot nights and midsummer dreams.

Fire Island is a long, thin barrier island off the Long Island coast, located around sixty miles away from Manhattan. Roughly thirty-two miles in length and unusually narrow in shape, with the northern and southern ends an easy stroll from one another, the island is comprised of around seventeen different vacation communities, each with their own distinctive character. Two of them, the neighboring communities of Cherry Grove and the Fire Island Pines, positioned roughly in the middle of the island's horizontal stretch, have a rich queer history. It was to the Grove and the Pines that I was headed.

Like any first time, it wasn't quite perfect. The trip had its share of stumbles and miscalculations. My friend Celine and I were staying in her friends' house in Point O' Woods, a private, family-oriented community a few miles west of Cherry Grove. From there we set off along the beach around sunset, armed with the hardy accoutrements of island living that had kindly been lent to us by our hosts. It was the first time I'd taken bug spray and a headlamp with me on a night out.

As we trudged through the evening sand on our way to Cherry Grove, cold and damp on our bare feet, our journey had the feel of an adventure. To our left stood something called the Sunken Forest, a lush nature reserve made up of American holly trees sunken behind the sand dunes. Rich in its biodiversity, the Sunken Forest is a living legacy of the environmental activism that took hold on Fire Island in the 1950s and 1960s. At this time of night, however, it would be full of ticks, and best avoided. This miniature odyssey along the beach made comically literal how entry into the gay world was a matter of crossing thresholds and traversing some rough terrain. The Sunken Forest acts as a buffer between Cherry Grove to the east and Point O'Woods and the other "straight" communities to the west, as if it prevented cross-contamination; as if the separatism that has long made a community like Cherry Grove unique arose from the island's topography.

We were soon to feel the special charm of such a place. After a slog along the sand, the Grove's lights were suddenly tantalizingly close, bright red and pink against the dark horizon. We took our headlamps off and put our shoes back on. We went eagerly up the steps onto the boardwalk, past an oceanfront restaurant with tables of men in nice shirts eating seafood and drinking wine, and wandered into the Ice Palace bar, where a drag show was in full swing, with a queen lip-synching to the Eurythmics.

A giddiness overcame us as we sipped beers and went out to the bar's pool deck to smoke a cigarette. We knew that this drink in the Ice Palace would be an initial stop on the night's longer route, but for a moment it felt like time stood still, as if we'd always been here, at home in a new place that was disarmingly familiar. Later, we walked along the wooden walkways that divide up the layout of Cherry Grove and stand in place of paved roads, with no automobiles allowed on the island besides utility and municipal vehicles. The same air of safety and affirmation permeated on the boardwalks. The eccentrically named cottages were adorned with fairy lights that looked inviting and kitschy; elsewhere there were plastic flamingos decoratively placed in the long grass and rainbow flags hanging from doorways. We said hello to the people we passed, mostly couples and groups of friends, who happily said hello back, an etiquette of geniality I associated most with rural or small-town life, compared to the urban huff or scowl. With its ice-cream parlor and gift shop, the Grove's downtown area did feel like a village, only with more drag queens and go-go dancers; quaint, with an edge of sexual permissiveness.

At the eastern end of Lewis Walk, the horizontal "street" that runs along the edge of the Grove and faces the Atlantic Ocean, the walkway's planks gave way to sand, and the houses were replaced by trees. Looking ahead at the dark passage leading towards more vegetation, I could tell from the excited lurch in my stomach that this was the entrance to the Meat Rack, the legendary wooded cruising ground that separates the Grove from the Pines. Tempted as I was to run straight in and explore this mythical free-for-all, there were other discoveries to be made. We took a direct route along the beach and carried on towards the Pines. On our left were the distinctive modernist mansions the community is known for, imposing geometric visions of glass and wood, with ocean views and swimming pools. Some of the houses had fences up around them, but that could hardly muffle the sounds of parties, the gentle thump of house music. To our right, we could make out the shadows of bodies writhing in the sand. Perhaps the Meat Rack was too busy tonight, or it was still unfashionably early to be seen there.

Before we went to one of the clubs at the Pines harbor, there was a beach ritual I wanted to perform. Roughly following a map on my phone, I was looking for a specific intersection, where Ocean Walk meets Crown Walk. This night in Fire Island was also a pilgrimage of sorts: it was somewhere near this point on the beach that poet Frank O'Hara was involved in a fatal dune buggy accident, in the early hours of a Sunday morning in July 1966. O'Hara's work had brought me not only to Fire Island, but to New York in the first place, where I had moved for an extended research trip to work on my PhD about American poetry and cruising. Discovering his poems as a confused student was a formative experience, offering me what felt like a new, private vocabulary for loving other men. As I scrolled to find the list of O'Hara's poems I wanted to hear in this moment, the excitement of our evening in the Grove gave way to something more melancholy, the buzz fading against the vastness of the ocean. After a pause, I played a recording of O'Hara reading "Ode to Joy," his voice tinny but unmistakable. In that moment, the utopian bluster of the poem's first line felt resonant: "We shall have everything we want and there'll be no more dying."

★ ★ ★

What did I want from Fire Island? I had gone there, in part, to commune with its ghosts. Just as O'Hara had scrawled James Dean's name into the sand during a visit on the same weekend in 1955 that the young actor died in California, so I had gone to the Pines in 2017 to write *Frank* in the sand. Now when I think back to that moment, I am reminded of the contemporary writers who have also met with some version of the poet on the island's shores. Like Jameson Fitzpatrick, who pays homage to O'Hara in her poem "A True Account of Overhearing Andy Cohen at Fire Island." This hungover recollection of spotting the reality TV star on the beach, written the morning after the speaker "took half a tab hoping to get some / advice from the ghost of Frank O'Hara," becomes a meditation on the visual imperialism of the Pines, as embodied by the tanned and toned men who move along the shore "with the ease of winners." In another Fire Island poem, British poet Sophie Robinson looks out in elegiac rapture to the sea, where the extremity of the waves and the rocks call to mind the mutilation of O'Hara's body, "my favourite alcoholic / the greatest homosexual who ever lived & died."

As these poems attest to, Fire Island entertains a peculiar psychic exchange between past and present, reanimating voices and shoring up stories. All of "gay life is stories," claims the writer Ethan Mordden in the introduction to his first collection of 'Buddies' stories, from 1985. "I have sat with friends," he writes, "on those long nights at the Pines, listening to the ocean dancing about our mysterious island," trading tales of "affairs, encounters, discoveries, weekends, parties, secrets, fears, self-promotions—of fantasies that we make real in the telling." Many such island stories have been lost. Vacation memories are often evanescent and sepia-toned, and Fire Island's archive can feel similarly fragile, a record of a seasonal community historically designed to evade detection. Its stories vanished, perhaps, in the moment of their utterance, consigned to the ocean breeze or the grave, along with the raconteurs, flamboyant and well-connected, who first told them. But a good many have survived, too, have been recorded through texts or artworks, or renewed in the retelling, through the lost art of dishing, and depend upon future generations for their posterity.

Of course, new stories are being made on Fire Island all the time, every weekend between May and the season's end in September. The renters who have bought summer shares, which entitle them to use a beach property for a set number of weekends during these months, come out to join their housemates. Old-timers and first-timers coexist. Memories are made at the tea dance, a somewhat ritualized afternoon dance-and-drinks party that dates back to midcentury Fire Island, or at the Underwear Party held on Friday nights at the Ice Palace bar. Quieter vignettes unfold as friends take afternoon walks along the shore, or convene on the deck for cocktail hours and long dinners. Solitude is also possible. So much of the time spent on Fire Island is about living in the present moment, though with a glance towards the near future: the particular promise of this weekend, this summer, this year. It is a place that has, on the surface, *everything we want:* the glamour of the high life, the comfort of coexistence, here and now, in this place. But the pull of the past is never far away either. Although it's possible to move through Fire Island without awareness of the weight and magic of its history, a closer look reveals its palimpsestic quality. Immediate pleasures are enfolded with a range of personal and collective memories: rich layers of art, texts and photographs produced by the many writers and artists who have made it their temporary summer home. Those storytellers will be our guides in the pages ahead.

After some moments lingering on the beach, Celine and I left our ritual and rejoined the grid of the Pines walkways. Although it was dark, we could still see the collision of the natu-

ral with the manmade. Flanked by extraordinary beach houses,
many of which were gated in the manner of Los Angeles mansions, lay a cranberry bog with trees and reeds poking through
the boardwalk. It is known, according to the sign planted there,
as Smokey Hollow, a name that felt distinctly eerie in the low
light. We carried on until we reached Fire Island Boulevard, the
long, horizontal strip that cuts through the middle of the Pines
and demarcates the ocean side and the bay side. We were walking west towards the harbor, where we planned to go dancing
in the Pavilion. The newest iteration of this nightclub, which
has been in the Pines since the 1980s, is a distinctive, two-story
asymmetric rebuild made of crisscrossing wooden beams. It reopened in 2013, after a fire destroyed the old building two years
earlier. On the way, we passed several people walking in the
other direction, most of them men, most of them shirtless. If the
atmosphere in the Grove had been one where amiable greet-
ings between strangers seemed appropriate, the mood in the
Pines could be best described as brooding, and we were quickly
schooled by a few botched *hello*s. As we walked along the tree-
lined approach to the harbor, the Pavilion materialized before
us, just past the empty ferry dock. We paid cover and went up
to check out the dance floor, pausing on the way to make the
most of the view from the club's balcony.

With the gentle hum of people walking by below, and the
twinkling lights from the surrounding bars and restaurants and
the yachts docked in the water, the harbor had the outward feel
of a marina somewhere in the French Riviera. The pumping
music from the next room was a reminder of its more raucous
energy. Arriving in the Pines just after midnight, we had long
missed the tea dance, which typically takes place in several sittings across different venues, beginning at the Blue Whale at
4:00 p.m. and finishing up at 10:00 p.m. at the bar Sip N Twirl.
The Pavilion was playing host to a group of DJs from the city
spinning disco and techno. On the dance floor, muscle queens,

all bulging pecs and techno whistles, swirled among twinks in speedos. This was where I wanted to be, but it was also over-whelming, and with my shirt still on, I was evidently not a Pines native, nor particularly at home on this dance floor. Unsure as to whether I would, in this moment, shrivel up or bloom, I did what I usually did, and turned to tequila.

Fire Island had seemed to me, in the weeks before I visited, like a climactic rite of passage in my gay journey. This was, after all, the island described in Andrew Holleran's 1978 novel *Dancer from the Dance* as a place for "madness, for hot nights, kisses, and herds of stunning men." It seemed like a natural extension of the world I had entered in the city. I had moved to New York some months earlier, to use the archives in the Public Library and NYU. By day, I was exploring the manuscript collections of some of the city's great gay writers: Walt Whitman, O'Hara and David Wojnarowicz, the subjects of my PhD thesis on cruis-ing. By night, my research took on a more practical dimension. I drank heavily, chain-smoked, and retreated to coffee shops to write hungover poems before my stints in the library. I was tick-ing off clichés, which included falling hopelessly in love with the city. I hadn't lost sight of what I was doing, exactly. If anything, my vision felt sharper and clearer. Play began to demand a devo-tion as serious as work. The gay bars of the East Village became the center of my universe; they were where I would go anytime I didn't have plans or just wanted an adventure. One sweltering Friday afternoon at the end of April, I moved my things out of an apartment-share in East Williamsburg, where I had stayed for the first month, and caught a taxi over the bridge to the city.

The new room was in a sixth-floor walk-up on Avenue D, a block away from the throng of East Houston Street. As a living situation, it was a little unconventional, though not by Man-hattan standards. The room was unventilated, save for a small window looking out on an alleyway, and going to bed meant climbing up a ladder to a mezzanine with a futon that sat around ten inches below the ceiling. The heat in the coming months was intense, and I slept less that summer than I ever had before. But it was cheap, for the area, and in Alphabet City, and therefore perfect. With the window open, letting in the nighttime soundtrack, I lay still under the ceiling for intense nights of almost-sleep. Sometimes (often) there'd be a stranger lying there next to me in the morning: a pickup from a nearby gay bar, a new friend I'd never see again. This was becoming a common occurrence. A joy, but also a need. Moving to New York had interrupted a new relationship that had only just started back in London. He and I had decided to put things on hold. On late afternoons we yearned across time zones, exchanging awkward non sequiturs over FaceTime.

I was not taking it well. Trying to numb the sadness of a thwarted relationship, of a life I had left unlived back home, I went looking for lost nights and chance trysts. The city's bounty, in this regard, seemed endless. I didn't know pain could be this fun, could feel this good. Why had I never behaved this badly in London? Though I didn't realize it at the time, in hindsight it was obvious that I had gone to New York in search of that elusive thing called "gay life." Like a lot of people, I'd always had a fantasy about living there, which only intensified after I graduated from college and moved to London. As any of my friends could tell you, moving there was all I could think or talk about. I spent much of my early twenties in London feeling lonely and tentative in my sexuality. I was inexperienced and intimidated by "the scene." I therefore pinned my hopes on the alternate life I might live in this other city. When the opportunity presented itself to spend six months in New York during my PhD, I applied straightaway for university travel funding and worked extra jobs for a year and a half to save money.

Entering the gay world of the city solo wasn't always a happy experience, but that seemed to me to be a part of the deal. Wasn't gay life, as the books I read had told me, supposed to be a bit sad? I had the sense, when lonely or hungover or postcoital, that there was something urbane about the abjection, a kind of melancholic glamour. If I'd told my adolescent self that this was where he'd be in ten years' time, he wouldn't have believed it. And this was my life, for a while. It tasted like happy hour well drinks and bleary-eyed Parliaments on early-morning walks along Sixth Street, past the bars of the night before. It had the feel of leather, or the many different textures encountered at a leather party. The unfamiliar scent of a stranger's pillow. The rough sensation of unexplained cuts on my forehead from the night before. This, it turned out, was the life I'd been missing out on, something I'd longed for and dreamed about during my slow crawl out of the closet. Though it soon became clear that I was getting swallowed up by the city, and forming unhealthy habits, I also felt, aged twenty-five, like I was living out my potential as a gay man for the first time in my life.

On the dance floor of the Pavilion that night in the Pines, I was still testing the parameters of my own relationship to the gay scene. Often I turned to the blind confidence provided by a few drinks, but on this particular night, the booze couldn't quite pierce through the feeling of being overlooked in a room full of people. What became clear, as the club emptied out about an hour later, much earlier than we had anticipated, was that this world had its own distinctive routine, its own norms that newcomers are unlikely to be versed in. Someone we met on the balcony explained that at this time of the night, the real fun would be happening at house parties. He was still waiting for his invite to one, hoping to be picked up. As Celine and I made the journey back along the beach while the sun began to rise, our excitement about the place had been dampened a little. Looking back now, I marvel at the naivety of assuming that this place would simply open up to us, immediately revealing the pearl inside the oyster. It would take more digging and planning than that. This place, which you have to take a train, another train, a bus and a ferry to get to, is not exactly somewhere one just shows up. And this simple fact—of the island's simultaneous proximity to and distance from the city, its requirement that you make the journey and cross the threshold into the unfamiliar—has long been, as I would discover, a crucial aspect of its allure.

The concept of utopia, writes the sociologist Henning Bech, is a "stock theme in the homosexual experience," shared among a community historically in pursuit of freedom and safety. But there is little consensus about something like a utopia; any place that is equal parts real and imagined is up for debate. Fire Island has all the qualities of this hybrid space—it can be pointed to on a map, and reached in a few hours from the city, but it is also, symbolically, a Xanadu or happy place, somewhere over the rainbow. But while fantasies are unrestricted, and in theory belong to anyone, vacation resorts do not. As novelist Toni Morrison once said, "All paradises, all utopias are designed by who is not there, by the people who are not allowed in." The history of Fire Island is to be found not only in what it has been—the glories and the pleasures—but also in what it hasn't been, or what it has failed to be, as a queer paradise that is, as Morrison has it, designed by absence as well as presence.

Many queer people today feel that Fire Island is not for them, that it's reserved for a select demographic, historically white, middle-class and cis-gendered, and structured around cachet and aspiration. Like most commercial vacation communities, the Grove and the Pines are exclusive by design. They do not traditionally cater to "day-trippers," and although the island's beach is a public space, the limited number of private properties can only accommodate so many people. Shares in them are expensive and often require personal connections. The fact that the Grove and the Pines have long provided respite from anti-gay oppression does not mean that they have also succeeded in undoing other imbalances of structural privilege. If its offerings

as a hedonistic idyll seem utopian in the abstract, the reality of
the island has often been different and more complicated. Esther
Newton, author of a definitive anthropological history of Cherry
Grove, wrote in 1996 that the community "is too white, too
middle class, and too middle aged to be a microcosm of America's diverse lesbian and gay communities." This remains true,
even if the demographics of both communities have changed a
little since then, and efforts are being made today to address the
blind spots and exclusionary structures of these communities.

In the course of writing this book, as a visitor to and an ob-
server of contemporary Fire Island, I have come to see Cherry
Grove and the Pines as providing unique insights into the nature
of community and liberation in twentieth- and twenty-first-
century America. Their histories, distinct but intertwined, shed
light not only on the challenges that queer people have faced
and continue to face, but also on the unique pleasures of escape,
and the vital need for inclusive queer spaces of our own. Rarely
have these communities been uniform in their makeup or worldview, encompassing distinctive desires and wants, different relationships to leisure, art and politics. Similarly, the figures you
will meet in this book—artists, writers and activists—came to
Fire Island in search of different things: sexual freedom, a sense
of shared culture and community, or simply space to work and
think. In the 1930s and 1940s, family units like that of Natalia
Murray, her young son, William, and her partner, the writer
Janet Flanner, or the queer artistic "throuple" of Paul Cadmus,
Jared French and Margaret Hoening (aka PaJaMa), found reprieve from the antagonistic gaze of the mainland and the moral
panics around sexuality that were rife in the period.

While many sought and found refuge in the Grove and the
Pines as they developed into the places we know today, not all of
them were endeared to what they found there. Ambivalence is a
recurring note in Fire Island's story, particularly in the recollections of W. H. Auden, who owned a cottage in Cherry Grove

in the late 1940s. The novelists Carson McCullers and Patricia Highsmith, who also moved in Auden's circles, both had friends among the Grove's lesbian literati. They commonly spent summer weekends there in the 1950s and 1960s, sometimes in the spirit of relaxation and convalescence, and other times to more tumultuous ends. James Baldwin usually went to Fire Island in the off-season, so he could avoid the crowds of the summer gay scene and find time to write. The community of the place was of less interest to him than the solitude it could sometimes provide, though he did socialize with existing acquaintances—including Frank O'Hara—if he happened upon them there.

While Fire Island had already attracted the movers and shakers of the city's gay and lesbian cultural scene in the postwar years, the events of the Stonewall riots in the summer of 1969 galvanized the liberation movement and brought a newly visible 1970s queer culture to fruition. Activists and writers like Jack Nichols reported from the frontlines of liberation, and looked to Fire Island as a space with the potential to be rethought as an alternative community, one that could match the radical fervor of the era. But the cultural boom of the 1970s took the island further down the path of glitziness, and attracted stars from the fashion and entertainment industries. Writers like Andrew Holleran, Felice Picano, Edmund White, and George Whitmore—members of the Violet Quill, a gay literary collective—wrote about life in the Pines in their fiction. In a typical summer of the era, Derek Jarman and David Hockney, Patti Smith and Robert Mapplethorpe could be seen passing through. Big names from the fashion industry, including designers like Roy Halston and Calvin Klein and journalists such as André Leon Talley, were also on the scene. The parties were legendary and the guest lists illustrious. For a time it must have seemed like a summer soiree that would never end. But when the devastation of the HIV/AIDS epidemic was first felt on the island in the early 1980s, activists and writers like Larry Kramer and Vito Russo railed

against political inaction in the communities, while younger
generations of gay writers bore witness to the legacies of those
that had already been lost.

The queer history of Fire Island suggests no neat arc from in-
nocence to experience, just as the queer history of America itself
has been volatile and changeable, and warns us against invest-
ing in linear narratives of progress. It is a remarkable thing that
Cherry Grove and the Pines are still in existence, still recogniz-
ably themselves. The particularly vibrant moment that they are
experiencing today, culturally and artistically, attests to the fact
that the drive towards assimilation cannot alone quell the appeal, nor the importance, of queer spaces. These communities
are, and always have been, works in progress. The self-reflection
demanded by the contemporary political moment can illuminate the path for Fire Island's future. In what follows, I tell the
story of how Cherry Grove and the Pines came to form one
kind of paradise, at once iconic and contested; both a radical
proposition, with a unique take on freedom, and an established
enclave with its own rules and hierarchies. But this story begins
long before the flash of a rainbow flag or the glimmer of a disco
ball. It begins with a spit of land on the edge of the Atlantic, a
sandbar still to be named...

PART ONE:

ORIGIN

(1882–1938)

1

A Spit of Land

ALONG THE SHORE, A FIRE IS BURNING AGAINST THE NIGHT
sky, a portrait of light. Is it signal or spectacle? A ritual, a wild-
fire? Wood, perhaps, caught alight by the wind, or swampland
combusting, its wet peat lit by lightning. It could also be whale
blubber, gelatinous and dense, burning down to a concentrated
oil. Maybe this fire is a false friend, a sign of life in the dark,
beckoning us towards the unknown. All that is clear is its viv-
idness in the distance.

Fire Island's name alone feels loaded with meaning; an evo-
cation, a burning bush. It suggests a tantalizing origin story, or
several: swamp fires, Native American signals to the mainland,
or fires lit by looters to attract unsuspecting ships to the shore.
The historical record doesn't confirm, though one theory suggests it came from a transcription error on a map.

Before the Dutch colonized the Long Island area in the sev-
enteenth century, Fire Island was inhabited by the Secatogues,
who exchanged wampum, a traditional bead from white and
purple clam shells, with European settlers. Along with the myths
surrounding the Secatogue origins of its name, there were tales
of pirates and shady merchants. By the middle of the nineteenth
century, Fire Island had a reputation as an outpost both dan-

gerous and quaint, a destination for nomads and fishermen, as well as vacationers from New York City and Long Island. The summer vacation, as we know it, first came to prominence among the elite classes. In the 1820s, reformers began advocating excursions into nature as a health-giving pursuit. Vacationing became a way to escape the dirt and diseases of cities and to enjoy the cleaner air of mountains or the healing powers of water. The mineral springs of Saratoga in upstate New York and a number of New England seaside resorts were among the first locations to meet this demand, and a nationwide vacation industry soon followed.

As the vacation became an integral part of family life, Long Island, with its bountiful coastline, was a prime candidate for development. It offered city dwellers a nearby reprieve, not only for the leisure classes who could afford to get away, but Manhattan's working poor, who took day trips to Brooklyn's Coney Island, home to a seaside resort and an amusement park, or went on outings arranged by social reformers seeking to save women and children from the oppressive living conditions of tenement blocks.

The beach also had transgressive potential, as a place where the body was exposed and emphasized, and cultural anxieties about this aspect coexisted with a continued belief in the healing capacities of water. Many of these late nineteenth-century summer resorts, argues historian Cindy S. Aron, "seemed to be providing space in which some of the rules of middle-class propriety were suspended, or at least relaxed." This entailed the mixing of men and women, who would bathe and swim together, while engaging in the culture of "flirting and courting." Such a sexually charged public space for members of the same sex was still a long way off, but the foundations for its eventual home were already being laid.

"Long Island is destined to be the producer of some of the most popular inland and seaside Summer resorts," predicted a journalist for the *Brooklyn Daily Eagle* in August 1880. Directly across the bay from the Long Island town of Sayville, he wrote, was "located an unpretentious but very popular resort known as Cherry Grove House," where the host served "roast clams, chowder and lager beer to the 'Queen's taste,' at moderate charges." Of course, in 1880, this old-fashioned idiom for perfection in taste had no double meaning, none of the coded association with gay male effeminacy that the word *queen* would come to bear. In fact, the category of homosexuality, as distinct from but connected to categories of effeminacy or gender inversion, was still nascent. But evidently this summer vacation resort, whose name was derived from the black cherry trees found there by its early proprietors, Archer and Elizabeth Perkinson, was already on the map by the 1880s.

For reasons that will become clear, 1882 is an important year for the shaky but appealing mythology of Cherry Grove, and of Fire Island's fate as a queer destination. One afternoon a few years earlier, over in Camden, New Jersey, a former editor of the *Brooklyn Daily Eagle* and longtime Long Island resident was reflecting on his own distant memories of Fire Island. In an entry dated June 4, 1880, from his 1882 autobiographical work *Specimen Days*, poet Walt Whitman, then sixty-one years old and often given to reveries about his life, experienced "a brief flash" that brought forth the "culmination of years of reading and traveling and thought." This particular afternoon vision gave him memories of "the wild sea-storm I once saw one winter day, off Fire Island," his own personal sublime. It is likely that this recollection is taken from the poet's younger years. West Hills, Long Island, where Whitman was born, is home to Jayne's Hill, the highest vantage point on the island. Although the family moved around frequently and left West Hills for Brooklyn when young Walt was four, Jayne's Hill was evidently a point of return. From the top of the hill, you could see for "thirty or forty, or even fifty or more miles," he wrote upon returning to

West Hills on a pilgrimage a year later in 1881. From there you could catch a glimpse of Connecticut to the north and the Atlantic Ocean, bordered by Fire Island, to the south.

Though he is often thought of as a poet of the city, a consummate documenter of the dawn of modernity in nineteenth-century New York, Whitman was equally devoted to Long Island's landscapes. In a piece published in 1857, effusively titled "Long Island Is a Great Place!", he wrote of its south side "the Great South Bay—the fishing and the fowling—the fishermen, the natives, the curious and original characters, so quaint, so smacking of salt and sea-weed—the sand-islands out in the bays—Fire Island—the wrecks and wreckers," another name for the pirates or looters associated with the island's dangerous reputation. Whitman, who published the first edition of *Leaves of Grass*, his life's work, in 1855, and revised it a total of six times, conceived of America as a yet-to-be-realized project, a democratic experiment in which everyone, from street laborers to presidents, and everything, from a leaf of grass to the city's mighty East River, warranted celebration. He advocated for physical and spiritual "adhesiveness," and the "beautiful and sane affection of man for man, latent in all the young fellows" through which the United States could be "effectually welded together" in a homosexual utopia.

Whitman would surely have loved what Fire Island became in the early twentieth century, a liberating world away from the din and spectacle of the city. His keen sense of the eroticism of outdoor spaces, the harmonious interplay of bodily pleasure and natural beauty, would later find echoes in the unfolding history of Fire Island's cruising culture in the wilds of the Meat Rack. As the scholar Michael Snediker argues, many of Whitman's most erotic poems take place on the beach, or in pastoral spots, and feature a speaker in solitude reflecting upon his own desires. Snediker calls these poems "proto-cruising moments," because they figure queer desire indirectly, making it legible only to those readers in the know. Of course, Whitman wrote a lot about actual encounters with strangers, too, the numerous men he would meet in bars and bohemian spots like Pfaff's beer hall in Greenwich Village, and along the Brooklyn waterfront. Sometimes he would pick up men on the street and write about them later in his notebooks, which are full of entries like "little black-eyed Post boy at ferry" or "Saturday night Mike Ellis—wandering at the corner of Lexington av. & 32nd st.—took him home to 150 37th street." On other occasions, he would share loaded glances with passing strangers among the crowds of Manhattan and go home to write poems addressed to them.

Whitman, whose extensive body of work also contained some overt celebrations of cruising and gay sex, is understandably envisioned as a radical forefather in gay American letters. But the temper of his later years makes for a somewhat uncomfortable fit. He left New York for Washington, DC, in 1862, where he worked as a clerk and a nurse during the Civil War.

After suffering a severe stroke in 1873, he traveled to Camden, New Jersey, to visit his brother and ailing mother, who died just three days after his arrival. In grief, Whitman ended up moving in with his brother on 431 Stevens Street and stayed in Camden for the rest of his days.

Despite his retreat from New York, Whitman remained prolific in the final years of his life; he continued to write poems and articles, and he gave frequent interviews. But it was in these years that his evident sympathies with racist, postwar pseudoscience became apparent. He expressed to his biographer a belief that the eventual dying out of African Americans and Native Americans was inevitable, a form of natural selection, in marked contrast to the abolitionist and egalitarian democratic project he espouses in much of Leaves of Grass. He seldom discussed his sexual relationships with men in these years, and when he did, it would be to downplay or disavow them. This was perhaps a sign of the shame that was coming to be associated with homosexuality. Although sodomy laws had been in effect in the United States for several centuries, the articulation of an identity related to particular desires and sexual practices would come later, and ultimately paved the way for social and legal recognition—as well as the collective identity of an enclave like Cherry Grove.

In January 1882, Whitman received a visitor in Camden who would himself become a part of Fire Island's mythos. This young Irish writer carried with him associations of excess and rule-breaking, and inhabited a distinctly gay sensibility in the guise of the aesthete, in contrast to the more rustic image of homosociality proffered by Whitman. Stepping off the SS *Arizona* at Ellis Island, Oscar Wilde cut a distinctive figure, dressed in a fur-lined ulster jacket and blue silk neck scarf. Asked the standard question by a customs officer, he is reputed (probably apocryphally) to have replied, "I have nothing to declare but my genius." Wilde's proposed four-month sojourn in America, during which time he intended to give a series of lectures, was soon extended into a yearlong tour that would help establish Wilde as one of the first modern literary celebrities. Traveling nationwide, he was a source of fascination to the American press, who revered and hounded him in equal measure, recording his every movement. His meeting with Whitman caused a stir.

The publisher Joseph Marshall Stoddard first made the suggestion that Wilde and Whitman meet, not least because such an exchange between an American elder and his European admirer would help to garner media attention. Wilde paid Whitman a visit at Stevens Street on January 18, and there was a full write-up of the meeting in the *Philadelphia Press* the next day, based largely on Whitman's account of it. "The Aesthetic Singer Visits the Good Gray Poet," ran the headline. Although the piece goes to great lengths to highlight the common ground they shared, as well as Wilde's admiration for his elder, having read *Leaves of Grass* with his mother as a child, the crucial differences between them are evident too. Whitman recalls that "I took him up to

my den, where we had a jolly good time." (Insert wink here.)
"I think he was glad to get away from lecturing, and fashionable society, and spend a time with an old 'rough.'" Although
Whitman was a bona fide literary celebrity, he also fancied
himself as one of the "roughs." His very identity as a poet was
defined in opposition to the artifice and excesses of fashionable
society. While Wilde turned up at Ellis Island in furs, ready to
be photographed, Whitman's most famous portrait, the fron-
tispiece image of the first edition of *Leaves of Grass*, shows the
author dressed in earthy drag: a simple shirt and trousers with
no suspenders, his hat slightly askew. Both of these identities
were constructions, of course, that spoke of their contrasting
ideas about beauty. While they drank wine and talked aesthetics, Wilde said, according to Whitman, that "I can't listen to
anyone unless he attracts me by a charming style, or by beauty
of theme." "Why Oscar," Whitman replied, "it always seems to
me that the fellow who makes a dead set at beauty by itself is in
a bad way. My idea is that beauty is a result, not an abstraction."

Although the two men reached a truce on this subject, it
is worth keeping in mind these divergent artistic sensibilities.
They did not openly discuss homosexuality during their meeting, at least not in Whitman's public account of it, but there are
moments in the newspaper write-up that feel suggestive. The
two men reportedly went upstairs to Whitman's "den," so they
"could be on 'thee and thou' terms," and Whitman remembers
that Wilde, a "great big, splendid boy," laid his hand on the elder
poet's knee. This account of the meeting leaves enough room
for us to wonder, wishfully perhaps, as to the exact nature of
the "jolly good time" these men shared. And in what is surely
one of the most tantalizing footnotes in queer literary history, a
friend of Wilde's from the 1890s recalls that he once told him,
"The kiss of Walt Whitman is still on my lips." The charm of
this story is not so much that it features two major writers col-
lapsing a generational and transatlantic gap, but that it features

two high-profile men sharing a hidden moment of intimacy. So when Wilde visited Cherry Grove six months later in July, during a summer break from his lecture tour, it seemed like a natural progression in his yearlong cruise of gay America.

But already this isn't quite accurate. Did Wilde really go to Cherry Grove? Could we really see his supposed visit, in 1882, as a cutting of the queer ribbon, a first step in the community's emergence into deviance? Wilde did sample a number of the getaway resorts that Long Island had to offer, including Long Beach, another barrier island off Long Island's South Shore and a popular bathing spot. Frank Leslie's *Illustrated Newspaper* published a piece on the Long Beach resort, and mentioned that Wilde had been a guest at the resort's "first-class Summer hotel." The piece even came complete with an illustration of a Wilde-like figure standing on the beach with his chest puffed and locks flowing. He is dressed in a svelte and fashionable bathing costume and poised to enter the ocean, while a female companion looks admiringly upon him.

Wilde had an effect on the Long Beach vacationers, though seemingly less as a heartthrob than a style icon. The *New Brunswick Daily Times* reported that a "surprising number of ladies came down into the grand promenade of the hotel to inspect Oscar's aesthetic makeup" and "followed him everywhere over the beach, even to the door of the cars when he took the train to visit Point Lookout, the new watering place, about four miles east of Long Beach, toward Fire Island." The Fire Island Wilde would have found that summer was in full swing, with its hotels overflowing. But there is as yet no primary evidence that Wilde ever actually made it there. The sole source for the story that he visited Cherry Grove was written by local Sayville historian Charles Dickerson. Dickerson claimed that, in local legend, Wilde wrote about Cherry Grove in his diary as "one of the most beautiful resorts" he had ever visited. But no diary from Wilde's American tour has ever been discovered, meaning there is no real evidence for this assertion, but that has hardly dulled its sparkle.

In writing this kind of history of a place, it's tempting to look for a point of origin around which to organize and narrate, to visualize Whitman and Wilde on Fire Island's beaches in the late nineteenth century like gay patron saints blessing its shores. But it also has to be acknowledged that, to the extent that they ever did, these writers brushed past this landscape more than half a century before it gained its reputation as an "alternative" destination. "A map of the world that does not include utopia is not worth glancing at," Wilde famously wrote in 1891. The map of Long Island did not include such a utopia then, not yet. But I still feel a compulsion towards the Wilde myth. Perhaps because, even in the face of available facts, the island feels sentient, attracting illustrious visitors, as if it always knew something of the fate it was headed for.

Wilde's and Whitman's influence has continued to impact Fire Island's culture and queer history at large. Take Craig Rodwell, the vice president of the New York chapter of the Mattachine Society (a pre-Stonewall gay rights group), who worked for two gruelling summers at the Botel, a yacht-club style complex at the Pines harbour, with a hotel, restaurant and bar, where an early iteration of the tea dance took place. Rodwell was working to save up the funds to open New York's first gay bookshop, which he did, on Lower Manhattan's Mercer Street, in 1967. Its name was the Oscar Wilde Memorial Bookshop. He named the store after Wilde because he was "the first homosexual in modern times to defend publicly the homosexual way of life." Or Jack Nichols, also a political organiser and journalist, who remembered incanting lines from Whitman on the beach at the Pines with his lover Lige Clark, who was killed in Mexico the year before. As founding fathers of queer cultural life, Wilde and Whitman offer resonances at once activist and elegiac, open and secret, just as they have been made to represent opposing factions of the queer sensibility. As the anthropologist Esther Newton argues in her seminal history of Cherry Grove, the gay liberation ideology of the 1960s and '70s was influenced by two forces: "the Declaration of Independence and Walt Whitman." Likewise, the long-standing gay tradition of camp, which emphasized "gender reversal, theatrical parody, and heightened sensation through drinking and sexual promiscuity," had a "flippant god" in Wilde. The kinds of queer utopia Wilde and Whitman dared to imagine were markedly different, but sensuality and intimacy were vital to both. To imagine them on the beaches of Fire Island just decades apart, each bearing witness to a rapidly changing urban culture, is to take the ultimate poetic license: to import into the island's origin story a politics that would not come to bear until much later. But it's a diversion in which I indulge, just for a moment. On returning to the vantage point of fact, at the turn of twentieth century, the picture looks a little different. A gay subculture was flourishing in the city, and Cherry Grove's leisure economy was developing, but it would still be another thirty or so years before these worlds would meet.

2

Chosen Families

IF IT HAD BECOME, IN THE EARLY DECADES OF THE TWENTIETH century, a go-to spot for the conventional family vacation, by the 1930s Fire Island was beginning to attract a different demographic of New Yorkers. Parties of unmarried men and women, described by locals as "groupers," were seen to be threatening traditional family life in communities across the island, including Saltaire, Ocean Beach and Cherry Grove further east. Ocean Beach, the de facto capital of Fire Island, was incorporated as a village in 1921, complete with its own school and police department. One of the earliest communities to get electricity, its relatively advanced amenities, compared to the rest of the island, attracted not only families looking for a wholesome, small-town atmosphere, but bohemians from the city and stars of the Broadway stage. A bizarre and presumably satirical 1935 column in the *New York Times*, about plumbing delays holding up the opening of the Ocean Beach jail, joked that the first prisoners to be locked up there would be singer Fanny Brice, her producer husband, Billy Rose, and the comedian Jimmy Durante, all of them regular summer residents. The village needed law enforcement, the columnist wrote, in order to crack down on the "rollicking hilarity"—a euphemism, perhaps, for a post-Prohibition taste for liquor—that offended "the sanctimonious nature" of its more conservative residents. Ocean Beach's many rules about public eating and undressing on the beach were devised to moderate the village's curious blend of the rigid and the raucous.

Because of its Broadway connections going back to the 1920s, Ocean Beach was likely to be the way in which many gays and lesbians working in the theater first heard of Fire Island. But if they were to find a space of their own, free to enjoy the idyllic setting without trouble from gawking families, they would need to find somewhere less developed than Ocean Beach, with its concrete boardwalks and municipal infrastructure. A place where the routine was still being choreographed. Somewhere, in fact, like Cherry Grove.

Cherry Grove in the 1930s was still a family-oriented place, but its rudimentary qualities—its lack of electricity and the absence of local governance or police—meant that it was to some extent out on its own. These were, as Esther Newton writes, "welcome deficits for those whose eccentricities or sexuality were on the other side of the law." The Grove's remoteness meant that groups of friends and lovers, whose behaviors and inclinations would be deemed outrageous or immoral under the scrutiny of mainland morality, could have a more authentic version of a summer vacation there, under cover of relative anonymity.

The dynamic between these "theater people" and the Grove's vacationing families was one of mutual suspicion. The epithet "theater people" accurately referred to the well-heeled set who worked on Broadway, but it also carried more deviant associations, not least the fact that Broadway's theater district and Times Square were an infamous hub for cruising and gay male prostitution. Lumped in with the theatrical types were people from the literary and publishing worlds, including a crowd with ties to a new weekly magazine that had been founded in 1925. With its particular mix of fiction, gossip, humor and commentary, *The New Yorker* was another byword for a certain kind of cosmopolitan sensibility. It would go on to feature short stories in the early 1940s that were set on Fire Island—another sign of the destination's growing popularity.

The queer parties who trickled through to Cherry Grove in the 1930s were also families in their own way, made up of individuals who were devoted to, and depended upon, one another. But unlike the Long Island families, these groups were distinctly untraditional, a mix of the subversive and the nuclear. Some of them even came complete with young children, like that of Italian editor and intellectual Natalia Danesi Murray. In the summer of 1936, she and a group of friends had driven out to Long Island along one of the recently constructed parkways in search of a summer beach spot. They ended up taking a speedboat from the South Shore town of Sayville to Cherry Grove. Murray went on to spend many summers on the island with her son, William, and elderly mother, Ester, first as a renter and later as an owner. The family of three lived together in Manhattan following Murray's separation from William's father, an American talent agent whom she first met in Rome. Her subsequent love affairs, however, were with women. William Murray's upbringing, much of which he spent surrounded by an eccentric coterie of adults, was anything but conventional, and he first went to Cherry Grove with his mother in 1937.

During these summers in the late '30s, William had the novel experience of being a heterosexual teenage boy enjoying vacation freedoms amid a burgeoning queer culture. As he grew into adolescence and experienced his own sexual awakening in pursuit of girls who came over on the ferry from Long Island, there were other boundaries being broken around him, albeit tentatively. It was still a "relatively innocent time," he recalled, and in the early years, "the gay community consisted mostly of older men who kept to themselves." The "drinking and partying" that went on at the hotel was still "evenly divided between straights and gays." Eventually, however, for reasons that will become clear, a new demographic of younger gay men discovered Cherry Grove as a cruising haven, though whatever they got up to was well-hidden, taking place behind cottage doors or in the "so-called meat rack," which in those days reportedly had a location that "shifted from night to night" between different boardwalks or in the dunes.

William was fourteen when his mother met the woman who would become her life partner. *New Yorker* columnist Janet Flanner was well-known for her *Letters from Paris*, elegantly written dispatches from the French capital that she wrote under the androgynous nom de plume Genet. She had been living in Europe since 1921 but moved back to the US on the eve of the Second World War, in late 1939. The two met at a cocktail party Murray was hosting at her Turtle Bay apartment a few months later. The encounter was brief, but memorable. Flanner was, after all, exactly the kind of guest who would make an impression; tall, worldly, and a storyteller dressed immaculately in a suit and with a cigarette permanently in her hand. Their second encounter came in July 1940, when they met again at a party in Cherry Grove. The two women fell in love over the course of that Fourth of July weekend, and they remained partners for life, even across great distances when Flanner moved back to Paris.

In 1975, just a few years before she died, Flanner wrote to Murray about chancing upon "a Kodak picture of you in a white long skirt on the back porch of the Fire Island house." "It must have been taken by me," she continues, "in the first week of our new love for each other. How we burned and so publicly. I could report on each motion of our bodies. I recall them all so vividly." Their host was "choked at the waste of oil in the lamp that I let burn all night when we lay awake." Like his mother, William was also "dazzled" by Flanner. She became not so much a mother to him as mentor and interlocutor, loving but harsh. When he went wayward at eighteen and "demolished

the interior of the Fire Island cottage during a two-day spree"
with a friend and women they picked up from the hotel bar,
the strength of Flanner's reprimand reduced him to tears. But
from that very first weekend, he remembered in particular her
radiance, the way she seemed "to be the center of attention, as
if a shaft of sunlight singled her out from among the crowd."

Flanner was a guest of the writer John Mosher that fateful
weekend. He was another member of the cosmopolitan entou-
rage that congregated in Cherry Grove in the late 1930s. He
was a colleague of Flanner's at *The New Yorker*, first as a short
story writer and later as a film critic. Upon his first visit to
Cherry Grove with his partner, he bought a cottage on the spot,
and vacationed there until his death from heart disease just six
years later, at age fifty. Mosher's witty short stories poked fun at
the mores of the city's middle-class—*The New Yorker*'s intended
readership—and his dispatches from 1930s Cherry Grove were
no different. Later, in the 1940s, Mosher's colleague Wolcott
Gibbs published in the magazine his own short stories about life
at Ocean Beach and went on to adapt them into the Broadway
play *A Season in the Sun*. Together, the works of these *New Yorker*
writers attest to the island's increasing visibility as a literary locale and a cosmopolitan reference point.

Mosher's greatest Fire Island creation was a character called
Mrs. Farragut, a seventy-year-old Long Islander who "keeps
house" for her son, a builder, during his seasonal contracts on
Fire Island. In one story, she stays in a cottage in the Grove during a cold March, "miles away from her own home at Ocean
Beach or from a spot where any sensible folk would dream of living." She observes the city people incredulously, and when one
of them approaches her to ask for a favor, she presumes it must
be for kerosene to light and heat the cottages. Running a vacation property in Cherry Grove at the time was no picnic. There
was no electricity, so light would come from kerosene lamps lit
on dark evenings, and any number of things could go wrong

with the houses, from stiff windows to potential fires. The distinction between locals and "groupers" from the city was often a matter of work and leisure; who got their hands dirty and who was just along for the ride. Mrs. Farragut's guests weren't after kerosene, in fact, but ice for "those everlasting cocktails they always had to have." Of course, for a satirist such as Mosher, this narrative situation was low-hanging fruit, but there was surely some accuracy in his depiction of Mrs. Farragut's conviction that "these feverish people [...] ought to be shut up in institutions," so that "sensible working people might then be able to get something done."

Mosher could only go so far in elaborating upon Mrs. Farragut's anxieties around the groupers, which come to the fore when she notes the "lady with an umbrella and with hair cropped in the back like a man's." These mostly unmarried urbanites were conspicuously different, not only because they seemed ill-equipped for necessary island labors, but because many of them flouted the gender and sexual norms of the era. With their cropped hair, eccentric conduct and love of liquor, they appeared opposed in every way to blue- and white-collar family life. Islanders such as Mrs. Farragut weren't usually invited to their drinking parties, but nor would they have been first on the invitation list to more traditional community events like the Sunday clambake. These newcomers depended upon one another for survival and affirmation. They too sought a summer reprieve, just like their traditional counterparts. But they met considerably more obstacles in the process.

Queer people often have an ambivalent relationship with the institution of the "family." For so much of our history, the phantom notion of family values has also been used as a stick to beat us with—a way to delineate our experience of the world as other, even to pathologize us. Almost a century after the Grove's emergence as a queer summer homestead, people are still disowned by their families because of their sexuality. It has kept us out of communities and classrooms. When the backlash of the religious right against gay liberation took hold towards the end of the 1970s, the infamous Anita Bryant spearheaded a campaign in Florida through an organization whose name sent a clear message: Save Our Children. The campaign sought to block a reform bill in Dade County that would ban discrimination based on sexual orientation. Bryant described homosexuality as a sinful practice that would always require the luring of new recruits, since it didn't involve reproduction, meaning that young children were not safe with gay teachers in their classrooms. Although Save Our Children was initially successful in its aims, its backlash against liberation galvanized activist movements throughout the country, and the controversy around it effectively ended Bryant's media career. This ideological conflict between queer and family values played out not only at the level of political organizing, but at shared vacation spaces. The conservative commentator Midge Decter wrote vitriolically in the early 1980s of being driven away from the beach at the Pines by the hedonistic, radical gays who had taken it over, so unlike the "sweet, vain, pouting" Pines gays with whom she had shared the beach in the 1960s. "Militant homosexuality," one reader wrote in response to Decter's essay, "has become one of the most destructive of ideological influences on the family in our society."

Conservative backlash against gay liberation was not a new phenomenon, but rather represented the resurgence of entrenched American attitudes about homosexuality that can be traced back at least as far back as the 1930s. So virulent were these attitudes that it's easy to forget about the queer subcultures that had flourished in Greenwich Village, Harlem and Times Square during the Prohibition era and earlier. They might have been forgotten altogether were it not for pioneering social histories like George Chauncey's *Gay New York*. The Village, Chauncey writes, "became the most famous bohemian community in the country," offering "cheap rooms to unmarried men and women who wished to develop social lives unencumbered by family obligations and to engage in work likely to be more creative than remunerative." Formerly Italian working-class, this community was reclaimed by these creative types in the early years of the twentieth century. For visitors, this bohemian enclave offered a modern spectacle of nonconformity, and gay men and lesbians integrated easily into the community's circles. In the public imagination, bohemianism and sexual deviance were often synonymous, and "in some contexts," writes Chauncey, "calling men 'artistic' became code for calling them homosexual."

Even greater freedoms were on offer uptown, in Harlem, which had taken shape as an African American enclave after mass migration from the South. In Harlem in the 1920s and early 1930s, gay men and lesbians inhabited a world of racially mixed speakeasies and "rent parties," gatherings in apartments where guests were invited to drink, dance and pass around a hat to collect money for the month's rent. They mixed with their white compatriots, who traveled uptown from the Village and other downtown neighborhoods, along with the middle-class white slummers who came to enjoy the jazz and the neighborhood's drag balls, which were frequented by thousands and reported on in the newspapers. Gender inversion, regularly cited by those attempting to pathologize homosexuality, was par for the course in this neighborhood during what became known as the Harlem Renaissance. Black cultural figures including Langston Hughes, Alain Locke and Bessie Smith were regulars of the scene.

The existence of these early gay and lesbian subcultures in cities challenges received ideas about the trajectory of queer history. There are examples of such spaces in Los Angeles, Seattle and the Twin Cities of Minneapolis and Saint Paul, to name just a few. The particular vibrancy of New York's gay ghettoes signals a period of relative permissiveness in the 1920s and '30s, during the era of Prohibition and the Depression, one that would not return until decades later, with the emergence of gay liberation. The notion of organizing politically around a shared sexual identity was yet to take shape in these decades, although the existence of the Society of Human Rights in Chicago, which was forcibly shut down by the police in 1924 and is thought to be the first US gay rights organization, shows the early rumblings of collective resistance. The gay scenes that flourished in New York between the two World Wars were also far from homogenous, demographically speaking. For one, the word *gay* as a descriptor of identity didn't come into regular usage until the 1940s. Before then, there was a much larger lexicon to describe the various kinds of sexual players who participated in the world of cruising, from married men to ostensibly "straight" sailors and soldiers to the working-class "fairies" who roamed the Bowery in lower Manhattan.

This world, however various and evanescent it was, offers insight into the early development of Cherry Grove. As Esther Newton puts it, the migration of gay theater people to Fire Island "is one of the clearest proofs we have" that sexual orientation was "becoming the basis for a complete sexual identity." The conservatism and crackdowns of the 1930s illuminate what these people were escaping when they boarded that ferry across the bay. The repeal of Prohibition in 1933 led to the establishment of the State Liquor Authority, which sought to control the moral order of the city and implemented draconian licensing policies. Bars catering to gay men and lesbians were rigidly policed, and either closed down after only a few months of business or forced underground, under the protection of organized crime groups who could afford to pay off the police. Alcohol and deviant sexual behaviors were deeply interconnected in the state imagination, as if one would inevitably lead to, or create space for, the other.

Gender and sexual norms were disrupted by the Great Depression; men lost their jobs, while women went to work in industries less affected by the stock market crash. A series of child murders throughout the decade caused a media storm surrounding sexual psychopaths. J. Edgar Hoover launched a war against sex crimes, writing in 1937 that the "present apathy of the public toward perverts, generally regarded as 'harmless,' should be changed to one of suspicious scrutiny." The definition of sexual psychopathy remained vague, argues author and activist Michael Bronski, "so that it could be applied as indiscriminately as possible," and laws were passed "throughout the country that implicitly targeted gay men. Homosexual behavior thus came under fire as a gateway transgression. If someone could so flout the natural and proper laws of gender in his sexual practices, what else might he be capable of? The "long-standing public image of the queer as an effeminate fairy," states Chauncey, "was supplemented by the more ominous image of the queer as a psychopathic child molester capable of committing the most unspeakable crimes against children." The sex panics of the Depression literalized the threat that homosexuality appeared to pose to the family unit. So it is no surprise that families vacationing at Cherry Grove during the 1930s were keen to distinguish themselves from the curious folk who were beginning to arrive there. They began to call themselves "the 'family' people."

Who would win this battle? There would be no showdown, no decisive conflict between parties that switched the Grove from hardy to theatrical, from straight to gay. As a rustic community growing into a holiday hamlet, the Grove seemed destined to follow the path of other Fire Island resorts. The gay men and lesbians who discovered it were not seeking to start a new kind of society. Besides the subcultural queer spaces being forged in the city, there were very few, if any, models to follow, and the notion of a gay and lesbian town was unprecedented. Any changes to the community in the mid-1930s seemed incremental, rather than irreversible. But there was a more sudden and random event that took place one afternoon in September 1938, whose devastation would literally redefine the structure of the community.

"She was not dressy and people who did not know her often called her crude," wrote the *Suffolk County News* on September 23, 1938, "but she was gay, she was carefree, and we loved her."

The obituary was for Cherry Grove herself, wiped out by a hurricane the previous afternoon. The newspaper's writers could not know that, when this "gay"—as in happy—and "carefree" outpost was resurrected from the rubble, its gaiety would soon develop an alternative meaning, and its reputation would verge on infamy. It is a curious thought experiment: to imagine that, had the Great Hurricane, as it is known in local lore, not wrought the devastation that it did, Cherry Grove might not have changed, or changed as quickly, into the place that it became. The story of Fire Island's relationship to queer life might have been an altogether different one.

The hurricane struck the island at 2:30 p.m. on September 21. One-hundred-mile-per-hour winds tore up the boardwalks. Cottages were either blown to bits or launched fully intact into the bay. While many evacuated before the storm hit, some of the Grove's more bohemian residents hunkered down in their houses and polished off the contents of their liquor cabinets while they waited for it to blow over. The damage was devastating, and the government intervened. Sand was dredged and used to build up the dunes, which were strengthened with grass and cordoned off by snow fences, the beaded wooden posts that snake through the sand and are a distinctive feature of the island's landscape. The majority of the Grove's eighty or so houses were destroyed, but some, like Murray's and Mosher's, as well as the community's only hotel, still run by the Perkinsons, remained intact.

Though they viewed the queer city folk with suspicion, the

old-time Grove property owners made a lot of money by renting to them. They now had to decide whether to abandon their
investments or try to rebuild. Many were forced to rent out
their personal summer homes in order to absorb the costs of rebuilding their investment properties. Others sold their lots altogether. Rental and property prices plummeted, and for a brief
period you could buy a summer house in the Grove for a song.
Empty lots were being sold for as little as $50. As the history
of queer neighborhoods the world over tells us, such enclaves
usually form, in the first instance, as a result of cheap rents in
run-down areas. Cherry Grove, which had historically been
working- and middle-class, became an even more attractive and
accessible prospect for queer people from the city.

Being for the most part Long Island people, the Cherry Grove
families felt a strong emotional attachment to the way of life that
had been fostered there. But while tensions between the remaining families and their queer neighbors continued into the 1950s,
"the hurricane," Esther Newton notes, "played a major part in
bringing the family way of life to an end." Many of the "frightened straights," notes John Jiler in his book on Fire Island and
hurricanes, went five and a half miles west along the shore to
Saltaire, which in the years after the hurricane came increasingly
to be defined as "a family place, as the emigrants were quick to
explain." Before the hurricane, however, some unconventional
households had already been setting up in Saltaire. In 1937, a
trio of artists, two men and a woman, all painters, rented a cottage there. They were Margaret Hoening French, her husband,
Jared French, and his lover, Paul Cadmus. Cadmus was well-
known in the art world because of the controversy surrounding
his 1934 painting *The Fleet's In!* The painting depicts a brawny,
colorful and debauched scene of sailors drinking, smoking and
soliciting women, while one of them is seemingly being solic-
ited by a blond male dandy, who's offering to light his cigarette.
The US Navy were none too happy with this depiction and got

the painting removed from the exhibition in Washington, DC, where it was showing, though this only increased Cadmus's public profile. The arrangement between Cadmus and the Frenches was somewhat typical of the time, though more complex than we might think. Jared's marriage to Margaret was not simply a cover-up of his love affair with Paul, nor an assimilation into the acceptability of the "straight" world.

Fire Island became a crucial setting for this ménage à trois. Art critics have even referred to them as the "Fire Island School of Painting," such was the influence of the landscape upon their work. During their summers, the trio produced an extensive series of photographs of themselves and others, sometimes using the images as models for paintings they would produce later. Because it was hard to tell, after the fact, who had taken which photograph, they used the collective moniker PaJaMa when the photos were shown publicly years later. Many of the PaJaMa photographs are beach scenes, shot on Fire Island or in Provincetown, and often feature fellow artists such as George Platt Lynes. Ranging from playful to poignant to erotic, the PaJaMa images blur the notion of singular authorship. They exploit, variously, the sense of isolation that can be experienced at the shore; or they feature an amorous assemblage of friends, lovers and theatrical personae, artfully arranged among the sands and the wilds of the island setting. They attest to the creation of an alternate, intimate world of open marriages and artistic collaborations; a place where sex and desire could be disentangled from the fixed social structures of work and traditional heterosexual kinship.

But most of all, the PaJaMa images attest to the queer affair of being isolated together, of operating in a minority, for Saltaire never became a haven for the unconventional. Content to work and play in private, the trio would nonetheless walk the long journey along the beach to Cherry Grove, Cadmus remembers, across the hard sand, "just to check the gay life there." Even before the hurricane, the Grove had offered the liberatory prospect of anonymity. It produced a "manic merriment" in its visitors, William Murray wrote. This joy was exemplified by one of his mother's friends, who, buttoned up in his "pin-striped business suit and a Homburg" hat, began to "divest himself of his protective disguise" as soon as the ferry left the dock at Sayville, and immediately brought out a "small silver flask" for maritime pre-drinks.

Now, on the eve of the Second World War, the Grove would come into its own, as a tangible cruising culture took shape. Still, the freedoms offered by Cherry Grove during and after its transition in the late 1930s were fragile. Vacationers were not totally free from snooping eyes or the agents of mainland morals. The French anthropologist Claude Lévi-Strauss, who lived and taught in New York in the early 1940s, visited Cherry Grove and saw it—with his ethnographer's eye—as a satirical place that "might have been invented by Swift"; a comic arena of "gay farcicality." He's right, in a sense. There is something irreverent and subversive about those early years in Fire Island's queer history, with its menagerie of satirists and alternative chosen families. It was a topsy-turvy place, populated by male couples who were "attracted no doubt by the general pattern of inversion." The island's geographical idiosyncrasy, as Levi-Strauss puts it, also makes it an "inverted Venice," where the land and sand dunes are fluid and moveable, and the canal system of boardwalks is solid. This quality defines the place's social identity.

But it's here that the anthropologist's account takes a nastier turn. He notes that "provisions are collected once a day from the one and only shop" in the Grove, and the "sterile couples can be seen returning to their chalets pushing prams (the only vehicles suitable for the narrow paths) containing little but the weekend bottles of milk that no baby will consume." This description invokes the melancholic figure of the absent baby and barely conceals its homophobia under the cloak of anthropological inquiry.

There may have been no babes in arms in Cherry Grove, but it was anything but a sterile place. Rather, its development as a sexual and artistic haven was marked by the movers and shakers who started congregating there during the interwar years and lived on their own terms. There would be so many more to come. Building from the rubble of a community in renewal, these early vacationers knew, like their successors, a fact that is one of the vexed birthrights of queer life: that family, at its truest and most generative, is not only or merely natural, but made.

PART TWO:

ENCLAVE

(1939–69)

3

Two People

COMING OFF THE BACK OF HOURS OF DRINKING AND dancing, the early-morning walk back along that beach that summer of 2017 seemed to take twice as long as the night before. Celine and I arrived again in Point O'Woods, while families were leaving their houses ready to start their Sunday activities. As the night's haze lifted to the sound of bicycle bells and children's laughter, this environment became increasingly surreal. The sun, beautiful and blazing, now felt antagonistic.

My first glimpse into the queer side of Fire Island had been intoxicating, but it suddenly felt very far away. There was no time to reflect on it now; sleep was urgent. When we woke, we went down to the beach, where we spent the rest of the day beneath a dusty gauze of moving clouds.

When I think back to that gray afternoon, a photograph comes to mind of a young man walking on the beach. Exactly where on the beach it was taken is unknown, probably at Saltaire. The man's eyes are fixed in the direction of the camera, and he's dragging a large black cloth—or it could be a fishing net, of the sort you could find washed up on the shore. The net leaves a trail in the sand, while behind him the shore is darker in hue, retaining the imprint of the previous wave—or it could be an interference in the image itself, a rogue patch of underexposure in the center of the photograph. The details of the man's face are hard to make out, but you can tell he is smiling. Like many of the images in the broader series to which it belongs, this photograph feels at once theatrical, morbid and quietly libidinal. Whatever levity is communicated by his youth and posture is offset by the languid black of the net and the peculiar dark aura around his body. Leaving aside the details from which you could, if you looked very closely, deduce its era, like the grain of the photograph or the style of the man's hair, the image has an ageless quality. What it captures is an island scene teeming with sensation, with desire somehow immanent in the landscape.

The man in the photograph is the writer Donald Windham, then aged twenty-one. Windham moved to New York in 1939, and by the early 1940s, when this picture was taken, he had fallen in with Paul Cadmus and his artistic set. In the summer of 1942, while Cadmus was away in Saltaire with the Frenches, Windham lived in his apartment on St. Luke's Place in Greenwich Village. It was a place to sleep and work for a young writer still looking for his foothold in the city. But as this picture shows, Windham would also spend summer weekends on Fire Island with the artists who were his friends and mentors. In fact, he continued going to the island for the rest of his life. That early photograph of him on the beach seems to anticipate something about his time there, for Windham would come to experience the island's multiple shades of life and death. It was on Fire Island that the great love affair of his life, with actor and editor Sandy Campbell, blossomed during the summer of 1943, and where it ended in 1988, when Campbell died suddenly at their summer home in the Pines, a community that did not even exist during the couple's first visits to the island. Windham's lifelong association with this place coincided with its blossoming as a unique enclave. By the time of his own death in 2010, he had witnessed all manner of historical events affecting the lives of queer people in America, from Stonewall and the AIDS epidemic through to the slow legalization of same-sex marriage across the states.

For Windham, who was one of the most underappreciated American writers of his generation, Fire Island remained a home, a place of retreat, where he could go to write and take stock of the cultural world he moved through. Indeed, Windham and Campbell's wide net of friends, peers and confidants included Truman Capote, Tennessee Williams, Tallulah Bankhead and Christopher Isherwood, to name only a few. Throughout his life, Windham wrote candidly about the ups and downs of fame and the wider literary world. He didn't experience the same levels of acclaim or popularity as many of his better-known peers, but his position enabled him to see more clearly the distorted—and distorting—metrics of literary success. It made him, perhaps inadvertently, one of the consummate biographers of his time; a writer who sensitively and expertly bore witness to the dramas of his milieu. In his own fiction, he wrote incisively about life in the South, where he was born and raised, and movingly about gay love and desire. His 1965 novel *Two People*, about the relationship between an American man and an Italian teenager he meets in Rome, inspires devotion among its too-few readers.

How did this boy from Atlanta, Georgia, who never received a college education and whose first job was in a barrel factory, come to move in such circles? Born in 1920, he was raised by his mother and aunt in a late Victorian house owned by the family. When it was sold, they were forced to leave, and soon fell into poverty. Windham was a voracious reader and naturally creative. When he wasn't rolling barrels across the warehouse floor of the Coca-Cola factory—a job his mother had secured for him after he graduated from high school—he began to mix with a local community of artists and writers. It was during this time he met Fred Melton (or "Butch," as Windham called him), a young graphic designer two years his senior. The two fell in love and moved to New York in 1939, after an intended one-week trip to the city became a permanent move. Over the next three years, they lived in various Manhattan apartments and worked odd jobs to stay afloat. Windham even continued a reluctant affiliation with his previous employer, selling Coca-Cola at the World's Fair in Flushing, Queens, during the summer of 1940. The pair built a social circle comprised predominantly of other aspiring artists and writers, and for a time, they shared a duplex apartment on East Thirty-Seventh Street with Tennessee Williams.

As it had been since the turn of the century, wartime New York was a sexually charged place for those who knew where to look. Regularly populated with soldiers and servicemen in town for a few days, the city's erotic traffic had surged. Curious recruits and old-hand cruisers alike knew that certain spots—particular bars, parks and streets—could deliver what they wanted. Windham explored the urban sexual playground a few times with Williams, particularly after his relationship ended with Melton, who had decided to get married to a woman he knew from Georgia. On one occasion, during a cruise gone wrong, Windham and Williams were attacked by a pair of sailors near Times Square. As bountiful as the gay demimonde was, the fact that it operated under the surface of detectability meant that the risk of violence or incident was never very far away. The antipathy towards homosexuality among the military— which viewed homosexual behavior, along with heavy drinking and soliciting prostitution, as morally noxious and unbecoming of servicemen—would eventually catch up with the sexual freedoms offered by port cities like New York. Police presence increased and, although they weren't the primary targets, gay bars were swept up in the anti-vice crackdowns that took place in urban areas near military bases throughout the early 1940s.

A remote place like Fire Island had a clear appeal in an increasingly hostile era. Williams stayed in Ocean Beach for three weeks during the summer of 1942, but according to him, it was "hardly describable as a retreat, Christian or otherwise." "I meant to get away from the world," he wrote in a letter, "but actually had more society than usual as all my New York friends flocked over for week-ends that lasted all week." When one of these friends left his bed in the middle of the night to try and climb into bed with Windham, who was also in attendance, Williams swiftly kicked the man out after a stern reprimand. He often found Fire Island lacking as a place to escape the world and write, and recalled that when the summer began, "the atmosphere of the place became even more hectic than Manhattan." But he was hardly opposed to its offerings either. As longtime Grove resident Audrey Hartman remembers, Williams was often known to show up at Cherry Grove parties.

Whether it was in the more permissive atmosphere of the Grove, or the traditional strongholds of Saltaire and Ocean Beach, Fire Island clearly offered space aplenty for frolics and transgressions, whether that was behind closed doors, or at a secluded point on the beach. Cadmus and the Frenches made several paintings that satirized the bourgeois social mores of Fire Island's communities, along with their PaJaMa images. As a regular companion and visitor on these trips, Windham was familiar with the place's liberating aspects, but the beginning of his love story with Campbell was not so freewheeling. That story would first begin, in a suitably complex fashion, with a triangle.

In his unpublished memoir-in-progress, Windham dedicates an entire section to the June 1943 trip to Fire Island with his beloved Sandy. It was during this trip, when they were staying in the Frenches' house in Saltaire, that their lifelong bond began to solidify. But it was also a time of rising tensions, for their meet-cute had been somewhat fraught. The pair met nine months earlier, through Cadmus and Lincoln Kirstein, cofounder of the New York City Ballet and editor of the magazine *Dance Index*, where Windham worked. Campbell, a handsome and boyish Princeton freshman, had begun a relationship with the thirty-seven-year-old Cadmus and became a regular fixture at St. Luke's Place. He and Windham soon got to know each other, unbeknownst to Cadmus. By the time of the trip to Saltaire, they had already hatched a possible plan to leave for California together to join Williams, who had moved there.

Although Fire Island was, in theory, the perfect setting for this burgeoning romance, Windham experienced its open stretches less as a romantic vista than as a perilous backdrop to his and Campbell's concealed intimacy. Campbell took a room with Cadmus, while Windham slept on the sofa. The island was less militarized than other coastal spots, but the fact of the war was still palpable. For one, the beach was off-limits at night, when the coast guard would patrol for enemy submarines. Cadmus, the Frenches and the clandestine lovers were thus forced to spend their evenings indoors, which only served to intensify the secluded chamber drama. Windham was anxious that his spark with Campbell was too conspicuous. Several times during the night, Campbell got up and visited him on the sofa for long stolen kisses, which ostensibly went unnoticed by the others. The days were spent eating lunches on the beach and bathing nude, as far away as possible from Saltaire's more conservative, and vigilant, residents.

Windham returned to the city alone that Sunday, and some weeks later, he and Campbell broke the news of their relationship to Cadmus, who eventually asked him to leave St. Luke's Place. During this fallout, Windham had a continued friend in Fidelma, Cadmus's sister, who was married to Lincoln Kirstein. A painter herself, she would often come to her brother's apartment while Windham was living there, to use it as a studio, and would then take the young writer home for dinner. The Kirsteins had an ambiguously drawn arrangement. They married in 1941, as an ostensibly conventional heterosexual couple, though Lincoln already took male lovers then and continued to do so for the duration of their marriage. Fidelma Kirstein appeared to be resigned to this fact—several of Lincoln's lovers lived with them in their apartment—but it no doubt took an emotional toll, and she was also prone to nervous episodes and breakdowns throughout her life. A talented artist who was frequently sidelined and underestimated, she was an object of fascination for Windham, and he never forgot her generosity. She would eventually become a literary subject for Windham as a protagonist in his 1951 short story "An Island of Fire," inspired by a trip they took to Fire Island in 1942.

"She is such a perfect character," Williams wrote to Windham in 1949 after reading a draft of this story. Fidelma becomes Miriam, an anxious amateur painter who rents a summer house with her maid, Effie. The setting of the story is undisclosed, but the title alone is suggestive, and mentions of Fire Island's distinctive poison ivy and landmarks like the Saltaire lighthouse. The story follows the daily life of Miriam and Effie; walking and bathing nude on the beach, collecting shells and drawing. When Miriam recounts that she and Effie, who is Black, received strange looks from the townspeople as they disappeared into the dunes to strip off for sketching, her brother and his wife laugh cruelly at her naivety. Miriam seems only glancingly aware of how unusual her attachment to Effie looks, seeming as it does to break the sexual and racial taboos of the time.

"An Island of Fire" provides a glimpse into this strange and rarefied world. Windham's stories, E. M. Forster wrote in the introduction to a collection of them, "are simply written, they do not shout or fuss" (and "they do not contain too much alcohol"). They attest to Windham's faith in "warmth"; his knowledge that "human beings are not statues but contain flesh and blood and a heart." "An Island of Fire" maneuvers elegantly between these tempers—the heat and "fire" of the summer setting; the suggested embers of lesbian desire, glimpsed only inadvertently, and the icy tundra of Miriam's isolation, stranded on her very own island. Miriam's benevolence—her affection for her Black maid, her insistence that "servants are people"—are mocked by those around her, as if her attempts at progressiveness are a strange quirk rather than a political position. Nonetheless, her affection for Effie, and her acknowledgment that, with only one other Black woman on the island, "it really would have been too lonely for Effie if she were entirely left out," still leave intact the power dynamic that governs every part of the relationship between these women.

Knowing how Fidelma's story ends—she died unhappy in 1991, in a nursing home Kirstein had put her in nine years previously—makes reading Windham's story all the sadder. But the story of Effie, or rather Elise, the Kirsteins' live-in maid, whom this character was based on, remains even more obscure than Fidelma's. She is not alone in being a marginalized and unwritten presence in the Fire Island landscape. As one of the earliest literary representations of the place, Windham's story gestures to forms of social exclusion that are hardly unique to this historical period, but remained, at the time, unquestioned. As a document of the island in the 1940s that is steeped in the lives of visual artists, "An Island of Fire" raises troubling questions about who is kept out of the picture, just beyond the frame.

If you walk from Cherry Grove to the Pines by daylight, along the sandy wooded stretch of the Meat Rack, you are likely to come across a boarded-up house. It stands at the westernmost edge of the Pines on the ocean side and has a "No Trespassing" sign clearly displayed by its entrance. Though it may look inauspicious compared to the modernist spectacle of Pines houses around it, this standalone residence is rich with history. Originally a bungalow, it is now raised on stilts and preserved by the National Park Service. Commonly known as the Carrington House, the property is comprised of the bungalow, which was built around 1912, along with an adjoining utility shed and a guesthouse positioned sixty feet to the west.

The Kirsteins rented this guesthouse for several summers in the late 1940s and early '50s. The trips were more about hosting weekend guests than they were about sampling the Cherry Grove nightlife. Lincoln appeared to refrain from going to the bars, perhaps out of a lingering sense of propriety, or a satisfaction with the presence of his regular lovers, who often came to stay. The couple used the time and space offered by the house to work. Lincoln planned for the ballet season ahead, and Fidelma drew and painted.

The Carrington House is named after Frank Carrington, the theater director and longtime denizen of Cherry Grove, who purchased the main house in 1927. Carrington eventually expanded the property by moving two abandoned outbuildings from the Lone Hill Lifesaving Station. This is why the Carrington guesthouse—which hosted a range of glamorous visitors including Katharine Hepburn and Henry Fonda—is often referred to in Fire Island folklore as the old coast guard station. Carrington, who was heavily involved in the queer theatrical culture of Cherry Grove, cofounded the community's Arts Project in 1948. He often rented the guesthouse to friends or acquaintances. For many years, this house was about as far east as the queer vacationers of Cherry Grove would venture.

What is known today as the Pines was largely an empty plot in those years, first purchased by the Home Guardian Company in 1925 but not developed until many years later. At the time it was already home to naturist groups and squatters, some of whom retrieved rubble from the wreckages of the 1938 hurricane and built their own huts. But this transient population was ousted in the 1940s to make way for property developments. In the early 1950s, boardwalks were laid down, leading to the construction of Fire Island Boulevard, the thoroughfare that bisects the Pines horizontally in the middle, and a basin was

dredged to form a harbor, with a ferry service quickly following. The inclusion of the harbor meant that the Pines was able
to accommodate the wealthier yachting and sailing crowd. The
lots tended to be bigger, which made space for grander houses.

If Cherry Grove was known as a hub for professionals from
New York's theater industry, the Pines would eventually garner a reputation as a kindred destination for the Grove's better-
heeled neighbor. During this early period in the community's
development, Frank Carrington also counted Truman Capote
among his guests. Then thirty, Capote stayed in the guesthouse
with his partner, Jack Dunphy, during the summer of 1955. One
of literary Fire Island's trophy stories is that Capote wrote, or
began writing, his novella *Breakfast at Tiffany's* in bed during
his sojourn here. Decades later in an interview, he recalled staying in this "cute little house" at a time when Fire Island "was a
very different place." There is something appealing about this
tale of composition; a picture of gay creativity, of the novelist-
as-dandy, and of Fire Island as a haven of leisure and inspiration.

The Carrington House sits just a couple of hundred yards
west of the Ocean Walk property that Donald Windham made
his summer home. He and Campbell purchased the house in
the 1970s, after a long time away from Fire Island. By then they
were a long-established couple. They lived together in Manhattan and spent many summers traveling around Europe, when it
was notably cheap for Americans to do so. It was when Windham was staying solo in Venice, back in the summer of 1948,
trying to finish his first novel, that he met Capote. They became fast friends, though over the years their friendship would
be strained by Capote's capricious and infamously difficult behavior as his celebrity grew and his drinking problem worsened.
When Capote died in 1984 of liver disease, aged fifty-nine,
Windham and Campbell had not seen or spoken to him for several years. The last time they spoke was during a heated phone
call they received from him at the Fire Island house. The couple

both chastised Capote for betraying Windham's trust and taking sides with Williams, whom Windham was in a legal dispute with at the time over the publication of an edition of letters. "I was completely undone," Windham wrote in his diary, his body shaking and his teeth chattering. "I don't know whether I regret having revealed my feelings or not. It probably won't mean anything to Truman either way."

In his memoir about Capote and Williams, *Lost Friendships*, Windham revealed himself as a stickler for facts, though this was less a pedantic impulse than an ethical one. "Stories about real people being in places they weren't, doing and saying things they never did or said," he wrote, "affront my sense of value." It is a challenge faced by any biographer, not to give in to the temptation to speculate neat or tidy narratives about what someone was thinking or feeling. Fortunately, Windham was an archivist by nature, and he drew on his extensive collection of notes and journals, many marked as being written in Fire Island. By the time he published the memoir, in 1987, Williams and Capote had both been dead for several years. But the Pines, in that era, had also become a graveyard of lost friendships, as gay men far younger than Windham were dying of AIDS at an alarming rate. The decimation of the island's gay community shed light on the fragility of the past, on how easily tales and stories could die with their protagonists. Whether consciously or not, Windham's deep dive into a past he shared with people who were now dead, and a gay literary world that had now disappeared, was a political act, at a time when bearing witness and remembering had gained a new urgency.

Windham only ever published one section of his long-term memoir project, at a time when he was still mourning the loss of his friend, the poet Tim Dlugos, who died of complications from AIDS in 1990, aged forty. If Windham had become familiar by then with grief, he was also having to adjust to a new reality defined not only by lost friendships, but the seismic impact of lost love. This memoir piece, simply titled "June 26, 1988," recounts in painful detail the day of Campbell's death in the Pines house. He captures vividly their daily Fire Island routine; eating breakfast on the deck, listening to music and feeling happiest when alone together. That day, they went for a walk along the beach in the pouring rain and later invited their neighbors over for lunch. As they ate, Campbell started to feel unwell and went to lie down. When he re-emerged a little while after, he seemed better, but soon gave a sudden jerk and went limp. His heart had stopped.

The day before, Windham had written in his journal: "People disappearing in life is more real to me than people disappearing in death." After several years of losing friends some time before their deaths, this statement had been true, he concludes, until that day in 1988. The Pines carried mournful associations for Windham in the years following Campbell's death, but it was also a site of remembrance. The house, for one, remained full of the couple's life together, not least the books that they had collected over the decades, many of which Campbell had had dedicated by the authors. In another unpublished piece, Windham recalls wearing Campbell's clothes after he died, his "beige and brown saddle shoes from Beans" and his corduroy trousers, just as Campbell had liked to do with his when they first met. Riding the Long Island Railroad from the city to the South Shore town of Sayville, where the Pines ferries depart from, to formally identify Campbell's body, Windham dressed entirely in his partner's clothes. "What happened to all that was in your memory that last day on Fire Island as it was in mine?" Windham wrote, in an entry addressed to Sandy after his death. "What happens to my memory and my memory of your memory when I'm gone?" Campbell's death threw into tragic relief Windham's anxiety about forgetting and being forgotten, though the fullness of the material the couple left behind, and the bequeathing of the Windham-Campbell Prizes, which each year offers substantial financial support to a range of writers, allows for the continuation of their legacy.

Windham still had numerous friends and correspondents and houseguests in his later years. By the time of his death in 2010, he had been going to Fire Island on and off for almost seventy years, a unique milestone among the people featured in this book. He was part of the very first generation to discover its potential as an enclave; first as a young man, visiting Saltaire with some of the earliest queer artists to incorporate the island into their practice; and later as a man in his fifties, happily coupled with the love of his life, who made in the Pines an enclave within an enclave, a restful home for two people, even amid the loudness of the community's sexual and cultural boom in the 1970s. This is why, when I think about the shape of Windham's remarkable life, the lingering image is that photograph of him in 1942 on the beach at Saltaire. Its composition seems to show us how remembering is an act, not a given. There Windham is, dragging the large net, collecting and carrying with him the various and unknown sediments of the shore while offering his gaze wholly to his beholder. There is a levity there, in the resemblance of the net to a gown or a veil, its slightly campy or drag quality, but also a quiet note of death, in how this black material evokes a shroud, or a mourning garb. Fire Island has long been a place where such contradictions are brought together; youth and death, glamour and grit. This interplay can be felt, the image tells us, in the landscape of the place. Other writers, present during the gestation of the island's communities, would discover this for themselves.

4

Body Fascism

I DIDN'T RETURN TO FIRE ISLAND THAT SUMMER. WE MADE THE trip back to the city after the weekend, and Celine flew home to London. I was keen to get back to my research and writing, but the first thing I found myself doing when I arrived back in Alphabet City was buying hair dye from the Duane Reade below my apartment building. I'd barely been back from Fire Island three hours and suddenly I was blond. Or bottle blond, that uniquely orange hue that's always much shyer of platinum than you'd hoped for. As any gay millennial will tell you, going blond is a sure sign of an impending crisis. I went straight out that night and arranged to meet a previous hookup for a late drink at a gay bar on Fourteenth Street. I don't remember a great deal, but I know that I didn't go home alone, and video evidence on my phone showed me butchering a Whitney Houston song in a neon-lit karaoke bar. I woke up the next morning disoriented and missing a bank card. Although I had fun, the next morning it was hard to shake the feeling that I was acting out, edging closer to an inevitable moment of rupture.

Being in the Pines had opened up in me a desire to feel embodied, to be connected with other bodies. It was a feeling I'd had on the edges of the dance floor in London gay clubs before;

a private sublime, as you stand watching all the different bodies in motion, that huddle of erotic potential. That the physiques in the Pines Pavilion had been impossibly sculpted only made the sensation more intense. It was a dizzying and excessive and not altogether pleasant feeling, perhaps because it reflected my own limitations and insecurities. I was frightened by the extent of the abandon I felt capable of in those moments. It is customary to talk about queer desire in relation to shame, as both a collective trauma and a private, individual legacy of repression. But I wasn't feeling ashamed of my desires. There was no moralizing voice telling me that what I was seeing or feeling was wrong. Rather, what I experienced in those moments was an anxiety about how I could fit into this scene altogether.

Shame and internalized homophobia, arising from without but felt within, are hardly the only factors precluding healthy and happy sexual lives. I'd always been insecure about my body, though for as long I'd suppressed my sexuality, I also seemed to suppress any self-awareness about being, or rather feeling, overweight. In the years after I graduated from college, I experienced a period of disordered eating. I lost a lot of weight quickly when I first became a graduate student. For a time, I lived on a diet of cigarettes, spinach and rationed teaspoons of peanut butter. Any time I knew I was going to be in the company of other gay men, I'd restrict further. If thin, then datable. The paradoxical consequence was that I wasn't in anything like the right headspace to be dating. The things I aspired towards—love, sex, connection—were made less, not more, attainable by the methods I thought would help me get them.

I worked over the course of a couple of years to change these habits and feel better about my relationship with food. By the time I went to New York, I was ready to take on the city's culinary clichés, the bagels and dollar slices and diner breakfasts, the famously large portions. I'd use the gym to stay in shape, and happily sweated away on the treadmill at my Alphabet City gym. I ate healthily during my daytime library stints so that I could have more indulgent evenings. Most importantly, it didn't feel as if I was working towards any particular end goal, other than trying to maintain a shape that felt acceptable to me.

The other people in the gym seemed to be taking it more seriously than I was—that much was clear just by looking at them. I expected the same to be true of the demographic on Fire Island, a potentially intimidating environment for someone with hang-ups about their body. But I hadn't been prepared for quite how much of a spectacle it would be. The Pines is a temple of athleticism: everywhere you look there are honed bodies displayed casually in the glory of the sun, adorned only in Speedos. Like most prerequisites, the prevailing physical aesthetic of the Pines is unspoken. The processes involved in sculpting such a body, the painstaking months in the gym, are anything but casual. Still, it seems, from an outsider's perspective, like a natural part of this habitat, effortless because it's so ubiquitous. And though it's not universal—there are people walking around in relaxed beach clothes too—you can't help but notice the trend as soon as you step off the ferry during peak season.

The Pines is no stranger to the term "body fascism," a concept that did not begin in the gay community but was increasingly used to describe the aesthetic of the Circuit in the 1990s, an international gay male party scene where the muscular bodily aesthetic is practically uniform. The "body fascist" is often synonymous, writes ethnographer Mickey Weems, with the "Circuit boy," who is frequently, though not always, imagined as the ideal of the "muscular White male body." If this look began in the 1970s, with the sexual revolution of gay liberation, the rise of gym culture and indeed the opening of gyms on Fire Island, it seems to have changed from a cultural trend to a collective trap that determined, implicitly, who was invited to the party. In a moment of campy satire, Andrew Holleran had already prefigured in *Dancer from the Dance* how the demands of the Fire Island body culture could become destructive. One of his characters "each spring contemplated suicide because he could not rise to the occasion—of being the most voluptuous, beautiful man on the island, the homosexual myth everyone adored." The particular features of this myth may change over time, or divide up differently into the physical types favored within the community. But these conventions can bring with them an increased risk of disordered eating, as well as "bigorexia," a form of body dysmorphia that involves building up muscle mass, sometimes through the use of extreme methods.

After going to Fire Island for the first time, my equilibrium had been shaken a little. Back in Manhattan, I could feel myself becoming more neurotic about my eating and exercise habits. It had piqued something in me, offered an aspirational vision. When I bleached my hair with a $10 bottle of blond dye, I was trying to replicate the kind of sun-kissed svelteness I'd seen gracing the early-morning dance floor. I wondered if I could change "tribe," to use Grindr-speak, and gain access to the prized terrain of twinkdom. But I was more of an "otter," or maybe a "bear" in training, with broad shoulders, a hairy chest and encroaching male pattern baldness. In pursuing the aesthetic of the twink—young, lean, clean-shaven—I would be attempting to mold myself to an archetypal fantasy that felt in no way native to me. Although I felt insecure that night in the Pines, to be white, able-bodied and vaguely slim is a form of privilege in a sexual marketplace that is experienced by many as exclusive and often needlessly brutal. Gay dating app profiles asking, notoriously, for "No Fats", "No Femmes", "No Blacks", "No Asians", speak to wider discriminatory attitudes towards Black, Brown, disabled, trans, and gender nonconforming queer people. Those who do not fit the dominant brand of white masculinity are frequently shortchanged by mainstream gay dating culture. You don't have to peer very far beneath the surface of the aesthetic in the Pines to see how the desire for litheness and muscularity can become nakedly ideological. How many people, I wondered, had felt this before on Fire Island? That insecurity peculiar to being among people who better embody the desirable—the hope that, at the end of the night, you won't be left dancing on your own.

It was in returning to the work of W. H. Auden that I reflected on how these discomforts were not unique to the so-called "body fascism" of the contemporary gay world, or to the 1970s club culture in which the associated aesthetic first became popular. When Auden summered in Cherry Grove in the late 1940s, the Pines was still an open plot of trees and vegetation that had previously been home to a nudist colony. He bought a house in the Grove in 1945, with his friends James Stern and Tania Kurella Stern, and for the next few years alternated weekends there with the couple. The poet's stays on Fire Island came at a curious point in his life. Soon after he moved to New York in 1939 he entered into a relationship with a younger man, Chester Kallman, and around the same time returned to his Christian faith. By the time Auden came to Cherry Grove, his turbulent relationship with Kallman had ceased to be physical. Fire Island seemed to reflect back at Auden his relationship to homosexuality and carnal pleasure, and his forays there were marked by familiar anxieties surrounding desire and the body.

With famously pasty skin and an aversion to the sun, Auden had never been particularly endeared to the beach. As his friend Christopher Isherwood remembers of a trip he took with Auden and Stephen Spender to Sellin, a small beach town on Rügen Island in Germany back in 1931, the poet "had no use for the beach and the sea." His "white-skinned body, when exposed, became painfully pink," so for "much of the day, he shut himself up in his bedroom with the blinds pulled down, ignored the summer, and wrote." Still, he came out of his room for long enough to have his picture taken with his friends on the beach, an image that Spender jokingly described as "the most famous photograph in the history of the world." Was Auden's aversion to the sun more than physiological, a matter more complex than complexion? Archetypal as this image may appear, of the pale and prudish Englishman shut up indoors while his more adventurous friends bathe and bronze, he was certainly no stranger to bodily pleasures. He had had plenty of sexual encounters with other boys at boarding school, and even more with fellow pupils at Oxford. After graduating, he moved to Berlin, where he cruised the city's bars and brothels and formed an obsession with Germany and Germanic culture.

But Auden detected something suspicious, even fatalistic in collective obsessions with the summer body. His first play, *The Dance of Death*, published in 1933, recalled not only the trip to Rügen two years earlier, but also Germany's *Freikörperkultur* ("free body movement"), which celebrated nudity, exercise, and sun worship as natural forms of invigoration. In the play, a sinister, silent dancer leads blinded members of the bourgeoisie, who are sunbathing on the beach, into a free-body-style cult that gives way to a destructive nationalism. Just as Auden's play anticipated the sinister equation of the strong, fit white body as social good, the nascent connections between the free body movement and Nazi ideology were already evident on the beaches of early 1930s Sellin. Stephen Spender remembered seeing dancers "doing exercises every evening in the woods," or lounging around "all day sunbathing" by "little forts" they built for themselves on the beach, along with a flag post on which they would "hoist a Nazi flag" and "gaze up in reverence."

Nor was this imbrication of body types and social purity movements unique to Germany in the early twentieth century. During Theodore Roosevelt's presidency in the 1900s, writes Michael Bronski, "manhood and the strong, athletic white male body were inseparable from America and patriotism," and decades later, there were fascistic echoes in the work of psychologist William Sheldon. In his work of the 1940s, Sheldon linked different male body types—the mesomorph (muscular), endomorph (soft and round) and ectomorph (tall and thin)—to distinct personality traits, and eventually arrived at the controversial claim that mesomorphs were biologically more likely to be involved in delinquency. Sheldon's ideas became widely known in the late 1940s, when he was made a professor at Columbia University. So much so, in fact, that they were satirized by the likes of Paul Cadmus, whose 1946 painting *Fantasia on a Theme by Dr. S* featured grotesque caricatures of the three types on the deck of a beach house, in a run-down resort setting that Cadmus said was based on Ocean Beach. Auden himself wrote a couple of short comic poems about Sheldon's ideas in the early 1950s that give us an intriguing insight into his double-minded views on such topics. Although his acerbic description in the poem of the "manly mesomorph" with "bulging biceps," whom "social workers love to touch," implies that there was something quack about Sheldon's enterprise, Auden was not immune to worrisome and even moralizing thoughts about bodies, their capacity for pleasure and destruction.

He was giving off endomorph energy by the time he reached the plumper years of his forties. It is a common note in accounts of his life that, as critic Richard Bozorth puts it, Auden "aged very quickly in the 1940s and '50s, both physically and temperamentally," and his "sense of his own ageing body was reinforced by the worship of youth that permeates gay male subculture." On the beaches of Fire Island, Auden was, for better or worse, at the heart of that subculture. Insecurities about his own body may account for some of his reservations about the gay world of Cherry Grove. In a letter written to the Sterns in the summer of 1947, he describes buying a new bathrobe to wear on the beach, feeling that "I am really too fat now to waddle around exposed." Needless to say, as a beach companion, Auden would surely have been quite the killjoy. But his complicated feelings about Fire Island ran deep, exacerbated, perhaps, by his increasingly dysfunctional relationship. Auden found himself exiled in a place that produced in him a deep ambivalence about what it meant to construct a community around acts of pleasure.

Auden first went to Cherry Grove in 1944. That summer, the Sterns were renting a cottage called Bassett's Roost and booked Auden a hotel room across the bay in Sayville, where he hoped to get some writing done. He moaned that the hotel's food was terrible and "served by sluts whose insolent clumsiness is all too American." But the benefit of his Sayville sojourn was proximity to the Fire Island ferry points. Cherry Grove in the 1940s was still in the process of rebuilding itself, and there was a great deal more open space around the houses, which were raised above the dunes on stilts and dotted along the boardwalks. There were some central amenities, like the post office, but the heart of Grove social life was the hotel, which had survived the hurricane and reopened in 1939 as Duffy's, a rowdier establishment than its previous iteration, with drinking, dancing and a mixed straight and gay clientele.

Auden's first evening in Duffy's that summer of 1944 must have appealed to him. The following year he and Sterns chipped in and purchased Bassett's Roost. The trio paid $500 in total—prices were still low after the hurricane—for the tar-paper-covered cottage on Main Walk, and renamed the property Bective Poplars, a composite of Auden's grandmother's estate in Staffordshire and Stern's family home in Ireland. Auden's arrangement of alternating weeks with the couple, who would sometimes rent a different cottage, meant that he could find some solitude, at least during the week, when there were fewer visitors looking to come and stay. The demands of his growing celebrity, however, could still reach him at Bective Poplars. He was frequently regaled by admirers, including a woman called Paula Schmuck, who shouted about how much she loved him

whenever they met at Duffy's and asked him to read the manuscript of her novel. On Wednesday, July 31, 1946, the photographer Jerry Cooke traveled to Cherry Grove to photograph
Auden for *LIFE* magazine. (The fashion and portrait photographer Richard Avedon, famous for his Harper's Bazaar cov-
ers, was also photographing Cherry Grove that summer.) The
pictures Cooke took of Auden present an idealized picture of a
typical summer weekday in the poet's island life. From them, a
tentative morning routine can be pieced together.

Auden rises early to meet the sun. He sits at his desk and
smokes the day's first cigarette while he glances over his open
notebook. He looks briefly around the room; suspended above
the desk is a large gas lamp, and on one of the walls is a map of
Pennines in the North of England, where he used to vacation
with his parents as a child. Barefoot and dressed in a comfortable cotton shirt and chinos, Auden leaves the house and sets
out on Main Walk, which connects Cherry Grove's network of
boardwalks. He drags a wooden trolley to the dock, where he
collects a brown paper bag of food supplies, a can of kerosene
and a copy of the *New York Times*. He pauses to sit on the dock,
his feet dangling in the bay. The water is perfectly still, a flat,
luminous sheet as far as the eye can see. He reads about unrest at
home and abroad: peace treaties are being discussed and drafted
in Europe; President Truman expresses horror at the lynching
of four Black men in Georgia. He is joined briefly by Tania,
and they sit and smoke together on the dock. The sun is burning through the morning clouds. Auden gets up and begins to
amble back with his trolley, a journey that takes just a few minutes, but not before stopping off at the Cherry Grove post office
on the way. He stands outside and reads the paper again. Then
he heads back to the cottage and starts writing.

On his desk are a lantern, a variety of papers, and the opened
envelope from the letter he just collected at the post office. He
uses a thick graphite pencil, and the glass ashtray by his side

fills steadily over the course of the morning. Later that day, he changes into a white-striped linen shirt and dark flannel trousers. He walks along Main Walk in the other direction this time, towards the ocean, and stops to chat with a small boy he passes on the boardwalk. He continues to the beach steps and pauses there too, the dune grass sprouting from the sand around him, as he looks out at the ocean. He walks to the water with his trousers rolled up and gets his feet wet. You could imagine this maudlin figure reciting the famous words of J. Alfred Prufrock, persona of his friend and publisher T. S. Eliot: "I grow old… I grow old… I shall wear the bottoms of my trousers rolled." He lingers for a while, smoking yet another cigarette, watching as the water draws in and goes out.

"I arrived to find the 'Life' photographer waiting," Auden wrote in a letter sent the next day from Fire Island, "who made me do the most absurd things like wading into the water and gazing soulfully out to sea. What will appear, I daren't dream of." The poet's splenetic camera-shy cynicism gives these images, which play at quotidian candor, a comic edge. All the more so when you consider that Auden's time on Fire Island was rarely as peaceful as these images suggest. Along with the usual demands of social life, there were the stresses of cooking and cleaning for oneself, not to mention fixing the numerous things that could go wrong in the house. Finding it a chore to cook more than one meal a day, Auden would get catering from Duffy's Hotel, and got local handymen to come and fix the porch screens and wash the floors. He was frequently joined during his summer stays in the Grove by Kallman, and neither of them seemed particularly house-proud. When Isherwood visited the house in the summer of 1947, he remembered a vision of flies buzzing over "unwashed dishes, uncollected garbage, unmade beds with dirty sheets and a vast litter of books and papers." Reliant upon the community's amenities, Auden knew all of the local gossip about the old-guard Long Island families, but he and Kallman must equally have been the subject of others' gossip too.

Auden and Kallman are an eternal source of fascination for biographers and critics, and there are whole books dedicated to analyzing their relationship. Kallman, an enterprising junior at Brooklyn College, was drawn to the elder poet when he first saw him give a talk in Manhattan in April 1939, just a few months after his arrival from England. Auden's lifelong and somewhat torturous devotion to Kallman is harder to grasp. Which is to say that it was not as simple, nor as predictable, as a tit-for-tat interplay between youth and power. Kallman was, by most accounts, truly striking to look at, with a Nordic appearance that was precisely Auden's type, although he had initially taken a shine to Kallman's classmate, who was also fair. So much so that when it was Kallman who called at Auden's apartment a few days after the talk to interview him for the college magazine, he reportedly stuck his head into Isherwood's room and proclaimed, "It's the wrong blond."

Nevertheless, the pair fell swiftly in love. Auden read and critiqued his young lover's writing and became friendly with his family, who were broadly supportive of the relationship. They discussed art and culture and went to the opera frequently. They had a passionate physical relationship. For the first few of years, Auden's life in New York was going well. He taught and guest-lectured at liberal arts colleges throughout the country and lived an itinerant life even within the city, where he moved from apartment to apartment. In October 1940, he moved into 7 Middagh Street, a writers and artists house-share in Brooklyn Heights that was known as February House and has since become the stuff of legend, occupied as it was by people like Gypsy Rose Lee, Richard Wright and Anaïs Nin. The following summer, however, things started to turn. In 1941, Auden learned that Kallman had another lover, an English sailor, who would be the first of many lovers and partners he had outside

of the relationship. This knowledge produced in Auden a jeal-
ous rage and a deep depression. Although the couple remained
together emotionally until Auden's death in 1973, the physical
side of their relationship was dulled almost as soon as it became
non-monogamous.

By the time Auden shacked up on Fire Island, he and Kallman were caught in the game-playing bind that would come to
characterize their relationship. They found ways, perhaps not
always consciously, of irking each other within the ambiguous
parameters of their dynamic. Kallman, for example, had a pen-
chant for rough trade, and brought a sailor back with him to
Bective Poplars. "Neither of them," Isherwood recalled, "was
at all interested in the beach or the ocean as such," for while
Auden spent most of his time indoors, "Chester went out chiefly
to cruise the population" of Cherry Grove, "which was wild
and barred no holds." While the Meat Rack was already catering to alfresco pleasure-seekers, the bar at Duffy's Hotel was a
lively indoor cruising ground. Where the cruisers ended up to
consummate the promise of their choreographed glances would
largely depend upon their accommodation situation. "At night,"
Isherwood remembers, "the noise from the bar could be heard
all over the colony, and couples stumbled out of it and threw
themselves down to screw on the sand, scarcely beyond the range
of the house lights." Auden's cruising was mostly confined to
Duffy's or the cocktail party circuit, though he couldn't be sure
if it was literary status that drew people to him. He was "very
flattered" at one such party, he wrote in a letter from 1947, because "the beauty of the island made eyes at me, much to the
fury of the other queens." But Auden feared that "this only
means he has a notebook of sonnets to his drugstore sweetheart
he is burning to show me."

Not all of Auden's relationships were based on transient encounters. His time on Fire Island also coincided with his love
affair with Rhoda Jaffe, a young woman who was Kallman's

contemporary at Brooklyn College and a member of the wider circle of young creatives that Auden often found himself with in the late 1940s. Jaffe was still married when Auden hired her as his secretary to type up his manuscripts, although the marriage had all but ended. They became romantically involved almost immediately. She was "earthy" and photogenic, Auden's biographer Dorothy J. Farnan remembers, an earnest, charismatic character, obsessed with psychology and prone to analyzing "all her friends, acquaintances, employers, and lovers when she was not analysing herself." Jaffe visited Auden at Bective Poplars a number of times during the 1946 season, and when they were apart he wrote her loving letters from Fire Island. They were clearly smitten, for a while, although the relationship confused many of their friends and onlookers. "I'm so looking forward to you coming," he wrote to her from Cherry Grove. "The bar IS going to be surprised."

How can we truly know what Auden felt for her? Jaffe apparently once described the poet to someone as being a "real man in bed." Auden, some years later, described his "affair with a woman" as a "great mistake" that did "not affect me at all," but rather felt like "sin" or "cheating," though we should perhaps remain wary of such moments of retrospective clarity, drawn from a writer's letters in the manner of evidence, which may be no less transient than the original events they comment upon. Perhaps Auden was simply tired of gay life, its physical and social demands, and chose to take shelter in a relationship that was in every way different from his and Kallman's. Whatever its complicated genesis, this relationship seemed to offer both parties a reprieve from the difficult transitional points they had reached in their romantic lives.

That said, Auden's sometimes domineering attitude towards Jaffe's looks sheds an unfavorable light on their dynamic, like the time, Farnan remembers, that he asked her to dye her hair blond at the end of the summer so it would stay light. Jaffe followed instructions and dyed her hair using something called an "ash-blonde vegetable rinse," but it went wrong and turned green. Auden was furious. In Farnan's memoir this reads as cutesy slapstick, but there is also something controlling and sinister at play in this anecdote. Was Jaffe Auden's lover, or lab rat? His protégé or his project? It seemed he was trying to reproduce in her, across genders, something of the flaxen youthfulness he had fallen in love with during the early years of his relationship with Kallman.

Auden had a number of female friends during his time on Fire Island, but he seemed somewhat blind to the complicated nature of their lives. Although he and Jaffe stayed in touch after their relationship ended, he was seemingly absent from her life when she committed suicide in the 1960s. Another of his friends from Cherry Grove, a married woman named Noemi Kenmore, with whom he may have had a brief affair, had a mental breakdown in the early 1950s, and Auden wrote to the Sterns that "I am at a loss to know what to do about her." His attitudes towards the Grove's lesbians, on the other hand, was outright hostile. The "dykes have multiplied this year here," he wrote to the Sterns in August 1947, when four of them were "arrested for nudity on the beach." Those arrested included Kay Guinness, who was among the group of lesbians that Esther Newton describes as the Grove founders. Auden called Guinness his "pet hate," though he also had it in for Alice Tiller, another of the community's early pilgrims, "because she looks like my mother gone to the bad." Auden's dislike of these women signals the limitations of his relationship to Cherry Grove as an inclusive political space. When a number of young men had been arrested by a local police officer the summer before for public nudity, Auden had written of them in a letter to the Sterns as his "sisters," when evidently the queer women of the community did not warrant such a title.

But Auden's sororal feeling for other gay men was also laced with criticism. Although he conceded that the actions of the "cop" busting these men for nudity was a "bore," he wrote that "I wish my sisters would stop behaving with provocative indiscretion and then think they're martyrs when there's a reaction." Tensions were rising in Cherry Grove, as the local families railed against nudity on the beaches and the local patrolman, Captain John Hawkins, cracked down on any signs of public transgression. This is the kind of political conflict that would come to define Cherry Grove, as an enclave whose freedoms were not given, but fought for. Evidently Auden didn't see himself as an ally in that fight, but it was against the backdrop of this moral atmosphere that he spent his final full summer on Fire Island in 1947, and later wrote a poem that seemed to ventriloquize anxieties about the kind of community that Cherry Grove had become.

The summer of 1947 was a busy one. The Sterns were vacationing in England, which meant that Auden had the run of the Bective Poplars and received many houseguests. Along with Kallman and his sailor, the Kirsteins also visited, and August brought the Cherry Grove carnival, which Auden attended in costume as Cardinal Pirelli, from Ronald Firbank's classic camp novel of the same name. In September, when the fun and games of the season were ending, he received some of his oldest friends. It was the first occasion that Auden, Isherwood and Spender had all been together since 1939, and so much had taken place in the intervening years, not least the war and its aftereffects. On the beach, the shirtless trio recreated a pose from a photograph Spender had taken of them on Rügen sixteen years earlier, but for Auden, the ebullience of that summer tableau, the sense of possibility, was gone. Although he returned intermittently in the decade that followed, Auden stopped going regularly to Fire Island after that summer. By the time he won the Pulitzer Prize for Poetry the following year, the first foreign-born writer to do so, *LIFE*'s description of him as a writer who "loafs through the summer at Fire Island, N.Y." was already out of date. He and Kallman replaced Cherry Grove with Forio, a seaside town on the Italian island of Ischia. It was cheaper and marked a more distinct separation from everyday life in New York. In a letter to Donald Windham, Truman Capote once described Forio as a Mediterranean version of Fire Island, complete with fucking and feuds between the gay American writers who congregated there each summer. Old habits die hard.

Auden's satirical, moralistic poem from 1948, titled "Pleasure Island," provides us with his parting missive on Fire Island. "People don't understand that it's possible to believe in a thing and ridicule it at the same time," he told a *TIME* magazine journalist who visited him at Bective Poplars in 1947, and this work attests to that dual gesture of belief and ridicule. It is a snapshot of a moment both personal and historical, of a poet plagued by what he saw as the uneasy fit between a life dedicated to writing and a culture that worships the body, with alienating and even morbid repercussions. The persona he observes in the poem—an unwitting writer who comes to the island hoping to find the time for "accomplishing immortal chapters" and "improving his mind," but who eventually "drops his book" and "surrenders his scruples"—is a ghostly cipher of his own character as a nomadic gay writer, torn between pleasure and more supposedly wholesome or sustaining persuasions. When asked about his solitude on the island by Oxford contemporary Maurice Cranston, who also visited him there that summer, Auden replied that if the intellectual life is one's calling, then it is better to stay celibate.

"Pleasure Island" arrives at a similar conclusion. It paints a picture of an erotic realm that Auden was simultaneously drawn to and repelled by, where the daily procession of "bosom, backside, crotch" along the beach signaled to him not only a site of temptation and sin, but a harbinger of death. Fire Island was, for the Auden of this poem, a godless place, far away from the "churches and routines" of respectable life; a deathly "place of the skull," populated by a "great gross braying group / That will be drunk till Fall." This unholy mingling of sex and death are illustrated in the way the "Lenient amusing shore / Knows in fact about all the dyings." These dyings describe not only the orgasmic little deaths of the Meat Rack, or a late-night assignation rolling out of Duffy's, but also actual deaths that were becoming a common fact of island life. Existing in the wake of the hurricane, which had cost several lives, the Cherry Grove of the 1940s was, in a sense, already reconstructed on the graveyard of its previous self, and further fatalities followed, some of them unexplained. Around the time that Kay Guinness and three others were arrested for public nudity in August 1947, a body washed up on the beach. Auden matter-of-factly reported it thus: "A body was washed up—no legs or arms—a month old." A couple of years later, in the summer of 1949, a young man named Robert Duff was found strangled in Duffy's Hotel. He had been sharing his room with his companion and patron, John Robbins, who claimed to have found him there with a bathrobe sash around his neck, and reports suggested the two men had stayed up all night drinking and arguing.

Robbins was charged with first-degree manslaughter, and it didn't take long for the press to set upon the Grove as a den of iniquity and danger. It was, as one headline ran, a war on "undesirables." Local families continued to write letters to the papers, blaming the murder on the culture of drinking, nude bathing and generally odd behavior that they had witnessed among the queer folk who now outnumbered them, but to little avail. Although the police increased their presence at Cherry Grove, and led a crackdown on public conduct, the queer renters and homeowners held strong, and the families who were scandalized by their goings-on decided to leave. It was a victory, of sorts, but this incident also offered a grim reminder of the ideologies that were at play not only in the conservative public imagination but,

more obliquely, among observers and participants like Auden
too. Auden's distinctive worldview, at once humorous, cantan-
kerous and ashamed, might render him an unreliable narrator of
this historical enclave, a place that was, for many of those who
made it their summer home, a sustaining and necessary form of
sanctuary. But the association between death and desire that he
identified on the shores of Cherry Grove has proved as stubborn
as the poet himself. In one way or another, it has haunted the
mythology of Fire Island throughout its history.

5

Like Water

THE "LIFE OF A RESORT," WRITES PROUST, REVEALS TO US HOW the "theatre of the world has fewer sets at its disposal than actors, and fewer actors than 'situations.'" The resort town of Cherry Grove in the 1950s was an assemblage of buzzing sets. From the bar at Duffy's to Pat's restaurant on the oceanfront, and the decks of beach houses, each was a stage for all manner of trysts, fallouts and amorous encounters playing out on repeat. It was a small but happening world, gay-friendly, ramshackle in its construction but glamorous in its clientele, made up of actors hailing from similar circles in the city: artists, writers, professionals, some socialites. Cherry Grove was starting to become notorious, and in clubs in the city, its name began cropping up as a euphemism in stand-up routines. The local shop even sold a tongue-in-cheek postcard that featured an image of two men in drag on the beach, with the caption "Mother thinks I'm at Ocean Beach." The community's roaring recreational culture was the most conspicuous expression of its deviancy. Social life in this boozy enclave, with its regular schedule of dinner parties, cocktail hours and nightly dances, was rooted in the cliquey, WASP-ish tradition of upper-middle-class sociability, and had been so since the late 1930s. But these lavish events became increasingly

open, Newton writes, to any islanders who "had something else
to offer—youth, good looks, or exceptional wit." Still, if coming to the Grove gave one carte blanche, sexually or socially, it
also exposed the perils of hard drinking, the complex motivations for which could not be escaped by simply taking a ferry.

It was at the bar in Duffy's Hotel, one afternoon in August
1950, that a group of women, who transpired to be in the Grove
at the same time, met up for a drink. Among them were the
novelists Carson McCullers and Patricia Highsmith, the writer
Jane Bowles, and the composer Marc Blitzstein. To be a fly on
the wall in Duffy's that day. "Like so many lesbians, then and
now" writes Jenn Shapland, author of a recent book on Mc-
Cullers, these writers' "paths and love interests intersected repeatedly" throughout their lives, even if they weren't personally
close. McCullers, then thirty-three, was Auden's former house-
mate in February House in Brooklyn, and had moved to New
York in her twenties to become a writer. Originally hailing from
Columbus, Georgia, she often retreated home to the South, and
made her career writing heartfelt novels about nonconformity
and conservative small-town life that are often described as
Southern Gothic. She cut a distinctive figure, with her cherubic
face and brunette bob, childlike stature and androgynous attire.
She was a hard drinker and chronically ill for much of her life,
suffering regular strokes. Highsmith, on the other hand, who
was then twenty-nine, and still a few years away from the mainstream success she achieved with her Tom Ripley novels, was
fairly well-known in the New York lesbian scene. Although she
is commonly remembered for her crime novels, her 1952 novel
The Price of Salt was a momentous publication in lesbian fiction.
She published it under a pseudonym, but it brought her much
recognition in the Village lesbian bars, where she could regularly be seen holding court, flirting, and propping up the bar.

"To Fire Island at 4pm," Highsmith wrote in her diary on Friday, August 18, 1950, "where I had contemplated being dead."

Recovering from a wisdom tooth extraction and seemingly scarred by her hallucinations under the influence of dental gas, Highsmith arrived on Fire Island with a woman named Ann. They stayed first at the house of a woman named Eloise, which prompted Marty Mann, an important pillar of the Grove community, to say, "You were a nice girl, Pat, when I first met you." Highsmith also stayed with her friend Rosalind Constable that weekend, who, according to biographer Joan Schenkar, was none too happy to find her in bed with Ann, the room "reeking of liquor, fornication, and unmade beds."

As the days went on, Highsmith was, as she wrote in her diary, in "worse and worse shape." You can imagine her, formidable and day-drunk, turning up at Duffy's Hotel, in her signature white shirt and dark blazer, her black hair tousled. After drinks with McCullers and company, she went to dinner at the house of her literary agent, Margot Johnson, and Johnson's then-girlfriend, Kay Guinness. Guinness, she wrote, kept making passes at her, and confessed to her that the relationship with Johnson was no longer a physical one. That evening marked the start of a monthslong flirtation. When Highsmith later told Johnson that she had been seeing her girlfriend behind her back, it brought their personal and professional relationship to an end. Johnson was a supportive, hardworking agent, twenty years her client's senior, and has been described to one of Highsmith's biographers as a "notorious lesbian and a drunk." She was in good company, at least.

Highsmith often fell into tempestuous and vexing dynamics with other women, romantically and professionally. She expressed a repulsion towards the feminist movement and was a known anti-Semite and racist throughout her life. Highsmith was hardly an ally to the cause of queer liberation, and her politics and private life have made her a source of fascination, as well as notoriety. That she was an alcoholic neither explains nor exonerates her character, but it illuminates, perhaps, some of the pain that existed behind it. That summer of 1950, she had just finished writing the novel that would eventually become *The Price of Salt*, or *Carol*, as it was called in later editions. This story of a love affair between Therese, an aspiring set designer working as a shopgirl, and Carol, a wealthy married woman, was historic for allowing its characters a happy ending, where most queer novels had to end in tragedy and suicide to get by the censors. Although they each move in different worlds, Therese among artistic types and theater workers in the Village, and Carol among the affluent environs of New Jersey suburbia, lesbian networks are intimated in both. Therese's initial connection to the theater world is through her boyfriend Richard—who, in a neat gloss on imposed heterosexuality, is anxious for Therese to read the work of James Joyce, rather than avant-garde lesbian forebears like Gertrude Stein—and at the end of the novel she has a brief flirtation with an actress. Carol, on the other hand, once had a romantic relationship with her best friend, Abby, though the revelation of this, as well as her affair with Therese, eventually costs her custody of her young daughter.

While the novel's ending suggests the possibility of future happiness for Therese and Carol, Highsmith hardly shies away from the difficulties of lesbian life in the 1950s, the shame and the hiding. *The Price of Salt* acquired cult status in the lesbian bar circuit, but this was at a time, Highsmith later wrote in an afterword to the novel, when "gay bars were a dark door somewhere in Manhattan, where people wanting to go to a certain bar got off the subway a station before or after the convenient one, lest they be suspected of being homosexual." While she was writing the novel, Highsmith was wracked with anxiety about how it would be received. "If I were to write a novel about a lesbian relationship," she wrote, reflecting on that moment many years later, "would I then be labelled a lesbian-book writer?" In 1950, such an epithet could be career-ruining, which is partly why Highsmith spent much of that summer reeling around in an alcoholic haze, plagued, Schenkar writes, by "waves of shame and fear at the thought of publishing a 'lesbian' novel that would wreck her career." She wrote in her journal, "I shall try to persuade Margot that the book should not be published now." Eventually, they reached a compromise: *The Price of Salt* would be published under a pseudonym, Claire Morgan.

One could imagine Therese and Carol spending a happy weekend in Cherry Grove, in a community of other ingenues and previously married women, redesigning their own realities, at some distance from regular society's gaze. Carson McCullers, who was twice married, unsuccessfully both times, to a man she knew from Columbus, pursued other kinds of relationships on Fire Island. She was a well-known figure and frequent visitor to the Grove and had been involved in the 1948 Cherry Grove Follies. This annual theatrical revue, organized by the nascent Cherry Grove Arts Project and often based around local in-jokes, was performed in the Grove's Community House theater, the long-standing venue for the Grove's drag shows. McCullers's third novel, *The Member of the Wedding*, was the subject of a satirical skit in the 1950 variety show. She was staying that weekend of August 1950 in the house of Marty Mann, with whom she was having a brief affair, although the extent of the relationship is unclear. Mann was an alcoholic in recovery and a key figure in Alcoholics Anonymous, which had been formed in Ohio fifteen years earlier and quickly became a national movement.

She lived in New York with her partner, Priscilla Peck, an art director at *Vogue*. While in the city they were known merely as friends or roommates, in Cherry Grove, they could be themselves. It was likely that they first met there in the 1930s. They were happy and committed life partners, but third parties like McCullers placed a strain on the relationship. Mann first met McCullers when she began guiding the latter's husband, a severe alcoholic, through AA's distinctive twelve-step program. McCullers developed an intense crush on Mann, a crush that "erupted" the weekend she came to stay with them on Fire Island. Although she remained friends with the couple and continued to stay with them in their apartment in the city, McCullers was a disruptive presence that weekend, and she continued to write impassioned love letters to Mann for a number of years despite the latter's request not to do so. It didn't help that McCullers was, if not an alcoholic, then a problem drinker herself. But she wasn't the greatest of Mann's worries.

Mann set up Cherry Grove's first Alcoholics Anonymous group, and was often on hand for support and sobering up. This group became an important part of the Grove's recreational ecology, and for many years was held in people's houses, rather than public buildings, to better protect the anonymity of its members. In the 1950s, Newton writes, the "pleasures of intoxication were cherished and unpleasant consequences disregarded," but many "who participated in Grove cocktail parties and spent weekend evenings at Duffy's bar eventually became serious alcoholics." It's little wonder that Highsmith and McCullers, among many others, drank hard and hid away. Although lesbianism was easier to conceal in public life than male homosexuality, the larger political atmosphere was frightening. Senator Joseph McCarthy's antigay witch hunts created a mood of secrecy and fear, although, as Newton observes, the "persecutions emanating from Washington were not seen as a direct threat to the resort."

While Marty Mann's work and private life could align on Fire Island, she had to hide the fact that she was a lesbian in AA circles. As a central member of the organization, she understood the importance of anonymity, and her impressive career depended upon concealing and suppressing her own identity. Eventually she and Peck had to leave behind their home in Cherry Grove; its association with homosexuality had become too strong, which created its own problems for the community. Just a month before McCullers and Highsmith made their way to the island in 1950, two men were stabbed and physically assaulted by a group of men from the mainland. Cherry Grove was becoming a badly kept secret, and while this attracted queer people from the city who sought to discover this haven for themselves, it also invited more antagonistic forms of scrutiny.

When Highsmith returned to Cherry Grove on a drunken rampage in the summer of 1953, local police raids, which targeted infractions such as public nudity and carrying open containers of alcohol, were becoming increasingly common. Highsmith was fortunate not to have been arrested after picking a fight with some women in Duffy's bar and getting into a violent brawl with them. It was the Fourth of July weekend, and Highsmith's lover, Ellen, a German woman with whom she had a tempestuous relationship, had just attempted suicide. The couple had had a blazing row the day before, and Highsmith wrote in her journal that Ellen had threatened to take Veronal, a barbiturate sleeping pill, and "insisted on having two martinis with me which she tossed down like water. I said go ahead with the veronal. She was poking 8 pills in her mouth as I left the house. I love you very much were the last words I heard as I closed the door." Highsmith fled the apartment, seemingly unfazed, and returned to find Ellen in a coma next to a suicide note. She took Ellen to the hospital and then went on to Margot Johnson's apartment, where she quaffed martinis, and decided to go to Fire Island the next day with her friend Jean. There, she tried to write, unaware if Ellen was dead or alive, though she found out later that evening that she had come around and her condition was stable. Highsmith got hammered in Duffy's bar, and the brawl at 1:30 in the morning left her with a severely bruised chest. It was a violent end to what was intended as an escape from the torturous situation with Ellen and her suicide attempt. She knew she wasn't going to Fire Island in the spirit of peace. "Ideal weather & connection & its heaven to be out here," she wrote. "I am escaping from hell." But Cherry Grove, with its nightly offerings of liquor and libations, was a shaky kind of heaven that weekend. There was, as Highsmith wrote in her diary after the bar fight, "Much drinking, naturally."

McCullers and Highsmith, and the other women and men they mixed with, were regularly surrounded by booze, perhaps for the simple reason that bars and parties were vital spaces for queer people to meet and socialize with their own kind. Cherry Grove was no different. But if the hard-drinking culture of the Grove led to many of its community becoming serious alcoholics, the question remains as to why drinking became such a part of its identity in the first place. The histories of alcoholism and of homosexuality overlap in intriguing ways. Right up until the 1970s, argues Audrey Borden in a book about gay and lesbian members of AA, "most physicians, psychiatrists, psychologists, and other medical scientists believed that alcoholism and homosexuality were etiologically—that is, causally—linked." The medical view of homosexuality as a disease, as opposed to a mere aberration, took hold in the pages of academic journals in the late nineteenth century, though it was not significantly disseminated until the 1940s. Much like the foundations of the Alcoholics Anonymous system, which treats addiction as an illness or malady rather than a moral failing, the disease model suggested, however wrongly it seems to us now, that homosexuality might be something that could be treated rather than punished.

Despite whatever "beneficent results medicine might promise," historian John D'Emilio writes, "by the mid-twentieth century it had in fact branded homosexual men and women with a mark of inferiority no less corrosive of their self-respect than that of sin and criminality." The framing of alcoholism as a disease makes more sense, and the aim of Mann and AA's other leading practitioners in the early twentieth century was to suggest that the stigma surrounding alcoholism could be reduced if it were understood as a pathological condition, although AA's faith-based approach has proved divisive. Alcoholism and sexuality are not comparable in any direct ways, but their trajectories in the public imagination have both been determined to a certain extent by the supposedly unshakable authority of medical discourses. And they are intersecting factors in the lived experiences of many. As the authors of one study of alcoholism and homosexuality from 1985 suggest, the gay bar is both locus and silo. The "most available milieu in which young people explore being gay," they write, is the metaphorical "sleazy part of town," where "they become exposed primarily to that segment of the homosexual world that is caught up, often compulsively, in the bar scene." If the historical predominance of queer spaces centered around alcohol speaks to a lack of options, drinking has nonetheless offered a way for queer people to explore their sexuality and even form a community around it.

Ever since I came to know myself as a gay man, I made the unconscious assumption that my own heavy drinking habits were linked to my sexuality. Or rather, to my relationship with my sexuality. It seemed to me that drinking just came with the territory, a natural crutch to turn to. I'd also consumed enough gay literature and gallows humor to think that my issues were merely part of a package deal. A problem drinker with disordered eating habits? So far, so gay, I thought. I looked at myself in the mirror, a man in his early twenties, and saw an identity defined by a lack, and a need to fill it. Drinking gave me a unique kind of confidence in nightlife spaces, numbing and sharpening simultaneously. It seemed to stave off whatever alienation I felt in bars or on dance floors (or inhibitions at the prospect of dark rooms). The act of going out became synonymous in my mind with drinking so much that I might lose control—blackouts were collateral. I'd give myself free rein. Although it existed at an entirely different historical moment, well over sixty years after I came of age, the boozy world of Highsmith and McCullers seemed entirely logical to me. Even stylish and romantic. A tableau of martinis knocked back over island gossip or probing conversations about aesthetics. From *Carol* to *Mad Men*, a glamorous sheen glosses the hard-drinking moment of midcentury urban life in America, and although queer culture had no natural monopoly over these drinking rituals, the solace of the bottle no doubt had a particular hold for people in hiding.

I still don't understand fully why I have the impulse to drink in the way that I do, but I do know that I find it much easier to have no drinks than just one. Often I might be a drink ahead of the people I'm with. I have real trouble ending the night once it's started. Memories of bad nights are as good an incentive as any to cut back. And although I remember my time living in New York as mostly joyful, and inordinately exciting, it had its fair share of bad nights; of scrapes and tears and lost possessions. I managed, for a while at least, to intervene in what seemed like a downward spiral. I tried to hold off drinking and partying so I could finish off my research and find some resolve. Perhaps that was why, when a stranger whose apartment I woke up in one Saturday afternoon asked me if I'd like to go out to the Pines with him that evening, I knew better than to say yes. I regretted that decision afterwards, but at least at that point in time it felt like there was some virtue in it.

Highsmith went back to Fire Island in the summer of 1959. She was then dating the young writer Marijane Meaker, who was developing a prolific career under various pseudonyms as a mystery and lesbian pulp fiction author. The pair met in one of Greenwich Village's numerous lesbian bars, and embarked on a love affair that would last a year or so. One August night, when Highsmith was returning to New York from Texas after a distressing visit with her family, the pair decided to escape to Fire Island and stay in the vacant beach house owned by Meaker's friends. The house was in Fair Harbor, a small community near the western end of the island, and far away from its increasingly infamous queer spots. There were "blissful days" in Fair Harbor,

Meaker remembers: "making love, sunbathing, reading, walking along the shore, cooking dinner for each other, and lingering into the night having drinks and listening to music." It was an idyllic and secluded routine, and in the privacy of the beach house, the couple were free from scrutiny. Highsmith's mother, who seemed deeply uncomfortable with her daughter's sexuality, had called just before they left for Fire Island and asked Meaker whether they were "going there to hang out with that Janet Flanner and her girlfriend." Illustrious lesbian personages like Flanner seemed, to people such as Highsmith's mother, at least, a byword for a particular kind of deviant milieu.

Meaker and Highsmith did go to dinner at Flanner and Murray's house in Cherry Grove on a Friday evening, and planned to stay with them overnight. It became clear, however, that they had misjudged the nature of the invitation. They were not expected as overnight guests, and after the four went out for a final drink at the Grove's new Sea Shack bar, Meaker and Highsmith found themselves stranded, still drunk from dinner. The jeeps that ran along the beach were not operating that late, and the hotel had no rooms available. Not wanting to put their dinner hosts out by waking them up, the couple slept on the beach in the rain. The next morning, learning that the beach taxis were halted by a storm until the afternoon, Meaker and Highsmith went to eat and take shelter in the Cherry Grove Beach Hotel, a new establishment built on the site of the old Duffy's, which was sold to an unnamed developer in 1954 and burned to the ground two years later. The new hotel, Newton writes, "never developed the rambling, gemütlich atmosphere that appealed to Grovers so much, and never regained Duffy's unifying function." It was a different establishment from the one Highsmith used to drink in, when queer encounters and boozy rendezvous were common but remained discreet.

Cherry Grove was starting to change. New houses were built and the town expanded, meaning there were more available rentals. New businesses, like the Sea Shack, or the Belvedere Hotel, the large, white, rococo mansion on the bay side, constructed by entrepreneur John Eberhardt in 1957, began cropping up. The erection of the Belvedere, an unmistakably gay feature in the Grove's commercial landscape, marked a shift towards openness in the way the community displayed itself. Several of the remaining Grove families took this shift as their cue to move on, but so too did old-timer gay and lesbian residents, who not only had wanted to preserve the private feel of the community's original iteration, but were also anxious about their own privacy and protection from exposure and persecution. A ready alternative had been offered in 1952, when a private development firm, the Home Guardian Company, began offering real estate lots in the new neighboring community of the Pines, named, like Cherry Grove, after the trees found there. The company initially touted the Pines as a family-friendly community, but this label wouldn't stick for very long.

Carson McCullers chose to spend her subsequent trips to Fire Island further east, a mile beyond the Pines, in the community of Water Island. Thick with shrubbery, only reachable from the mainland by a private ferry, and comprised of fewer than fifty houses, Water Island feels more like a remote artists' colony than a vacation destination. A beacon of this community in the late 1950s was the house of arts patron Morris Golde, who regularly had visitors from the city's cultural scene (including, as we shall see, Frank O'Hara). A "simple modernist house" perched on top of a ridge, remembers the art critic Douglas Crimp, who spent time in Water Island some decades later, Golde's house looked "westward to the Pines" but offered something quieter and less developed. McCullers visited this house several times in the early 1960s with Mary Mercer, her former therapist and close companion. They were hosted there not by Golde but by the younger playwright Edward Albee, then thirty-five, who often rented the house as a place to write.

Recovering from a double operation in the summer of 1962, which involved surgery on the joints in her left hand and the removal of her cancerous right breast, McCullers, forty-five, ventured to Water Island in August to visit Albee, who was working on a stage adaptation of McCullers's 1951 book *The Ballad of the Sad Café*. "This summer," she wrote in a piece for *Harper's Bazaar*, "I spent part of my vacation with Edward Albee at Water Island, a small community on Fire Island. I had already loved his work, so with this vacation I was well prepared to love him as a person." It certainly seemed like the kind of stay that incubated tenderness and mutual understanding. (She would visit Albee at Water Island again in 1963). The two writers stayed up late into the night discussing their craft, while Albee read the first draft of his script to McCullers. They also explored the landscape of the island. "At night," McCullers continues, "he would point out the stars to me. When I think about Edward I always think about stars and starlight."

It feels apt that McCullers turns to metaphors of the stars to remember her time at Water Island. To look at the stars, in a place where the sky is clear and open enough to see them, is a consummate space of reflection. The moving parts of one's life come together in the form of a constellation, random but ordered, if only after dark. Their stargazing surely had particular pertinence for McCullers, who was still convalescent and fragile. Water Island was also a place, despite its name, where one might go to dry out. Like McCullers, Albee too had his own problems with drinking. Alcoholism is perhaps the central subject of his most famous work, *Who's Afraid of Virginia Woolf?*, which he was also working on that summer. In her *Harper's* piece, McCullers called the play, which she read while at Water Island, "as luminous as the stars," characterized by the "dark brilliance that, to me, is peculiar to the genius of Edward Albee."

Reflecting on Albee's craft, McCullers repurposes the language of stargazing; it is against the cosmic backdrop of darkness, after all, that we recognize the brilliance of the stars. The effusiveness of her description is a common trope in speaking about art and artists, where appreciation risks yielding to a potentially damaging romanticism about the darker aspects of queer and creative life, not least the addictions. It is unclear whether Albee and McCullers were too industrious to drink during their shared vacations at Water Island. Or whether, conversely, their industry depended upon lubrication. McCullers never publicly addressed her own problems with drinking, but her alcohol dependency surely contributed to the panoply of illnesses that led to her death. She died in 1967, aged fifty, of a brain hemorrhage, in the hospital in Nyack, where she had lived with her mother for the past two decades. By this time, she was bed-bound and totally paralyzed on the left side of her body, but her celebrity, and taste for liquor and cigarettes, had remained undimmed.

Around six months before her death, McCullers had gotten her hospital bed moved to a room in the Plaza Hotel in New York for a short visit, where she held court and received admirers and interviewers. She told Rex Reed of the *New York Times* about the numerous film adaptations of her work that were forthcoming, and, candidly, about how she was in the end disappointed by Albee's version of *The Ballad of the Sad Café* when she saw it on Broadway, because he "has his own genius and I thought he was just cooling his heels working on something of mine." The same *Times* piece vividly paints McCullers in her final months, incapacitated but incandescent, "sipping a bourbon toddy from a silver goblet, smoking endless cigarettes" while she "sat up in bed, thin and frail, like a quivering bird, with dark, brilliant eyes and an aura of otherworldliness about her."

Although they were both queer writers who drank hard and published often and resisted the traditional paths for the women of their generation, Highsmith and McCullers were very different figures. While Highsmith is remembered as politically controversial even in her time, McCullers is often thought, Jenn

Shapland writes, as being ahead of it, because of her "empathetic writing about gay men, interracial love, racism and disability" in midcentury America. They moved, nonetheless, through the same world, and the theatrical world of the resort town, made up by the various sets of Cherry Grove and other Fire Island communities. Over the course of several weekends and weeks and in the 1950s and early 1960s, McCullers and Highsmith, like many queer women of their generation, lived out their respective traumas in various corners of this enclave. They deadened them with drink and with fists, and nursed them during walks along the beach and evenings looking at the stars. They weathered breakups and arguments and illnesses, though they did not by weathering end them. And the island could provide perhaps only momentary forms of reprieve. But it made an apt site for their contradictoriness, as a place itself made up of contradictory elements: of revelry and respite, fire and water. And as the 1960s dawned, that mad and mythical decade in American history, movie-like in its tumult, the whole country was changing. It was only a matter of time before the Grove, now notorious, and the Pines, a haven-in-progress, began to change with it.

6

Over the Rainbow

I CAUGHT THE SUBWAY WITH SOME FRIENDS FROM Chinatown on a Sunday morning, subdued and hungover, my chest tight with emotion. Earlier that week, the man I was seeing from London and I had broken up on Lexington Avenue as he climbed into a taxi to JFK airport; tears streamed down both our faces.

On that Sunday morning, we took the subway all the way to its final stop at Rockaway Park in Queens. We walked along a promenade that took us to the main beach complex, where there were food and drink stands and public bathrooms. Like a lot of the beaches in Queens and Brooklyn, the Rockaways don't have the feel of a resort, but rather a residential neighborhood that comes alive in the summer months when city-dwellers descend on it for day trips. It wasn't a particularly sunny day, not compared to how hot it had been in the days before, but it was warm enough to sit on the beach. I was feeling pathetic enough that I didn't mind the grayness. It was good to be away from the city, away from the cycle of drunken forgetting that I'd established in the last forty-eight hours. I had a hair-of-the-dog michelada from the beach's Venezuelan arepa bar, and we found a spot nearby to sit looking out at the ocean.

I was feeling introspective and invisible, barely tuned in to the conversation my friends were having. I took myself off for a solitary walk along the beach to get my feet wet in the splash of the tide. I didn't wander far. I looked east, imagining I might be able to make out the shore of Fire Island, and then west, imagining I was looking towards the city, trying to make out its limits, though my geography was totally off. The water looked unforgiving, waves lapping in the breeze. I looked around at the shrubbery running along the shoreline, and could see bodies congregating quite a bit farther down the beach, though I didn't think much of it. On a more inquisitive day, I might have clocked that distant spot as Jacob Riis Park, the best-known queer beach within the city limits. Like Coney Island, Riis Park was designed with democratic aims in mind, to provide shoreline access to all New Yorkers, especially those who could not otherwise afford summer vacations. In the late 1940s, gay men began to colonize the eastern part of the beach for congregating and cruising. Riis Park was not without a police presence in this period, and numerous men were arrested there, but this did not stop it from becoming one of the city's established queer spaces, fragile but fit for purpose, and sexually freer than the other beaches in the metropolitan area. More diverse members of the queer community could come to shed their clothes and have their own kind of seaside excursion at this cheaper and more accessible alternative to Fire Island.

By the 1960s, both beaches had not-so-secret reputations. They were both mentioned in a pseudo-anthropological cover story run in the *New York Times* in 1963 about the growth of "overt homosexuality" in the city. For the beachgoers reading, this fear-mongering report was no doubt sinister, but also a work of overwrought comedic gold—nothing in it was news to them, after all. It certainly got a laugh out of Frank O'Hara, who mocked it in a letter to his friend, the poet John Ashbery, particularly the journalist's account of cruising, in which he quotes

a verified homosexual describing the "look that lingers a frac-
tion of a second too long." Both of them were readily familiar
with the erotic routine being described on the city's streets and
beaches. In a letter from a few years earlier, O'Hara had tried
to lure Ashbery back to New York from Paris by invoking the
languid and sandy pleasures of Riis Park beach—known among
gays in the 1960s as "Screech Beach."

O'Hara worked as a curator at the Museum of Modern Art,
a champion of the Abstract Expressionist painters whom he
also called his friends. He had climbed the ranks there after
getting a job selling tickets and postcards in the front lobby in
1951, just after he moved to New York from graduate school in
Michigan. Poetry was his vocation, if not his profession, and he
wrote prolifically amid busy workdays and sociable evenings.
He was a chameleonic presence—a fixture not only at institutional champagne receptions but at downtown parties and on
the dance floors of gay bars—and a cutting and charismatic figure. Manhattan was his habitat, a lively backdrop to his own
ebullience. O'Hara had a relatively conservative childhood in
Grafton, Massachusetts, and spent his college years at Harvard,
where he enrolled on the GI bill after a brief stint in the navy
during the war. O'Hara's love of the city did not preclude his
desire to leave it on the weekends during the summer months.
During the decade and a half that he lived in New York, O'Hara
regularly spent time on the beach, from day trips to Riis Park
to monthlong stays in the Hamptons. Unsurprisingly, Fire Island was also on his radar.

On his first trip to Fire Island, O'Hara was thinking a lot
about mortality. It was early October 1955, and he was staying
with Morris Golde in Water Island. The week before, on the last
day of September, the country had been shaken by the death of
twenty-four-year-old actor James Dean in a car crash in California. O'Hara was drinking in the Cedar Tavern that day, a bar

in Greenwich Village that was frequented by many of the Beat poets and Abstract Expressionist painters, when he received a call from his roommate (and sometime lover) Joe LeSueur. "I immediately phoned him there," LeSueur later recalled, after hearing about Dean's death on the radio, "as though the troubled actor had been a close friend of ours."

This was of course a large part of Dean's appeal—his availability to many moviegoers, who saw elements of themselves in his brooding burlesque of nonconformity. Tough-guy stars like Dean and Marlon Brando held a particular currency as renegade icons, and their looks—leather jackets and coiffed hair—were widely emulated among teen rebels and gay men alike. The Hollywood-inspired "jackets and hair-dos," wrote Paul Goodman in his 1960 study of youth and delinquency, were "profitable for the garment industry and drugstores." The "flash and style" of this look came, in part, from Cherry Grove, populated as it was by fashion designers and trendsetters, and while these garments made their way from the "good haberdashers to the popular stores," the "ego ideals of the homosexual designers are the young toughs who finally wear the fashions." Toughs, after all, were a particularly desirable type in gay male culture. It was not uncommon to see Brando and Dean lookalikes on display at the city's cruising spots, hustlers offering masculine sexual fantasies for a price.

O'Hara had a capacious, even obsessive love for Hollywood movies more generally, not only for the male heartthrobs but for the female divas and starlets who graced the screen in the Golden Age of the studio era too. For him, cinema was a collective experience at once quotidian and magical. And while he moved in decidedly avant-garde circles, he held a lifelong torch for the populist glamour of Hollywood cinema. One of the charms of living in New York was surely the feeling of never being very far away from that glamour, from movie premieres and the happenings of Broadway, even if you're spending most of your evenings in Village taverns and dive bars. Fire Island was also buzzing with stars of stage and screen during this period. The surrounding area was well-known in show business not just because of Cherry Grove's notoriety, but because it was home to the Sayville Summer Theater, a playhouse where the renowned practitioner Erwin Piscator ran drama workshops and productions. The young Brando performed there in the 1940s, just before he got his first break on Broadway, and in the years to come, numerous stars would frequent the area on their way to Fire Island. Earlier in the summer of 1955, some months before O'Hara's visit, Marilyn Monroe came to stay in Ocean Beach at the house of the acting coach Lee Strasberg, director of the world-famous Actors Studio in New York. The local press went wild for her, though she was there—just like anyone else—to read and sleep and get away from the bustle. And in another of the hard-to-file stories about his sexuality, James Dean himself spent a summer "as a 'professional house guest' on Fire Island" to help his career, or so he once told a friend from college.

Still, it wasn't Water Island's proximity to movie stars that O'Hara appreciated that weekend in October 1955, but rather its quiet and celestial clarity, as McCullers found at the same house some years later, with Edward Albee. The island's stillness offered a landscape in which to process that strange grief we feel for people we never knew. Never knew except, of course, on the endlessly intimate level of the imagination. The island's vistas felt cinematic; the sky's rainbow like "a nickelodeon soaring over island from sea to bay," as O'Hara writes in one of his elegies for Dean. Between the martinis and the steaks consumed that weekend, he went swimming in the "dolorous surf" and contemplated not only Dean's death but the parameters of his own life, a life active and joyful but punctuated by melancholy. He went for a "cold last swim" (it was October) before returning to the city, which "flatters meanings of my life I cannot find, / squeezing me like an orange for some nebulous vitality."

The water, in its vast and unforgiving coldness, rendered everything else meaningless and transient, mere mainland trivia. As O'Hara well knew, these moments of reflection could only last so long. Though he mused upon the borders of mortality, it was the call of life, hectic and glitzy, that beckoned him back each time, leaving behind only his poems for Dean—typed on paper, and written in the sand—as the evanescent records of a moment.

It is both too convenient and dubiously superstitious to draw posthumous links between events; between O'Hara's elegiac repose at Water Island, on the one hand, and his own death on the same beach, a mile or so west, eleven years later. But it is still hard to shake the feeling that O'Hara's trips to Fire Island were punctuated by the sense that his own days were numbered. Perhaps this is yet another condition of retrospection, intensified by the gauzy recollections of those who were there. "I seem to remember," LeSueur writes, "seeing him trace" an obituary for Dean in the sand. "I say 'seem to remember'" for "the simple reason that I may have imagined it so intensely, seeing Frank on his knees in front of Morris's beach house, more like a child playing in the sand than a man of twenty-nine, that in time it became a reality, something I actually witnessed." An image—real or imagined, perhaps a bit of both—of childlike levity evoked in the light of lives—Dean's, O'Hara's—stopped short.

It's hard to piece together the exact details of O'Hara's time on Fire Island. He was an itinerant character, whose relationship to preserving his own work was irreverent, with now-iconic poems once stuffed away and hidden in sock drawers. After he died, friend and poet Kenneth Koch found "A True Account of Talking to the Sun at Fire Island," a poem O'Hara had written in the summer of 1958 when he visited his friend Hal Fondren at the house he rented in the Pines, as LeSueur remembers it. Or was it at Fair Harbor, in the house that Fondren actually owned? Many of the details regarding this trip and the composition of the poem are unclear, so much so that it has been a source of intense speculation on the part of writer Kent Johnson, who has proffered the theory that Koch wrote this poem himself and slipped it into O'Hara's oeuvre after his death as an elaborate creative gag. Whatever its provenance, the poem gives us another vivid portrait of a consummate O'Hara figure, positioned on the beach in the act of self-reflection. He wakes one morning and has an imagined dialogue with the sun, a sage and soothsayer, who tells him that it's:

> easier for me to speak to you out
> here. I don't have to slide down
> between buildings to get your ear.
> I know you love Manhattan, but
> you ought to look up more often.

Fire Island was, for O'Hara, an open-sky reprieve from the heat of everyday life in the city; a heat that gets trapped between buildings, consumes your time, instantiates tunnel vision. Fire Island was a place where joy and hedonism could be meaningfully balanced with rumination.

Hedonism for O'Hara meant cocktail parties more than it did casual sex. He certainly cruised and had love affairs—often with his friends, or with younger men, like the dancer Vincent Warren, and often to torturous or unrequited ends—and those experiences gave rise to some of his tenderest and most beloved works. But he was also "adamantly opposed," LeSueur suggests, "to the gay ghetto principle as exemplified by Cherry Grove," or "any gay gathering where straights were excluded—in other words, a way of life that promoted compulsive cruising, misogyny and homosexual separatism." O'Hara was the life and soul of the party—"I have been to lots of parties / and acted perfectly disgraceful," he wrote in one poem. He was at home in the company of bohemian heterosexual couples as much as he was amid the effete repartee that characterized much of the gay male culture of the time. Even into the late 1950s, some years after its development, the Pines still had a profile distinct from the theatrical "gay ghetto" energies of Cherry Grove— well-heeled, peaceful, and discreet rather than "disgraceful." O'Hara seemed to take solace in it, beguiled more by the land-scape and atmosphere than the explicitly erotic forms of libera-tion that it offered. He built sandcastles in the knowledge that they would be washed away, and talked to the sun knowing that what goes up must come down.

In early May 1959, the Cherry Grove Beach Hotel received an illustrious guest. Filling the gap left by Duffy's only in the sense that it still provided accommodation, this iteration of the hotel was, by most accounts, unappealing. James Baldwin wrote to his brother of his "grim, inland room with a gas heater" in this "enormous, hideous hotel," where he was staying some weeks before the Fire Island season began. It was an inauspi-cious venue for his labors. He had gone there to work on a draft of *Another Country*, his novelistic ode to bisexual and interracial love, which he compared during his stay at the hotel as a baby "pushing itself out." Baldwin, who often left the city in search of places to write, was seeking from the island the peace and quiet he needed to finish the novel. May would be one of the only habitable times of the year when such serenity would be possible. Although there were multiple options in the New York area where he could go to write, the remoteness of the Grove and its lack of a social life during the week, characterized by the cultural and carnal pleasures that made it unique, seemed to appeal. He wrote to playwright Lorraine Hansberry that he didn't, thankfully, know the people who came out on the week-ends. His particular therapy was a combination of writing and walks along the ocean. This was the man, after all, who wrote in one of his earliest essays that "I do not like bohemia, or bo-hemians, I do not like people whose principal aim is pleasure."

It's safe to presume that Baldwin wasn't spending all his writing breaks in the Meat Rack.

Baldwin's aversion to pleasure wasn't born of stridency so much as seriousness, a mark of his political commitment to art and ethics. Casual sex, with women or with men, seemed to him a distraction from the cause of truth, meaningless without the hard-won spiritual alibi of love. There "are few things on earth more futile or more deadening," he wrote, "than a meaningless round of conquests." It's little wonder that Baldwin remained suspicious of the white gay world, which often either excluded Black men or fetishized and objectified them. To be a Black man in America, he argued, "is also to be a kind of walking phallic symbol," envied and desired by white men both straight and gay. Born and raised in Harlem, he trained as a preacher in the Episcopal church as a teenager but moved downtown in his twenties to Greenwich Village to join its circles of artists and writers. His entrance into the Village in the 1940s was also, he recalls, his entrance into the "gay world." It was not an altogether happy one, characterized by gay men acting as "imitation white women," and engaging "speculations concerning the size of his organ: speculations sometimes accompanied by an attempt at the laying on of hands."

White gay men who held progressive beliefs about racial equality still engaged in primitivist fantasies and offensive talk about the sexual prowess of Black men. Frank O'Hara had numerous sexual liaisons with Black subway clerks and hustlers, and frequently referred to the desirability of the Black men he encountered in letters to his friends. Another poem he wrote "near the sea" at Fondren's Fire Island house during the summer of 1958 obliquely referenced these desires. An expression of solidarity with the "French Negro Poets" during the time of the Algerian War, O'Hara's speaker in this poem envisaged a kind of interracial, intercultural domination, calling to the "spirits of other lands" to not "spare your wrath upon our shores."

There had not, historically speaking, been many Black visitors to the island's shores. Like a lot of the city's queer spots south of Harlem, Cherry Grove was majority white, much more so even than those found in Manhattan's downtown neighborhoods, which were naturally more integrated because of the urban traffic of overlapping communities. The Grove, on the other hand, was not a place easily found. You needed time, money and inclination. Nonetheless, with its growing reputation and commercial expansion in the late 1950s, the increasing appearance of nonwhite day-trippers revealed the racist prejudices of some of the older gay and lesbian residents, who were now faced with a choice, much like the one that faced the conservative straights they had once ousted, twenty years earlier, about whether to leave or stay. Many of them retreated further into their cliques and cottages, which were largely concentrated on the western side of the community. But the Grove's "record of white exclusionism," Esther Newton writes, "has been no worse than in heterosexual resorts, and probably better than most." With the exception of a cluster of neighborhoods in Sag Harbor, a small bayside town in the middle of the Hamptons where Black New Yorkers bought up property in the 1940s, many of the vacation communities in the Long Island area were historically white-owned and racially exclusive. While Black luminaries like Langston Hughes, Lena Horne and Duke Ellington visited Sag Harbor as esteemed guests in the company of their own community, "Grove African-Americans," Newton suggests, had historically "fit into one of three categories: hotel and restaurant workers, entertainers, or friends/lovers of whites who were renters or property owners."

Baldwin went to Cherry Grove under his own steam, though it is likely he heard about the resort via the white gay literary circles he moved in. His growing reputation as a writer and public intellectual indeed had much to do with his dexterity in different worlds and among different groups of people. He was both a

New York native and a cosmopolitan citizen of Paris and Istan-
bul, cities he decamped to regularly. He was a literary novelist
who counted Henry James and Miles Davis among his influences, and a journalist and orator who spoke out with eloquent
rage about the realities of race and oppression in America. You
only have to watch a few minutes of him holding forth in tele-
vised debates with racist politicians or pseudo-scientists to see
that Baldwin's gift was not only his intellect, but his delivery, his
emphatic charisma. He had flirted with the idea of becoming a
playwright and an actor in his early twenties, after he moved to
the Village, and once took a theater class in which he met and
befriended Marlon Brando, just a few months before the latter's
stint in Sayville, in fact. "Brando," writes Baldwin's former assistant and biographer David Leeming, was one of a number of
men whom he "loved but did not approach as a lover," and the
two remained friends "through the civil rights days and after."

During his Fire Island stay, Baldwin was working on a talk
that reckoned with his ideas about creativity and popular culture, which he delivered a few weeks later at the Tamiment Institution in Pennsylvania, in June 1959. He was passionate about
theater and cinema throughout his career, and the author of several plays and adaptations of his novels. Many of his friends and
peers were in show business, and he knew that Broadway and
Hollywood were two of the most effective structures that could
be used to reach large audiences with the urgent messages that
animated his writing. But he was suspicious of mass culture in
general, believing it a distraction from unbearable realities that
must, nonetheless, be faced. In the talk, he conceded that life is
perhaps "not the black, unutterably beautiful, mysterious, and
lonely thing the creative artist tends to think of it as being; but it
is certainly not the sunlit playpen in which so many Americans
lose first their identities and then their minds." Of course, he is
railing here against the nefarious opiate of the masses—cheap
Hollywood fantasy and trash television—but there is something

telling about this image of the "sunlit playpen": a confined space
of oblivion, warm and light and naive, where players renounce
seriousness but in turn loosen their grip on life itself.

Was Fire Island to Baldwin not, in both literal and figurative
ways, a sort of "sunlit playpen," one in which he carved out a
space for his own "lonely" and "creative" retreat? It takes little
imagination to wonder how such an analogy might have come
to him, looking out of the window of his pokey hotel room
onto the curious scene of this makeshift beach town, a pleasure
island warming up for its season in the sun. It was and is, after
all, a place where people lose their "identities" and "their minds."
To leave behind the baggage of a deviant identity, to lose your
mind to intoxication; these were both important elements in
the Grove's modus operandi. But if the white members of the
island's queer community could shed the pejorative associations
of their being and simply be queer, untrammeled by the pry-
ing and judgmental eyes of conventionality, most Black people
had no such luxury. They could not, as Baldwin well knew, so
easily fit into a mostly white, middle-class queer world. This
was to him an unforgettable and cautionary fact, another reason
not to be beguiled by the excess charms of the "sunlit playpen."

In the autumn of 1963, Baldwin returned to Fire Island, staying this time at Lee Strasberg's Ocean Beach house, to work on
his play *Blues for Mister Charlie*, which was mooted for a Broadway run in association with Strasberg's organization, the Actors
Studio. On this visit, Baldwin's troubles were both personal and
political, inseparable from what had proved to be a tumultuous
year for the civil rights movement, and he was plagued by the
question of his own role to play in the struggle. That year, he had
traveled nationwide for speaking engagements, been the subject
of documentaries, and met with members of the government in
the hope that they would do something about the civil unrest
in the South. As Black political thinking became increasingly
polarized, between the nonviolence of Martin Luther King Jr.

and the separatism of Malcolm X, Baldwin remained torn. He was given an ambivalent reception as a public figure too, as if his literariness carried a whiff of impotence, and exposed homophobic presumptions about the countenance of the movement's figureheads. "He is not, by any stretch of the imagination, a Negro leader," reported *TIME* magazine in May 1963. In search of any number of euphemisms for gay, the journalist wrote that he "is a nervous, slight, almost fragile figure, filled with frets and fears. He is effeminate in manner, drinks considerably, smokes cigarettes in chains, and he often loses his audiences with overblown arguments [...] Nevertheless," it was conceded, "in the U.S. today there is not another writer—white or black—who expresses with such poignancy and abrasiveness the dark realities of the racial ferment in North and South."

At the end of August, some weeks before he went to Fire Island, Baldwin participated in the historic March on Washington, the peaceful mass demonstration in the capital where King gave his "I Have a Dream" speech. Baldwin marched with other celebrities like Harry Belafonte and Charlton Heston, and there is a striking photo of him and Brando at the march, smiling and youthful. But the hope of that afternoon quickly faded in mid-September, after a horrific bomb attack on a church in Birmingham, Alabama. Four Black schoolgirls were killed. Baldwin's play, a composite story of racism in the South that was loosely modeled upon a series of false accusations, murders and lynchings that had occurred in the preceding years, had gained even greater urgency. Although he retreated to the very edge of his vexed country, on the brink of the Atlantic, in order to write, Baldwin was never very far away from the events in Washington, DC, or Birmingham, Alabama, during those solitary and feverish nights.

There is a diary entry, dated only a few weeks before Baldwin's sojourn to Ocean Beach, that captures the curious political mood of the queer parts of Fire Island that year. It is by the

British playwright Noel Coward, who was taken by a friend to the island for the Labor Day weekend. "I don't really think I shall ever go again," he wrote. "It is lovely from the point of view of beach and sun and wearing no clothes, but the atmosphere is sick-sick-sick." Coward was horrified by what he saw. "Never in my life have I seen such concentrated, abandoned homosexuality. It is fantastic and difficult to believe. I really wish I hadn't gone. Thousands of queer young men of all shapes and sizes camping about blatantly and carrying on—in my opinion—appallingly."

It's unclear whether Coward, who was then in his sixties, genuinely had "always" felt, like many gay men of his generation, that "a large group of queer men was unattractive," or whether he was just anxiously aware, like all diarists, of who might come to read his words. In any case, he doubled down on his disgust at this "welter of brazen perversion." The male gathering he witnessed on Fire Island was to him "more than unattractive, it's macabre, sinister, irritating, and somehow tragic." He then follows up this self-hating critique with a self-aware addendum: "For the benefit of future historians who might avidly read this journal, there has been a large 'Civil Rights' march on Washington during which both Negroes and whites behaved in an exemplary manner and nobody got hurt." It should come as no surprise, given his feelings about the island's carryings-on, that the Washington march inspired in Coward a similarly conservative politics of respectability, where nonviolence was "exemplary," and anything riskier an aberration.

For most of those on Fire Island that August, talk of the March on Washington would have been in the air and on the airwaves, particularly since the introduction of household electricity at the beginning of the 1960s to previously isolated communities like the Grove. But for some visitors to the island, like Baldwin, this was not a peripheral news story about something happening elsewhere; it was impossible to ignore what was happening in the nation's capital and throughout the country. The white gay men and lesbians who vacationed on Fire Island in the 1960s belonged to a persecuted group, no doubt. They risked losing their jobs if they were outed and were still forced, for the most part, to lead double lives. But the very existence of gay ghettoes like Cherry Grove and the Pines attested to a level of structural privilege that was simultaneous with this status of alterity. These places offered, at least, some form of respite. "I think white gay people feel cheated," Baldwin told an interviewer many years later, "because they were born, in principle, into a society in which they were supposed to be safe. The anomaly of their danger puts them in danger, unexpectedly." For Black queer people, the "sexual question comes after the question of color; it's simply one more aspect of the danger in which all black people live." During the island's peak season in the summer of 1963, he had been in Paris garnering expat support for the Washington march, and as the summer faded, he continued to work on putting into words the rage and despair of the moment.

The 1960s were a political time on Fire Island. The most political aspect of island life up until this time had involved local priorities and questions about how the land was regulated. Although most plots were privately owned, the island was vulnerable to the jurisdiction of the state government, and in particular the infamously tyrannical urban planner Robert Moses, who wanted to build a destructive highway along the middle of the island to increase access. Through the coordinated grassroots efforts of the island's communities, Moses's plans were scrapped, and the island won the protected status of a National Seashore in 1964. There would be no more automobiles, nor excessive state intervention. Around the same time, more local battles were being fought, but with significant and far-reaching implications. For one, a younger generation of Grovers would soon be calling time on repressive attitudes like Noel Coward's. Seismic changes were brewing. What Coward saw as "brazen perversion"—camping around on the beach and cruising in the Meat Rack—was wholeheartedly embraced by the younger gay men who made the Grove their summer home. Restrictions placed on these freedoms would no longer be tolerated by this generation.

Throughout the 1950s, the invasion of gay bashers from the mainland had been a problem, and so too was the Suffolk County police crackdown on gay cruising in the Grove. The police resumed their raids of the Meat Rack in 1964, and entrapped and arrested numerous men on the charge of public indecency. The raids continued into 1965, sweeping up men from the Grove and, for the first time, the Pines as well. The New York chapter of the Mattachine Society stepped in and fought back. After the Mattachine activists protested against this and papered the beaches with flyers on legal and civil rights, the raids came to an end, though what Esther Newton describes as the "antipolitical" spirit among the Grove's older community members meant that their valiant and successful efforts were not altogether appreciated. The original Mattachine Society was formed in Los Angeles in 1951, an event that is commonly seen as the birth of the modern gay rights movement, and it subsequently split into discrete chapters that were concentrated in urban centers throughout the country. With its early roots in Communist thinking, the Mattachine name was synonymous with advocating for the rights of America's sexual minority. Its founding members, historian John D'Emilio writes, "affirmed the uniqueness of gay identity, projected a vision of homosexual culture with its own positive values, and attempted to transform the shame of being gay into a pride in belonging to a minority with its own contribution to the human community."

A gay politics focused on pride and resistance had long been percolating. In the summer of 1966, the Mattachine staged a "Sip-In" at Julius' in Greenwich Village in order to protest the State Liquor Authority's antigay laws. The laws against gay bars in New York prohibited any bar in the city even from serving patrons who were suspected to be gay, which meant that any visible or behavioral signals, from wearing full drag to being, as the saying went, a little "light in the loafers," could be policed. Members of the Mattachine, including the New York chapter president, Dick Leitsch, and Craig Rodwell, founder of the Oscar Wilde Memorial Bookshop, strolled into Julius' and made their sexuality known, aware that they would be denied a drink. Like the Mattachine's intervention at Cherry Grove a few years ago, this was an orderly, choreographed intervention intended to raise consciousness. But by the end of 1960s, after countless acts of state aggression and raids of New York gay bars, peaceful protest would no longer be enough. It was at the same time becoming evident to civil rights thinkers like Baldwin, who had initially remained cool to the ideology of Black nationalism, that racial oppression could not be combatted by peaceful means alone. If the country's racial and sexual minorities were to successfully carve out and protect their own spaces, they would need to take things into their own hands.

In May 1965, Baldwin returned to Fire Island. He absconded to a friend's house in Cherry Grove with his assistant, David Leeming, so he could work, uninterrupted, on his short story collection, which was due to publish later in the year. One evening, they went to one of the Grove's restaurants and bumped into Frank O'Hara. Baldwin and O'Hara had met before, at literary gatherings back in the city, and they stopped in the Grove to chat. O'Hara invited the men for drinks at the place he was staying in the Pines, and the three of them caught a dune buggy down the beach. The cocktails and the conversation, Leeming remembers, lasted until dawn, and a good deal of it was about their shared love of Henry James. Baldwin and O'Hara evidently clicked. They had similar interests and mutual friends. That conversation could well have been the start of a new and fulfilling friendship, but it is unlikely that they ever saw each other again. The following summer, O'Hara was struck by the same kind of vehicle that had brought them from the Grove to the Pines, on roughly the same stretch of beach. Leeming's recollection, through the haze of the night's many drinks, is our only trace of this meeting of minds, of two luminaries from similar but different worlds, both shored up, off-season, on this spit of land.

Tensions between racial and sexual identity in the city's artistic community were brewing. Shortly before O'Hara and Baldwin's meeting on Fire Island, the talk of the town had been that playwright and poet LeRoi Jones had moved to Harlem from the Village, changed his name to Amiri Baraka, and joined the Black nationalist cause, a decision prompted in part by the assassination of Malcolm X. Given the flippant treatment of racial politics in gay bohemian circles, and its place as the racist butt of campy jokes, it is little wonder that Black writers and artists gravitated uptown to Black creative enclaves. Although his commitment to the cause was steadfast, Baldwin was divided between these two neighborhoods, and symbolically between their associated sensibilities. Many Black nationalists treated him, and other gay Black men, with suspicion. In the little-known 1968 novel *Mr. Ladybug*, published pseudonymously by a writer called Becky Crocker, its author unknown, and set in a fictionalized version of Cherry Grove, a Black gay resident of the island community is given the nickname "Uncle Tom," the satirical implication being that Black gay men were viewed by their own community as race traitors.

Baraka himself was one of the first dissenting voices who critiqued Baldwin, and subsequent comments from members of the Black Panther Party became increasingly homophobic. Baldwin was well aware, Leeming writes, that people on both sides of the struggle, the nonviolent Dr. King camp and the Black nationalist camp, "were wary of his own reputation as a homosexual," and some of the attacks by the latter were virulent, a sign of the masculinist views at the heart of the movement. Many Black homosexuals, wrote the Black Panther activist Eldridge Cleaver from prison in 1965, "are outraged and frustrated because in their sickness they are unable to have a baby by a white man," but still "they redouble their efforts in take of the white man's sperm." Black men loving white men, Cleaver supposed, was ultimately an emasculating form of self-hatred, a "racial death-wish" that "is manifested as the driving force in James Baldwin." Against such attacks, Baldwin's more temperate theology of love, of queer and interracial sex shot through with the virtues of understanding and interpersonal reckoning, barely stood a chance. It would still be another few years before the solidarity between different groups fighting for racial, sexual and gender equality would be meaningfully acknowledged; it was in 1970 that Black Panther leader Huey Newton called for the party to unite with "the various liberation movements among homosexuals and women." What took place in the intervening years, right at the end of the 1960s, was groundbreaking for the queer community.

O'Hara, meanwhile, never got to see the spoils of Fire Island's vibrant next chapter. On a late July weekend in 1966, he went with some friends, remembers J. J. Mitchell, who was one of them, "for a 'sortie' into the night life of Fire Island Pines, only fifteen minutes down the beach" via taxi. They had gone to "look at the animals," the gay revelers at the dance held at the Blue Whale, a central new fixture of the Pines harbor. The Pines Yacht Club and Botel, where the Blue Whale now stood, was first built in the late 1950s and owned by Peggy Fears, an ex-Ziegfeld showgirl, who ran the hotel with her girlfriend, the model and actress Tedi Thurman. When the wooden complex burned down in 1959, it was rebuilt using glass and aluminum. Fears sold the complex in 1962 to a group of buyers that included the model John Whyte, who later bought out his partners and took the building over. He opened the Blue Whale bar in 1964, which was known for its signature cocktail, a mix of blue curacao and gin. Whyte had recruited esteemed singers like Jimmie Daniels to perform there, and cultivated a glamorous nightlife. (Even hardworking Baldwin was spotted there for drinks from time to time.) It would be from Whyte's miniature empire on the harbor that the legendary party culture of the Pines would grow.

O'Hara and his friend J.J. Mitchell were the last two standing that July night. They stayed in the Pines drinking stingers until the early hours. When they got tired, they went down to the beach to hail a taxi back to Water Island. It lost a left tire and broke down after just a few minutes. While the party waited for another taxi, O'Hara wandered towards the back of the broken-down vehicle to look out over the water. At the same moment, twenty-three-year-old Kenneth Ruzicka, who was driving down the beach in a jeep, crashed straight into the middle of this scene, having been blinded by the headlights of the stalled taxi, according to his testimony. O'Hara, unable to move out of the way in time, was struck by the jeep and fell into a coma. He died in a Long Island hospital the next day, aged forty.

It feels unsavory to speculate about the nature of this death, and whether to class it as a freak accident or an intentional incident. Some scholars of his work have long felt that "it is time to forget all about Fire Island and the so-called 'killing'—or instinctive suicide—of Frank O'Hara." But the fact that he died on the beach at Fire Island continues to bear, in all its randomness, some kind of mythical weight. That night provides a point at which O'Hara's own legacy, as a beloved gay poet, meets with the history of a place that would become synonymous with a new kind of sexual citizenship. For his readers and imitators, his is a queer voice that emanates from the brink, at once candid and mysterious, just shy of the liberation years. The *Village Voice* ran an obituary for him on August 11, 1966. A young poet was quoted about his views on O'Hara's eternal wattage: "No matter what he did, he never lost that movie star quality." Just a few days after this obituary was printed, the new gay world that eluded O'Hara could be glimpsed west along the beach from the site of his death. Mattachine Society activists were present at Cherry Grove, posting blue mimeograph posters, with advice for "homosexuals" about what to do if they were arrested, a prime example of homophile activism and a signal of the politicized atmosphere of resistance and revelation that was just around the corner.

Three years later, another death haunted Fire Island, albeit less directly. Judy Garland had connections to the Pines, mostly through the composer Jerry Herman, who owned a beach house there, and a few days before her death (in London) from a barbiturate overdose, there had been plans for her to fly over and convalesce on the island, though of course this never came to pass. Garland was the consummate gay icon of the era. Her death resonated in the island's community, just as she herself had predicted. "When I die," she once quipped, according to her daughter Liza Minnelli, another island favorite, "I have visions of fags singing 'Over the Rainbow' and the flag at Fire Island being flown at half-mast." "She was right," remembers the activist, historian and film fanatic Vito Russo. On the day of Garland's funeral, June 27, 1969, flags on Fire Island were lowered in her honor. It even became a campy joke that it was grief for Garland that catalyzed what was happening back in the city that same night, outside the Stonewall Inn in Greenwich Village.

But the loss of an icon and the fight for civil rights were totally different events, overlapping by coincidence but distinct in their implications. The Stonewall Inn had been mafia-owned since 1966. Police raids were not uncommon, but tip-offs paid for by the bar's owners meant that most could be preempted and the bar's patrons warned via flashing lights in the dance floor area. On this particular evening, the patrol wagon was late in arriving to transport arrested patrons, which meant that while people were being hassled and frisked by the police inside the bar, a crowd of those who had been released, along with bystanders, began to form outside. A butch-presenting lesbian woman was dragged violently out of the bar by law enforcement and implored the growing crowd to do something. As the police huddled out inside, now-mythic objects—bricks and rocks, gasoline bombs and burning garbage—were thrown and windows were smashed, in a protest that continued for several days and nights. Perhaps some of the protesters hassled by the police that first night did go to Garland's memorial service earlier in the day. But the ensuing rebellion by a diverse crowd of gay men, lesbians and self-identified drag queens, most famously Marsha P. Johnson and Sylvia Rivera, who today might identify as trans women, ran far deeper. It was about a much older grief, after years of persecution and scrutiny. The events of that night, and the days following, were an expression of solidarity within the community and an act of resistance against the state. That night in 1969, far away from the sleepy, funereal rituals of Fire Island, something radical was happening on the streets, unfurling and extending into the early hours of the next day, and the days and the years and the decades to come.

PART THREE:

HALCYON

(1969–79)

7

Homecoming

THE CHANGES FORGED BY THE EVENTS OUTSIDE STONEWALL
would alter life on Fire Island forever. The freedoms that had
long been developing—bars that offered safe spaces to drink and
dance with kindred spirits, sandy stretches with the potential for
cruising—could now continue without the persistent threat of
police intervention. But while Fire Island's queer culture could
now grow and develop in a manner different than before, this
new era still presented problems, issues that arose outside, within
and between these communities. Both communities came to be
distinguished, in a sense, by their relationship to gender and its
performance. Cherry Grove, being much older and historically
more outrageous, had been associated with a thriving drag and
cross-dressing culture ever since the early Arts Project shows
were first performed in the late 1940s. In the 1970s, this aspect
of Grove life became an established part of the local and annual
traditions that make it distinctive to this day. The Pines, being
the option usually favored by those who didn't want to be outed
by their choice of vacation destination, saw a flourishing of gay
male culture that incorporated a new masculine aesthetic. One
example came to be defined as the "butch clone" look, a term
used interchangeably with "Castro clone," denoting the main

gay thoroughfare of San Francisco. This look would typically feature a toned body and a workmanlike getup, complete with "short cropped hair and a trim moustache, a flannel shirt, and 501 brand jeans."

It has never made sense to speak of Fire Island in absolutes, and the Grove and the Pines were never quite the same trajectory, either in terms of their demographic or their atmosphere. In the postliberation years, they splintered off further through the consolidation of the distinctive cultures, rituals and patriotisms that are the subject of this chapter, island particularities immortalized in the work of some of gay literature's earliest stars, such as Edmund White. Some of those who spent time on Fire Island in this period, like the writer and activist Jack Nichols, or British artist Derek Jarman, sought to glean from it a more rustic, imaginary version, but any such vision would go unrealized. As leisure towns first and foremost, both the Grove and the Pines were already built around commercial infrastructures, and each had a somewhat ambivalent relationship to the gay liberation movement. Instead, it was the local politics of who was allowed in or out, and the political differences between the communities, that became most apparent in the postliberation decade.

A cherished annual event held in Cherry Grove and the Pines every Fourth of July harks back to, and makes light of, one such conflict. And so it was that in the summer of 2019, two years after my first trip to Fire Island, I stepped off a water taxi with my friends Celine and Astrid, a little late, a little sweaty and flustered. We were swept up into the crowd moving along the harbor, and people were congregating around a large double-decker ferry that was stationed at the dock. Red, white and blue confetti wafted through the air above the boat. The passengers were more eye-catching still, a fluorescent vision of pink and purple garbs, towering blond wigs, and the yellow high-vis jackets worn by the stewards, who were welcoming the boat's passengers onto the red carpet laid out on the dock like a cat-

walk. As each queen walked out onto the dock, they were announced by Panzi, the veteran emcee of this event, armed with
a megaphone, in a pink bouffant wig and a flowing rainbow-
striped gown. We made our way closer to the dock and joined
in the cheering that accompanied each new queen, a cheer so
regular that it became instead a continuous hum of applause,
interspersed with whoops.

We had caught a water taxi from Ocean Bay Park, a community four miles west of the Pines by boat, where yachts docked
in the marina displayed sails branded with the Trump 2020 logo.
I tried to imagine, not without some pleasure, what the owners
of those boats would make of this Pines spectacle, filled with
outlandish drag queens and shirtless gays in droves. Is this the
future that liberals want? Draped over the side of the boat was
a tacky but poignant Pride flag, its slogan an adapted version of
the opening words of the preamble of the American Constitu-
tion. "We the People…means everyone," it read—and next to
it was the American flag made up of the colors of the rainbow.
This nautical drag ball was a celebration of the present, a re-
assertion of the inclusive principles that were celebrated in the
city the previous weekend during WorldPride, which marked
the fiftieth anniversary of Stonewall. It was Independence Day
done the Fire Island way, a celebration free from bourgeois heterosexual morality.

But this event is also deeply rooted in the island's history. The
story begins in the summer of 1976, when the Cherry Grove
Arts Project introduced a new fundraising initiative that involved the crowning of one of the community's drag queens as
the Homecoming Queen, who would attend events and pre-
side over the wider Grove community. This playful queering
of the American high-school tradition, which has historically
been a way of inscribing heterosexual adolescent norms (with
the simultaneous election of a Homecoming King), is a classic
Cherry Grove gesture. It is a cherished tradition that contin-

ues to this day, and it is not uncommon now for professional drag queens who are known and loved in the Grove to launch whole Homecoming Queen campaigns at public events and on social media. The ritual became more subversive still in 1994 when, for the first time, the title was given to a woman. Cherry Grove regular Joan Van Ness, who presents as butch in every-day life, dressed up as a drag queen named Queen Scarlet. By re-performing a feminine transformation usually undertaken by gay male "queens," Van Ness "wore the clothes of her op-posite gay gender," argues Esther Newton, and her victory was a "bid for inclusion and visibility within the landscape of gay male symbolic and social power."

Back in 1976, its inaugural year, the Homecoming Queen title was given to Thom Hansen, drag name Panzi, who had been coming out to the Grove since the early '70s. The scene was thus set for the Grove's response to an incident that took place in the Pines some weeks later. Another Grove drag queen, Terri Warren—who a number of Grove community members suggest would now be described as a trans woman—went to John Whyte's Blue Whale restaurant for dinner one evening. Whyte turned her away because her attire was not in keeping with the respectable family-friendly atmosphere he wanted for his establishment. When word of this got around the Grove, a plan was hatched to teach the Pines a lesson. Panzi and a group of Grovers in drag, including Lyn Hutton, who dressed as a man in leather, took a water taxi to the Pines to ambush the harbor and make some noise. On the trip over across the water, the queens—there were at least nine of them, and maybe more—had no idea what to expect. When they arrived, they were greeted with cheers by the onlookers at the Pines harbor, who clearly got the joke, bought them drinks, and treated the Queen with an appropriately royal reception.

With its theatrical bombast, the Fourth of July rebellion was fun at heart, but there was a righteous aspect to the spectacle. It was a rejection of the transphobic respectability politics at play in Whyte's encounter with Teri Warren. Drag queen and Invader Rose Levine named the event the "Invasion," in the spirit of other activist happenings of the 1970s, and it came to symbolize a point of political contention between the communities. Esther Newton suggests various ways to think of the Invasion; for one, as a metaphorical conflict between England—the eccentric, traditional land of the Grove, complete with its own Queen—and America, as embodied by the flashy, competitive energy of the new money Pines. Alternatively, Newton continues, the Grove could be thought of as analogous to "the dowdy immigrant parents of affluent, scornful, and Americanized Pines offspring." Whatever its framing, the Invasion came to symbolize distinctions both aesthetic—ramshackle queens versus the Pines' male beauties; and generational—the Grove's middle-aged and elder queens versus the young Pines upstarts. Passed down through generations, with Panzi always at the helm, the Invasion has become a lighthearted but vital fixture of the Fire Island calendar. By the 1980s, over a thousand people would congregate at the Pines harbor to watch it unfold, and the double-decker ferry had its own security provided by the local police.

Attending the Invasion in 2019, it was hard to miss the number of police officers around, who ticketed people carrying open containers of alcohol on the boardwalk, as well as straight day-trippers, who were not, historically, a welcome presence in a queer enclave whose freedoms were hard-won. The widespread love of drag in contemporary culture, as exemplified by the success of *RuPaul's Drag Race*, would seem to account in some way for the pronounced heterosexual presence at an event like Invasion. But the accessibility and commodification of queer culture is not just a contemporary phenomenon. In Cherry Grove in the 1970s, it was a problem. The late '60s interventions by the Mattachine to drive away the police from the Grove was hotly followed by an influx of ogling and overreaching straights, whose presence threatened to ruin the freedoms and integrity of the community. In the late '70s, a committee held a public meeting on the topic and later created the Ad Hoc Campaign to Save Cherry Grove, which included some of the original Invaders.

Straight people could not simply be turned away, despite efforts to flyer visitors at the ferry dock with questionnaires about why they were there. Although they had before been an antagonistic presence, in the end it was agreed that the police would return to Cherry Grove to curb the ill-effects of the tourist boom. Even gay and lesbian trippers were seen as part of the nuisance. The ad hoc committee's rise to community power did not in the end create an atmosphere of successful gay separatism, or a return to some apocryphal vision of the Grove as it used to be. How had these many visitors, straight and gay, heard about Fire Island in the first place? Cherry Grove previously possessed an infamy that amounted to a conspicuous wink. The Pines had a reputation as a classy, family-friendly spot where gay men could do as they pleased behind closed doors. But in the 1970s both communities were placed firmly on the map. Fire Island would no longer be an open secret, but a place to be.

In the summer of 1965, Shel Silverstein went to Cherry Grove to cover the ways of this "high camp summer resort" for *Playboy* magazine. It was an atypical assignment for Silverstein, who was already by then a beloved children's cartoonist. A lot of the gags in his images predictably punch down at the Grove's eccentric citizens—an old-timer considers going "straight" now that homosexuality is no longer controversial, a drag queen is described as a "gay deceiver"—but in their whimsy, they don't feel a world away from the self-deprecating ethos of this "summer fairyland," even if they were drawn and written by a "straight John," as the copy for the piece put it. In fact, Silverstein wasn't the only beloved Jewish children's author on Fire Island that summer. While he was in Cherry Grove, reports scholar Golan

Y. Moskowitz, Silverstein spoke with Maurice Sendak. Sendak, a gay man, typically summered further west, in the Jewish, family-oriented community of Seaview, where the novelist Herman Wouk had established a synagogue in 1952. He felt safe in Seaview as a Jew and as a gay man not publicly out for most of his life. (Cherry Grove was no longer an incognito choice.) But, Moskowitz argues, the famous orgiastic "Rumpus" sequence of his best-loved book, 1963's *Where the Wild Things Are*, which Sendak began writing on Fire Island, suggest that he was familiar with the sexual freedoms on offer farther down the beach, even if he always returned to the more respectable surroundings of Seaview afterwards.

While the mainstream media caught on to Fire Island more slowly, the burgeoning gay press had already highlighted the pleasures of a place like Cherry Grove. The emergence of a gay press in the late 1960s, in the form of early activist and homophile magazines, was an important way of spreading information and building a national movement. In 1965, *Drum Magazine*, a Philadelphia homophile publication that was known to be racier than its other East Coast counterparts, ran a detailed piece on the gay mecca of Cherry Grove, complete with a photo shoot featuring hunky male models posing against the island's wild landscape. The writer Leo Skir, author of the 1971 gay novel *Boychick*, published a series of Cherry Grove travelogues in 1966 for *Tangents* magazine, another homophile publication, under a nom de plume. He paints a picture of Cherry Grove as both wild and restricted; lavish costume parties would be held in people's extravagantly named houses—one was called MGM (Much Gay Madness)—but men could not dance together in the hotel bar unless women joined them or they were in a group formation, like the Madison or the St. Tropez. Where houses were presided over by "whitehaired men [...] affluent, assured," and "mixing martinis," the hotel dance floor drew a racially mixed crowd of teens and older men alike. But the costs even then could prove prohibitive for creatives and activists. Skir began one travelogue by keeping a diary of the trip's expenses—$2.65 for a one-way train fare (in the hope of "meeting someone with a car to bring me back home,") $0.75 for the taxi to the ferry, and $2.00 for the ferry—but stopped counting when the hotel charged the high season rate of $15.00 (around $125 in today's money), for a shared room.

Two books published in 1968 also introduced readers to life in Cherry Grove. The figure of the straight visitor to Fire Island is used as a comic trope in *Mr. Ladybug* by the pseudonymous Becky Crocker. The novel is structured around the conceit of a straight-laced schoolteacher from the Midwest, who is duped into renting a house in a fictionalized version of the Grove one summer and fails to understand the increasingly risqué things she witnesses there. This novel and Alexander Goodman's introduction to the place, *A Summer on Fire Island*, were part of a quickly proliferating catalog of island life portraits. The Grove also had an outing on-screen in Stan Lopresto's *Sticks and Stones*, which was filmed there during the Fourth of July weekend in 1969, less than a week after Stonewall. The film shows an assemblage of gay and lesbian types—the leather queen, the show queen, the naive first-timer, the butch—attending a Fire Island party. In this curious film, endearing in its ropiness, the characters travel to Cherry Grove from the city via train, car and ferry, exchange barbs and quips in the gay vernacular, and let their hair down, but it hardly feels idyllic. The film opened at Andy Warhol's Garrick Cinema in Greenwich Village in January 1970, some years after Warhol shot his own film in Cherry Grove, 1965's *My Hustler*.

A few days after the Invasion in 2019, I took a protracted amble through Cherry Grove on my way to an engagement in the Pines. That week, I had been working in the archives of journalist and activist Jack Nichols, whose 1976 book *Welcome to Fire Island* provides a detailed tour of the Grove and the Pines communities and their idiosyncrasies. It was a Sunday morning, not quite brunch time yet. Nights before were being slept off. The boardwalks were extremely quiet. A couple of people were going for jogs along the boardwalk or heading to the beach for an early swim. Others were heading back to their houses with bags of groceries. Nichols's descriptions of the Grove from the 1970s were superimposed on what I could see before me. The houses, he wrote, are "wooden, quaint without ostentation [...] sometimes reminiscent of America's past"; some are standing "on stilts ungainly, but determined in a lackadaisical way to remain intact." Naming the houses is a long-standing Grove tradition, reminiscent of British rural dwellings. Some of the house names, like Balmoral, or W. Highland, appear to nod to that. Other names, like Christopher Street, are more obviously gay in theme, in keeping with the Grove's local color. Although the names of the houses often change with the handover of ownership, there is something oddly timeless about the tradition, much like the Grove itself, which has adapted and modernized but doesn't seem all that different, on the surface, from the bucolic spot described by Nichols.

Nichols, who was involved in the Washington chapter of the Mattachine Society and described *Welcome to Fire Island* as an anarchist-inspired book about community politics under the guise of a travelogue, saw a political aspect in the Grove's old-fashioned eccentricities. "To appreciate Cherry Grove," he wrote, "is to know that it is a prototype of what America might yet become: a neighborly community." But for any island community to fulfill its potential as a space for friendlier, alternative living, Nichols argued, it would need to evade the municipal clasp of the town of Brookhaven, whose local government did nothing for these communities but charged them high taxes. Secession from the mainland and absentee landlords, Nichols argued, was not for the purpose of making these communities more private or exclusive, but for returning to their original, ungoverned state and building a new cooperative from the ground up, of the kind espoused in anarchist circles.

Gay communes began cropping up throughout the US in the 1970s, as part of the activist windfall of the post-Stonewall era. The Gay Liberation Front's Men's Collective described these experiments as a natural part of any liberation project, because any "group which calls itself radical and revolutionary must concern itself with providing an alternative way for people to live and work together than the competitive, role-oriented model which heterosexual capitalist society offers us." Many of these communes, like the aptly named Stonewall Colony in Alpine County, California, were based upon visions of mud, free love and living off the land. Like their non-queer counterparts, many of them were ideologically complacent and failed for this same reason, and they were not visible parts of the gay world in the way that urban enclaves and villages were. Larry Mitchell's 1977 cult book, *The Faggots & Their Friends Between Revolutions*, an anarchist fairy-tale-cum-manifesto, is unusual in its focus on communal living as one of the spoils of gay liberation. Illustrated by Ned Asta, the book is inspired by Mitchell's and Asta's experiences at the Lavender Hill commune in Ithaca in upstate New York, where everyday life was defined by non-monogamy and gender-fuck drag.

From Nichols's very first visit to Fire Island in the summer of 1969 with his lover Lige Clarke, another activist and journalist, it was precisely its commune potential he noticed; the "free nature" and the unbridled offer of an idyllic "paradise for lovers." As he got to know the Pines and the Grove better, it was the ad hoc committees, community initiatives and anything-goes reputation of the latter that struck Nichols as exemplary of a new kind of society that might be created there. In reality, Cherry Grove had already become too commercialized for these kinds of pastoral and separatist fantasies to take root. Although many residents were opposed to the commercialization of the town,

signaled by their negative reaction to wildly popular nights at
the Ice Palace bar, feelings of separatism were less a product of
political ideology than protectiveness over the sanctity of this
hideaway. In fact, some of the older generation of Grovers, who
were used to living their double lives in the city and on the island, were decidedly cool towards the movement, which advocated coming out of the closet as a political act. The Grove's
radicalism seemed to be cultural rather than political. Although
the community neglected to join up with the activist cause, it
remained, with its embrace of the lopsided and the zany in their
many forms, truly unlike anywhere else.

That morning, I walked through the middle of the Pines along
Fire Island Boulevard. The houses there are much bigger and
more private, separated from the street by large gates and long
walkways. If the Grove's development in the 1970s saw a dou-
bling down on its eccentricities, the Pines came into its own as
a more luxurious space, where fantasies could be fulfilled and
reenacted. One's body, like one's house, would become a monu-
ment to exceptionalism. As put by the photographer Tom Bianchi, whose sun-kissed Polaroid images of Pines from the 1970s
and '80s are a central feature of gay Fire Island's iconography,
over the years "more and more gay men found gyms and trans-
formed themselves into our sexual fantasies." While the masculine "butch clone" look was popular sartorially, in the Pines it
also mattered what was underneath your clothes: pecs, abs and
whole-body definition.

One of the houses I passed along the boulevard had a banner
with the logo of *Just for Fans*, an adult entertainment site where
users subscribe to the content of their favorite performers. The
use of Fire Island as a setting for contemporary, subscription-
based pornography feels like a natural extension of a much longer
tradition, and the Pines, with its modernist mansions and pool
decks, has been a prime location in particular. The people who

lined up outside the Fifty-Fifth Street Playhouse in Manhattan back in December 1971 for the opening of Wakefield Poole's gay adult film, *Boys in the Sand*, were to see, perhaps for the first time, an otherworldly landscape of untold pleasures. *Boys in the Sand* took its name from Mart Crowley's hit 1968 play about a group of gay men, *The Boys in the Band*, which premiered off-Broadway three years earlier, in a theater three blocks west of the Playhouse.

Unlike the troubled queens of Crowley's chamber drama, the men in Poole's film exhibit no reticence about their sexuality and desires, and the film was hailed by critics as a refusal of the closet. The chic, heady visuals flickering on the screen of the Playhouse that winter represented a brave new world of positivity and sexual freedom. The film belonged to a category that Ryan Powell calls "liberation porn," a mode of gay '70s cinema that was "utopian in that it sought new futures," but also proposed "a continuum of imagination and actualization, offering trial utopias to be experimented with." With a narrative suspended between fantasy and reality, *Boys in the Sand* was a landmark porn film, distinguished by scenes of beach and poolside frolics, interracial sex and a close look at the sleek interior spaces of the Pines' houses. Audiences gay and straight flocked to it, got off to it, in the dead of a New York winter, and in the process learned of a hot summer enclave just miles away. In turn, porn films like this one offered a blueprint for new kinds of sex. In Patricia Nell Warren's best-selling novel *The Front Runner*, about the love affair between Billy, a twenty-year-old college athlete, and his coach, the pair have passionate sex on the Fire Island beach, as if in homage to the "endless gay films featur[ing] love scenes on the beach." "Talk about boys in the sand," Billy jokes, as they are caught by the "swirling foam" of a wave.

Neither the Grove nor the Pines had a monopoly on sex and eroticism. As a 1972 *New York Post* piece by the writer Albert Goldman identified, there was plenty of promiscuity, hetero-

sexual pick-ups and swinging to speak of in other Fire Island
communities like Ocean Beach and Ocean Bay Park. But it is
when "you get out to the gay reaches," Goldman wrote, that
"you really start to feel as if you're living the future"; for there,
unlike the drunk and "screwed-up" straights found elsewhere
on the island, the homosexuals are "healthy, intelligent and on
top of their scene." The Pines, in particular, was a place possessing the "calm" of "people who have made it," successful fashion
designers and creatives who have "rounded on the realization
that life must be ordered and harmonious and benevolent if it
is to be happy." This is a harmony that relies upon "very strict
rules about what you can and cannot do or wear." "People were
free," remembers the fashion journalist André Leon Talley, who
visited and photographed the Pines in the 1970s, but there were
still norms and standards. He and designer Manolo Blahnik were
sartorial outliers in their capes, "anti-Fire Island citizens but
weekend guests." With the right connections, the Pines wasn't
a difficult place to penetrate, but fitting in was another matter.

To whatever extent Fire Island seemed to journalists in the
early 1970s to signal new frontiers of license and liberation, what
Goldman called the "Fag Futuristic," there was also something
paradoxically quaint or old-fashioned about them. No one understood this more perceptively than a young writer from Ohio,
who moved to New York in the 1960s after college, in pursuit
of a boy, and made ends meet by working publishing odd jobs
and writing freelance book reviews. Edmund White first went
to Fire Island in 1965 and vacationed in the Pines for numerous summers after. It was there that he wrote what would become his debut novel, *Forgetting Elena*, which was published in
1973. The novel is narrated by an amnesiac who has woken up
on a mysterious island and must try and reorient himself in its
culture, one characterized by eccentric rituals and a pervasive
sense of propriety. White's novel captures how a community
like the Pines could be baffling for the uninitiated. Although

he was a Fire Island regular for a number of years, he also observed it, like many of the writers who have made it their subject, at a certain literary distance, armed with a similar curiosity he held at the time about the customs of Japanese culture. The "rituals of gay men" on Fire Island, he recalled many years later, "rhymed in my imagination with the rituals of medieval Japan or Versailles," as if the late dinners and dances belonged to some gay courtly realm, new but also old, and obscure to those who didn't know the rules.

In fact, these rituals came into being in the early 1970s, exactly at the time that White was writing the novel. They were structured around the ritual of the tea dance, which added a European resonance to the cosmopolitan court of the island. The tea dance, or *thé dansant*, an amalgam of the Victorian tradition of afternoon tea and dances hosted by French society ladies in colonial Morocco, was a popular export to America in the early decades of the twentieth century. A social event often involving food and refreshments, live music and ballroom dancing, the tea dance was a way for eligible singles to meet and connect on Sunday afternoons at a respectable hour. Tea dances held a particular currency for gay men and lesbians in the postwar years because they offered aboveboard spaces for socializing, even if dancing could only happen between members of the opposite sex. One of Esther Newton's interviewees remembers attending a Sunday afternoon *thé dansant* with other lesbians at Duffy's Hotel, implying that some variation on the gay tea dance had occurred on Fire Island since the 1950s. Other islanders see John Whyte as the originator of this happy hour tradition when he took over the Pines Botel in the mid-1960s. It wasn't until the 1970s, however, that the tea dance became its most unrestrained self, a gay island institution.

The bar attached to the Cherry Grove Beach Hotel had been flailing for a while, and among locals it had earned the name the Boom Boom Room on account of its loud jukebox. (A popular gay bar in Laguna Beach, California, also had this name, first colloquially, and then officially, which suggested the interconnectedness of the national gay bar circuit in these years.) Along with the Grove's Monster Bar and Restaurant, purchased by Joe Scialo in 1969, and the original iteration of the now-iconic gay bar in the Village, the hotel bar became a central spot in Fire Island's own claim to disco history. At the the start of the new decade, it was taken over by disco aficionado Michael Fesco, who renamed this hot and sweaty establishment the Ice Palace, after F. Scott Fitzgerald's short story, and introduced a number of new features to drum up business. One of these was the Sunday tea dance, inspired by the 4:00 p.m. serving of tea and crumpets Fesco had previously witnessed in a London gay bar. On a Sunday afternoon during the 1971 season, he arranged for one of the Grove's drag queens to serve crumpets and tea from a silver service, while the bar's DJ spun records. It was a hit with the islanders, so much so that Fesco remembers competitors in the Pines picking "up on the idea within three or four months." The drinks and dance party known as tea went on to become a central Fire Island ritual, with venues in Provincetown also taking up the tradition. Dinners and cocktail parties would be organized around its numerous sittings. In the Pines, Low Tea would take place on the deck of the Blue Whale from around 4:00 to 8:00 p.m., while High Tea happened from around 8:00 to 10:00 p.m. at the Pavilion, after which people would head to their house or someone else's house for a late dinner. (Some version of this routine is still in place today, seven days a week during the peak season.) In the 1970s, Pines partygoers would head out after dinner, around one, and go dancing at the Sandpiper discotheque until the early hours.

This was a routinized way of life. A summer vacation in the Pines was, for some, anything but. The demanding social calendar allowed, of course, for hungover afternoons on the beach, or spontaneous hookups in the Meat Rack, but even those acts of soaking up sun or having sex were part of a larger program of imbibing. In keeping with the tenor of the post-Stonewall moment, many of the gay men in the Pines in the early 1970s had indeed "come out," and like their debutante ancestors, from whom this phrase was borrowed and repurposed, they were also coming out into a form of high society. And like any high society, it was hierarchical, even feudal, with homeowners at the top and, at the bottom, the houseboys, the cute twentysomethings who were employed to perform household chores but were otherwise free to enjoy the island during the week, when the professionals went back to the city for work.

Of course, there is an alternative way to view this hierarchy, jokes Ethan Mordden in one of his Fire Island stories: "Those who rent are the proletariat, those who own houses are the bourgeoisie, and houseboys form the aristocracy." Looks, as much as land, were a vital currency. In *States of Desire*, his 1980 travel guide to gay America, White wrote that, on the afternoon tea decks of the Botel, the "best-looking men in the city are assembled." Movie stars, models, European royalty are there; "here's my doctor talking to my lawyer." Crucially, the "money represented on the deck, if calculated in terms of dentistry, plastic surgery, gymnasium fees and clothes bills, not to mention the price of renting and maintaining a house, is formidable."

What you made of this "spectacle of gay affluence and gay male beauty" surely depended on your security within it. Populated by advertisers, fashion designers, interior decorators, and other visually minded people, the aesthetic pressures of the Pines seemed to come with the territory. White, who self-identified "as a person of average looks and average income," remembers the particular sense of inferiority it could instill. The Meat Rack, though no less ritualistic, was at least more anonymous, and therefore more democratic. Perhaps this had something to do with its wildness, the wooded, labyrinthine foil to the clean architectural lines of the Pines. Like the dangerous, derelict piers on the West Side of Manhattan, which provided a cruising space that was at least marginally more diverse and democratic than the Greenwich Village bars, the Rack was an arena where no words need be spoken, no money passed over for drinks, nor clothes be worn. The demographic of men cruising there was still made up, in part, of the tea deck's affluent beauties, but the terms of exchange in the bushes were different. One's happiness in the Pines was also a question of attitude. In addition to the gregarious princes and professionals, there were those who merely wanted to stay at home and enjoy the peace and respite the island could afford them. André Leon Talley remembers that "stay-at-homes" was a commonly used term the summer he visited; Calvin Klein was known as one of them. Many of the island's artists were stay-at-homes, not unlike the figure of the painter White identifies in his travel guide, who "lives on the island for the entire summer," peacefully working on his deck and emerging "only for groceries and midnight skirmishes." David Hockney spent a month in the Pines in the summer of 1975 with his friend, the curator Henry Geldzahler, and loved the place. He filled a whole album with photographs of men he captured on the beach. But he still stood out somewhat, walking around, writes Peter Adam, "dressed in white baggy trousers and matching white jacket, looking rather too smart for this place," or at least too covered up.

Not all the visual creators who visited found the Pines pleasing to the eye. The summer before, in the 1974 season, Derek Jarman could both be found wandering at tea and in the dunes. Jarman wrote in his journal that the island's scene had "a deadly, well-heeled monotony," populated by "ad-men and lawyers," "tanned Ambre Solaire, work-out muscles, and faces wrinkled by over-exposure to the December sun-ray lamps," with the tea dance made up of "muscle-bound fantasists." Ever a naturalist, Jarman found greater potential in the Meat Rack and on the beaches, particularly after he was kicked out of the house he was staying in for bringing someone home and playing around with him in the pool. Sleeping rough, Jarman would spend "every night wandering" and observe how "power, privilege, even good looks, certainly money, disappeared in the dark." In the mornings, he would "sit by the sea-shore watching the sun rising," where the "world had a purity that one never encounters in 'civilised' surroundings." His Super 8 film from this visit, simply titled *Fire Island*, bears witness to the landscape's ecological glory.

For artists of a certain temperament, there was an ugliness to the Pines' resolutely manmade beauty, a carnal excess that sat uneasily. One of Edmund White's friends, a young and controversial photographer who split his time on Fire Island between the Pines and Oakleyville—a rustic and secluded cluster of houses a mile west of Cherry Grove, past the Sunken Forest—felt much the same, though he found it hard to resist the lure of the Pines. "If I'm not there I think I'm missing something and when I'm there, I'm not sure it's really what I want," the thirty-two-year-old photographer Robert Mapplethorpe, famous for his explicit images of the male body, told a local Fire Island newspaper. "It's sexually obsessive, and in that situation it's hard for me to think of anything else but that." Sexual obsession was one of Mapplethorpe's subjects, and the appeal of a place like the Pines would seem obvious, although the black-and-white portraits he shot there of friends and peers are more casual and restrained in atmosphere.

Oakleyville, at first glance, has the feel of a remote cul de sac. Mapplethorpe's lover and patron Sam Wagstaff preferred it to the Pines, and eventually bought a house there. Wagstaff, who was twenty-five years Mapplethorpe's senior, spent happy summers with his younger lover photographing one another nude in the sand and among the shrubbery and mixing with Oakleyville's small creative milieu. The art curator Sam Green also lived there, and artists including Peter Hujar, Paul Thek, and John Lennon and Yoko Ono came to work there as studio renters or houseguests. The artistic temperament there was more experimental, whereas the Pines was more mainstream, and Mapplethorpe throughout his career was suspended between these sensibilities, the avant-garde impulse nurtured in private, and the art world celebrity of international renown. So was his friend and former lover Patti Smith, a punk-poet who became a rock star, who visited Oakleyville, where Wagstaff photographed her in the woods in 1973, and the Pines, where Mapplethorpe photographed her on the boardwalk a year later.

Early one July morning in 2019, a few days prior to my Fire Island trip, before heading uptown to the library for research. I went for a coffee in Greenwich Village. When Patti Smith walked into the café ten minutes later, I could barely contain myself. A longtime fan, I knew better, of course, than to disturb someone trying to mind their own business and drink their morning coffee. But the opportunity was too providential to pass up; this was research, I told myself. In 1972, when she was still trying out a career as an actor, Smith starred in an off-Broadway play about a family of misfits on Fire Island. *Island*, Smith told me, a play she hadn't thought about for years, was about a different kind of people from those who frequented Fire Island's more well-to-do and expensive parts. Set in a house somewhere between Cherry Grove and Ocean Beach, farther west than the civilized climes of the Pines, it featured a chaotic family of in-laws, ex-husbands and rebellious teenagers who congregated there for a summer vacation. The play's writer and director, Tony Ingrassia, had cast Smith in her role as a "speed-freak," she remembers, because he thought she was an amphetamine user in real life. She was skinny and often typecast in this kind of role. The play ends, funnily enough, with an invasion on the Fourth of July, when a flotilla of destroyer ships emerges on the horizon of the Atlantic. The Pines Pantry is closed and boarded up, and the revolution is coming. When civilization breaks down,

Fire Island, and a place like Oakleyville in particular, seems an ideal destination in which to forage and try to start again.

But in reality, the island's settlers showed no signs of being ousted. There would be no starting again. Oakleyville was not actually a colony, but a primitive cul-de-sac discovered by art world figures looking for an alternative to the cruising and cocktail party circuit of the city and the Pines, its urbane island counterpart. Scattered across the two main queer communities, as well as their quieter subsidiaries, Oakleyville to the west and Water Island to the east, the dramatis personae of Fire Island in the 1970s is practically dizzying. New people were coming and going all the time: first-timers, emerging artists, drunk day-trippers. Between the postwar veterans and the new cohort of gay-lib baby boomers, there were at least two generations mixing, each with different attitudes towards sex and society. Drag queens mixed with Broadway directors, Long Island locals, activists and straight or sexually fluid members of the jet set. Beneath the sheen of daily tea in the Pines, there was a hidden dance of sensibilities. The slogan I saw that day on a flag at the Invasion, "We the People…means everyone," was a principle that has come to be celebrated in New York and around the world every June, in proud commemoration of what happened at Stonewall. But during that same period, in the years when gay liberation began more fully to unfold, the precise category of Fire Island's "people" was a little harder to agree upon.

Mapplethorpe's Fire Island photographs, like the portrait of Patti Smith in a headscarf on the boardwalk or David Hockney yawning on a pool deck, "not of boredom" but rather "out of excess of life," in his own words, are resonant images of an illustrious era. But there is another more symbolic image, featuring no human subject, that most effectively captures some of the contradictions of the times. It is a simple black-and-white image of an American flag seen in the Pines. Raised high up by a flag pole, the stars only barely conceal the sunlight burning through the fabric, while the stripes resemble waves, with the flag billowing in the wind. Most strikingly, the flag is frayed at its ends, it torn edges outlined against the blank gray sky.

Shot in 1977, exactly two hundred years after the Stars and Stripes became the nation's chosen standard, Mapplethorpe's simply titled *American Flag* speaks most immediately to a country in tatters, reeling from the cumulative effects of the Vietnam War, the Watergate scandal, and an economic downturn. But it could also be read as something more defiant, a broken beauty, a symbol, in fact, of Fire Island itself, and its own ambivalent claim to patriotism. These makeshift municipalities had reached, in the 1970s, what is commonly thought of as their golden age. Even then, you only had to look closer to see that these communities were likewise frayed at the edges. But a sentiment of allegiance survived. The Invasion, with its sending-up of the kinds of exclusion associated with the mainland, takes place, after all, on the Fourth of July, just as the Grove's own version of Homecoming draws upon another kind of Americana. The flags raised above houses in both communities, in hues of rainbow and red, white and blue, signal a belief in what Esther Newton calls gay nationalism. Like Mapplethorpe's flag, tattered and wind-struck, the topsy-turvy queer nation made up by the Grove and the Pines remained defiant and precarious in the face of the fractures, fashions and political flux that threatened to endanger its unique status. And there were yet other stories of unity in this era, special but fragile, still to be told.

8

Loving the Dances

FOR THREE DAYS AT THE END OF JUNE 2019, NEW YORK CAME to its knees in celebration. On the Friday evening of World-Pride and the fiftieth anniversary of the Stonewall riots, the West Village was inundated. I'd rarely seen so many queer people in one neighborhood before. The scene was bathed in dusk, lit up by streetlamps, fairy lights and the glow of phone screens capturing the moment. En route to a night of dancing, we passed the Stonewall Inn, where a crowd of people had congregated. Many of them weren't particularly bothered about getting in—the line extended a whole block—and a street party was unfolding outside the bar. Whitney Houston's "I Wanna Dance with Somebody" rang out from a large speaker. All around us, that intricate intersection where the city's grid system gives way to the mosaic of Christopher Street, Seventh Avenue, West Fourth and Sheridan Square, stages were being constructed and railings put in place. The scaffolding for Pride was being raised, but the party had already started.

Whitney's 1987 hit felt like an apt anthem for the anniversary. Stonewall began with dancing, after all. Even if what was at stake came to feel much bigger in the course of the fifty-plus years since, those events effectively politicized the right to dance with "somebody who loves me," whomever that may be. Claiming the right to dance, an act that stands for a whole host of freedoms, gained greater urgency in the years leading up to June 1969. It is hardly surprising that dancing defined the 1970s, the decade of both gay liberation and disco.

While the tea dance presented Fire Island's own spin on the phenomenon, there were gay dances in the city that were more obviously political in theme. Of course, one didn't have to be expressly political to go to them. When the artist John Button was asked some years after Frank O'Hara died about what the poet would have thought about gay liberation, he replied: "Oh, he would have thought it was silly, but he would have loved the dances!" Button himself had been at many of these dances— he was involved in creating a mural for the venue where they took place, an iconic but short-lived venue in SoHo known as the Firehouse.

The disused firehouse had been taken over in 1971 by the Gay Activists' Alliance (GAA), which was formed by members who broke away from the more antiestablishment Gay Libera- tion Front and advocated for gay civil rights. Every Saturday, weekly dances at the Firehouse were attended by hundreds and sometimes even thousands, who paid two dollars entry for a good time, and helped to keep the organization afloat in the process. The dances were described as a heavenly "cross between Woodstock Nation and Dante's Inferno." Until it burned down in an arson attack in 1974, the Firehouse had provided a sense of balance, a symbiosis between politics and pleasure—it was a community center by day and a discotheque by night. The apocryphal spirit of Emma Goldman, the oft-misquoted anar- chist of the early twentieth century, seemed alive and well: "If I can't dance, it's not my revolution."

In the Pines, it would still be some years before the ethos of the political dance took hold, at a legendary 1979 beach party held to raise funds for a new fire truck. That party would seem,

in many respects, to be a climax of the hedonistic and liberatory decade that had come before. But on the island, political
involvement and the pleasures of the dance floor did not go naturally hand in hand in the intervening years. The island's dancing establishments were essential spots in the history of disco. As
Tim Lawrence shows, elements of disco culture were arguably
born out of the rivalries between the Ice Palace in the Grove
and the Botel and the Sandpiper in the Pines, a one-story, driftwood building on the harbor that functioned as a restaurant in
the early evening and a discotheque by night, flooded with up
to six hundred dancers on weekends. The model-turned-disk-
jockey Tom Moulton innovated the form of the extended mix
and the mixtape in the summer of 1972 when, sick of hearing
DJs botch the transitions between two-minute songs, he put together a tape of nonstop music and handed it to the owners of
the Sandpiper. Other places began to follow suit.

The island's discotheques were vibrant churches of music and
movement, and with the advent of Moulton's mixes and their
imitations, the early-1970s vogue for funk and soul—he remembers seeing "all these white people dancing to black music"
during his visit to the island—gave way to that elongated and
danceable mode we know as disco. But although they attracted
dancers gay and straight to the island in droves, these summer
parties offered something harder to reach, literally and metaphorically, than the GAA's community dances back in the city.
At the Firehouse, prominent members of many of the era's activist groups could regularly be seen, including Johnson and Rivera, who had set up their own activist organization, the Street
Transvestite Action Revolutionaries (STAR). The Fire Island
discos were commercial enterprises that served the needs, desires and newfound freedoms of a community, but they were
not exactly hotbeds of radicalism.

Someone who understood this intimately was Andrew Holleran, real name Eric Garber, whose eulogy for the era's dance

floors, 1978's *Dancer from the Dance*, is still for many the island's gospel—the "Great Pines Novel." Born and raised in Florida and a graduate of Harvard, Holleran moved to New York in 1971 after short stints in the army, at law school in Philadelphia, and at the Iowa Writer's Workshop. Like many of the gay men who moved to the city in the late 1960s and 1970s, what he found there was a place of unprecedented freedom: a mecca of sex and drugs, dancing and socializing. He spent a number of years in the city temping while he wrote fiction on the side. In fact, being a gay man on the scene in this era was a vocation in itself. The "body [...] the thing that had not seemed important at Harvard," had now become "crucial"; while at college he would have been pondering over a Henry James novel, now he found himself "wondering how to combine brewers' yeast with my morning milkshake because I needed the extra protein for the body-building I was doing at the gym."

It was around 1972 that Holleran first went to Fire Island. During his first two summers there, he worked for a bus company that operated a service from midtown Manhattan to the Sayville ferry dock, trips made notoriously boozy by excitable islanders eager to reach the licentious shore. Working this job allowed Holleran to stay with other workers in the Pines property known as the Bus House. There he made close friends and learned the ways of gay life. The house apparently once bore a mocking sign that said something like "Fire Island Academy of the Arts," a satirical nod to the fact that it was usually the body, not the intellect, that won out there. Fire Island hardly lacked an intellectual culture. In the late 1950s, when James Purdy's cult novel *Malcolm* was published, one islander remembers how men "bronzed on the beach as they read the novel [...] in order to be prepared for the discussion that would invariably dominate conversation at that evening's social gatherings." But for all the literary and theater queens in attendance, it was not chic to overintellectualize in 1970s Pines society. As Ethan Mordden's narrator writes, in a story featuring a thinly fictionalized depiction of Holleran, his friend, on Fire Island, the "beguiling but often irrelevant data of talent and intelligence that can seem enticing in the city are internal contradictions in a place without an opera house or a library."

Naturally, amid the dances and the dinner parties, the afternoons drying out on the beach and the dropping of pills at twilight, there wasn't much time left for politics either. As the narrator puts it at the end of Holleran's novel, recalling a gay liberation march in Central Park at which he recognized no more than "four or five faces" from that "sea of humanity," many gay men were "at the beach, darling; they couldn't be bothered to come in and make a political statement." The statements to be made on the island were quite consuming enough, it seemed. It was there that one cruised and camped and went on show at tea and along the beach, in the hope of attracting the gazes of known and unknown faces; four or five, perhaps, or maybe many more.

There was also a trend for gay men's erotic lives to relate, even in small ways, to their activism; the tearing down of boundaries and ripping up of rulebooks. There would be extensive foot traffic in any given Pines house-share: renters, their friends or houseguests, and the more transient visitors encountered on the dance floor or the boardwalk, who were swiftly ushered into the bedroom. For the more populated houses, where privacy was at a premium, the Meat Rack provided not only an alfresco frisson, but a practical public alternative for consummating the stirred-up desires of brief encounters. In some houses, everyone was in on the action anyway. The underrated 1973 film *A Very Natural Thing* shows a young gay couple who venture to Fire Island for the weekend and have an orgy with their housemates on the living room floor. One of them is into it, the other less so; casual group sex doesn't match his idea of a committed relationship.

There were plenty of monogamous couples treading the

boards of the island's gay scene. But as queer sexuality emerged from the shadow of repression and traditional models of kinship, confining yourself to one partner was not the order of the day in the sex-positive '70s. The city had ample orgiastic possibilities, not least in the basement darkrooms of its bars and clubs, and Fire Island was particularly synonymous with sexual license and multitudes, whether in the wild terrain of the Meat Rack or in some grand modernist home overlooking the ocean. Casual sex and nameless sex, sex "good" and "bad"; these were part and parcel of liberation's bounty. Perhaps nowhere else on earth quite offered so many sexual opportunities in such a concentrated space, flanked by the boundlessness of the Atlantic.

There were, as the saying goes, so many men, so little time. Time itself signalled trouble in paradise. Each year the seasons would change and the island would wind down for another year, a welcome relief after months spent in its pressure-cooker environment. But each year one also got older. Was there an expiration date to the dream of limitless sex and intimacy, the conviction that casual encounters were not meaningless, or rather, that they needn't be meaningful by traditional (straight) standards? Would promiscuity mean the same thing at age fifty, or forty, as it did at thirty? And at what age does one become a doomed queen—that old gay trope—the love-starved solitary who hides his loneliness behind camp humor? Aging in—or, in fact, out of—a community driven by youth, beauty and availability could be difficult for the men who tried to keep up. Even the beauties who spent the spring months in the gym in readiness for the island season could be sick with worry, like Holleran's suicidal character, Frank Post. To be sexually liberated on Fire Island was no plain sailing.

Think of a dancing ocean of chiseled men; bobbing, swishing, punching the air; an atmosphere close with the heat of bodies, leavened by a breeze off the ocean, and you can begin to feel the force of Holleran's central metaphor, a pastiche of a line from Yeats. How can we know the "dancer" from the "dance," the one from the many? Or, indeed, the One. Disco extricated dancers from the need for a partner or a fixed formation. To dance in a discotheque was to be suspended within the collective, a space of diffuse romantic possibility, where the line formation of the Hully Gully had become all but obsolete for the erotically minded. The formality of aboveboard group dances had been replaced by a mode of movement whose relationship to sex was much more explicit. In the search for a partner on the dance floor, some form of physical intimacy, however transient, was guaranteed. As Donna Summer sings to her dance partner on the 1978 hit "Last Dance," a connection on the dance floor is a momentary truce; it needn't mean that "you're the one for me." And yet, it was a search that could easily beget exhaustion. Love and liberation seem not like bedfellows but anxious antagonists in the eyes of the doomed queens who populate *Dancer from the Dance*. And there was surely no better soundtrack for this mood than disco music, which so expertly blends euphoria with hidden melancholy. The men in Holleran's story dance to disco as if their lives depend on it, like a form of worship scented not with incense but the early-hours tang of sweat and poppers. At a climactic party on Fire Island, when the DJ plays a lovelorn funk hit hazily remembered from their disco youth in the earlier years of the decade, it viscerally evokes, in the way that only songs can, the time that has passed and the time they have lost.

By the time Holleran left New York to visit his family in Florida, where he got the idea to write his tale of men jaded by years of bed-hopping and drug-popping, disco was itself beginning to wane. The genre was now yielding a diluted product, lighter and samey, in the ears of the purists, a category that included the men who had been dancing on Fire Island for the better part of the decade. Holleran was one of them. In an essay published the same year as his novel, he lamented the sudden vanishing of original disco numbers, those "songs that went inside you" and "spoke of things in a voice partly melancholic, partly bemused by life, and wholly sexual." As the genre became ubiquitous, and began to sound different, the music slowly ceased to be the collective libidinal lifeline it had once been. Even its association with darker moods, as in 1977's angry-young-man drama *Saturday Night Fever*, starring a young John Travolta and soundtracked by the Bee Gees, served only to hasten the genre's commercialization while erasing its Black and queer roots. This was one of the nerves that Holleran's novel struck: the sense of a decade and a world beginning to unravel. Among the cerebral, well-bred Ivy League men who had made their lives in this milieu, there were those who wondered if its pleasures, which had sustained them in their sentimental educations, were in fact an illusion, likely to disappear at the sight of a buck and a larger culture newly eager to consume what had once seemed like theirs alone.

But as the Village People sang in their sunny disco tribute, "Fire Island," it was still a place of free love, a place where you might meet the men of your "wildest fantasies." (In a knowing aside in the song's bridge, they also warn: "don't go in the bushes.") Whether you were on the island for a season, a weekend, or just a day, you were promised a kind of fun you couldn't have in many other places. Whatever your poison— uppers, downers, or simply an ice-cold glass of rosé—the island's delis, dance clubs and dealers had you covered. Recreational drugs were already a part of the gay scene in the 1960s, but in the 1970s, drug use on Fire Island was amplified. A typical night might begin with several bumps of cocaine at the club, before taking a quaalude to mellow out the rest of the night and remain in the hypnotic, sensual state promised by the dance floor. Ecstasy pills were also popular. Amyl nitrate, or poppers, and weed were so ubiquitous as to seem prosaic. Overdoses and accidents were not irregular, a morbid feature of life on the island, a place that could swallow you up if you weren't careful. The narrator of Holleran's novel recalls details like the "summer some nameless ribbon clerk died trying to sniff a popper at the bottom of a pool." Fire Island was indeed known "among certain crowds as Dangerous Island," dangerous because "you could lose your heart, your reputation, your contact lenses." But for the most part, a stay on Fire Island was, to quote the Village People once more, a "funky funky weekend." If you were young and attractive and had money to spend, even more so.

Clothes and drugs came in and out of fashion each year. As Eric Laurence and Richard Danvers put it in a piece for *Christopher Street* magazine, "a bathing suit and a pair of rubber clogs" were all the clothes one needed as a day outfit. More variety was found among clothes on show at evening events; you might see "black tie seated next to denim, and/or leather chaps rubbing against bar legs." In the 1979 season, they continue, "blue denim pants were interspersed with painter's pants of turquoise and lemon yellow; white athletic shirts yielded gradually to day-glow green and magenta." Theme parties were the other places to dance and dress up for, to cruise and be seen. Sometimes unfolding over whole days and nights on the pool decks of ornate beach houses, these were classier affairs than the eccentric costume parties that had been held in Cherry Grove for decades, but they were no less lively. They were a crucial part of the social season, and grew more ambitious and large-scale as the decade wore on.

Some of the decade's hottest disco records were first spun at these parties by in-demand DJs who were either resident in the community or hired from the city. Particular Pines houses had reputations in the late 1970s for their high-concept costume parties. A jungle-themed "Hot Safari" party came with life-size images of jungle animals arranged in the garden. Another Broadway and movie-themed party, remembers Pines resident Ron Martin, welcomed "six muscular men in white linen loincloths carrying a rolled carpet above their head," which they swiftly unfurled to present "a resplendent drag-version Cleopatra."

In the summer of 1978, the Sunrise party was held at a distinctively designed house whose front facade was in the shape of a television, complete with a huge square glass window. As an early iteration of what would become a Pines fixture, the improvised dance floor on the sand and the gauze canopy seem now a little lo-fi. Ultimately, these events were precursors to a party that defined not only the decade, but the community, which had gone from being a mixed gay and straight community in the early 1970s to a place where gay men were the predominant population and held political and cultural sway. This event, a victory for collaboration and cohesion, was a first for the Pines. And it would not be the last dance of its kind.

Being in effect a hamlet, with provisions and services in miniature, the Pines had only a small, volunteer-run fire department. True to its name, fires are not uncommon on the island due to a combination of factors, including vicious winds and the precarious timber construction of the oceanfront. Numerous establishments on the island have burned down in suspected arson attacks, like Duffy's in Cherry Grove in 1956, but a similar number have been razed by freakish accidents and spontaneous fires. It was evident in the late 1970s that the Pines needed a new fire truck, but it lacked the funds to buy one. When the idea for an all-night fundraising party came up at a department meeting in the summer of 1978, plans quickly developed, and the mostly straight members of the fire department began to collaborate with the gay men who had already developed quite a reputation for throwing elaborate summer bashes.

The party, simply named "Beach", was scheduled for the following summer. It was an ambitious event, ten months in the making, and required an unprecedented level of trust and collaboration from different parts of the community. Longtime

Pines resident and "Beach" co-organizer Ron Martin, who began serving on the Fire Island Property Owners' Association in 1978, the youngest gay man on a mostly straight board, remembers the divisions that needed addressing, or at least papering over, if the party was to be a success. The relations between gay and straight residents were the community's most obvious fissure, but as in the Grove, there were also concerns about the influx of day-trippers who came to enjoy the tea dance and other island rituals, something that even led owner John Whyte to cancel tea at the Blue Whale for several years.

A related issue was noise. Over the course of the 1970s, the Pines had effectively become an epicenter of disco music. The ability to dance until late to loud music was one of the community's defining cultural characteristics, but this didn't stop older homeowners and some members of the Property Owners' Association from launching an anti-noise campaign, or at least trying to educate revelers on what constituted considerate amounts of noise. Nightlife establishments like the Sandpiper were targeted. Divisions grew. The Fire Island Pines Businessmen's Association held an anti-anti-noise rally in September 1977 and made the point that if "people can't dance at the Sandpiper or the Botel, they are going to attempt to play disco and party music at home," leading to more noise. With the culture of elaborate house parties, this tendency was of course already in full swing. The real issue was where such in-fighting and sensitivity to noise would lead. "One thing leads to another," read a poster advertising the rally. "Who knows what other parts of our care-free lifestyle are in danger of attack?" That the 1979 extravaganza went ahead without opposition from the anti-noise contingents is testament to the diplomacy of its organizers, and the wise preemptive decisions, Martin remembers, to stage it at the easternmost part of the Pines beach, where the dunes would muffle some of the noise, and to limit the number of tickets to three thousand, sold only within the community.

The right to dance had once again become political. Like the ongoing battles in cities over noise complaints and protected status of nightlife cultures, the tension around noise levels in the Pines was a matter of values. The aim to raise money for the fire truck was a cause that spoke widely to the whole community, and though it was attended by movers and shakers of numerous persuasions, in execution, the beach party was truly a victory for the gay disco contingent. Paying $20 for a ticket to what promised to be the party of the year was the kind of political gesture that everyone, even those gay men less endeared to the presence of activist causes during their summer vacations, could get behind. Some younger gay men were equally at home on the frontlines of a march and the fringes of the Pines, frustrated by the political indolence of the moneyed homeowners and older men, as well those, of a similar age, who were left cold by the day's dominant causes.

In his 1980 novel *The Confessions of Danny Slocum*, the writer George Whitmore observed how activists behaved off duty on Fire Island. The narrator spots one of his political friends one night on the Sandpiper dance floor, shorn of his usual activist getup, and wearing "lemon-colored painter's pants and a shocking-pink athletic shirt, a plastic belt and blue suede dancing shoes." This admittedly horrific-sounding outfit illustrates how strange it was to see the man "consorting so enthusiastically with the very milieu he's always seemed to resent so—as exemplifying all the ills of gay life: ingrown, artificial, hedonistic, uncharitable, moneyed." Whitmore also pokes fun at the apoliticism of the Pines in his 1980 play *The Rights*, set on the deck of a Fire Island beach house one August. Larry, a classically doomed queen in his late forties, arrives at the holiday home of his ex-boyfriend, who is now a successful screenwriter and has a handsome younger boyfriend named Buddy, who lives off Paul's wealth and is completely unmoved by gay politics. In Terry Miller's *Pines 79*, another Fire Island play staged in New York the year after Whitmore's, men in their midtwenties and early thirties are no less damning about the bore of political engagement, and describe an *Advocate* fundraising party in the Pines as a "seminar" and "all a bunch of nonsense." "Most people would be better off taking a course in irresponsibility," one quips.

Felice Picano, another of the Violet Quill writers, remembers the island in the 1970s, when he was in his thirties, as a more charitable place. "No matter how 'out' you were among family and at work," Picano recalls of his immediate social circle, "we were staunchly supportive of gay rights and gay politics. Benefits for various gay causes were hosted at the Pines every other summer weekend, considered chic, and well attended." Perhaps this was the ultimate Pines formula—give back, but make it fashion. It is a hallmark of a given social class and milieu that fundraising takes place in the form of benefit galas, the kinds of events to which guests are drawn by factors beyond mere altruism, even if the outcome is ultimately the same. These events were different in style from the fundraising dances at the GAA Firehouse, but not in essence. "Beach", which was raising money for the fire truck, and thus was a different kind of firehouse party, was a successful composite of local positive, grassroots collaboration, and unbridled glamour, which was provided as much by the musical guests and aesthetic arrangements as by the natural beauty of the setting.

Not since the urban gay subcultures of the 1920s had there been a space for the queer community to move communally together, in a public sphere within a public sphere, and with such style. The '70s dance floor seemed to offer something hopeful and novel. This spirit of possibility was there at the start of the decade, in 1971, when Marvin Gaye's antiwar soul anthem "What's Going On" was the song of the summer, the same year that the New York law prohibiting same-sex dancing was relaxed. Dancers in the Sandpiper "began to feel comfortable dancing in one another's arms," and hugged and swayed to "the warmth of the music, the romantic sounds," as one Pines-goer remembers it. And it was there too at the end of the decade, this time not in the Sandpiper but in the sand itself, at the party to end all parties, a celebration of Fire Island's primary ritual of togetherness on an unprecedented scale.

Picture a beach at midnight. Colored mosquito nets, red, white and blue in the moonlight, draped over large tent poles in the form of eight scattered pavilions, are gently billowing in the wind. Archive images of the Pines are being projected onto a screen. Fine cheese, charcuterie and cookies are being served at various stands. Wine and champagne, and perhaps additional forms of chemical encouragement, are on offer. Artworks are being auctioned in one tent. In another, there is a casino, where people are playing blackjack and roulette. Calvin Klein is in line for entry. There are so many people, dressed, or rather un-dressed, to the nines. An exposed and toned abdomen is the chosen outfit for men tonight.

Just outside, people are congregating by the snow fence to get a vicarious slice of the action. They may not be inside, but they will be close enough to hear the sound emanating from the party's centerpiece, a makeshift wooden dance floor that has just opened. It is thrumming with activity, flanked on all sides by enormous speakers. The crowd anticipates the next act to come on stage, their eager faces illuminated by light tow-ers surrounding them. The stage is elevated above the dancers, equipped with a robust DJ booth. The entertainment is about to begin. Over the course of the night, three of New York's best-known DJs on the gay scene, fixtures on the island and in the city, will spin records together. Breakout stars, like the sixteen-year-old French-Canadian singer France Joli, whose single "Come to Me" will become a huge hit in New York in the weeks following the party, share the bill with bigger disco stars, like The Ritchie Family, who fill the headline slot at

3:00 a.m., and Bonnie Pointer, who follows at 5:00 a.m., when the party shows no signs of abating. There was once a dream of getting Donna Summer, Queen of Disco, as the headline act, but scheduling conflicts meant that it was not to be.

In the makeshift casino-cum-piano-bar, you encounter a handsome man tinkling on the keys, smartly dressed and curly-haired, with deep brown eyes and a striking face, the image of a crooner with notes of feyness. It is Paul Jabara, the Lebanese-American singer, songwriter, actor, island regular and key figure in disco history. In 1978 he won an Oscar and a Grammy for his song "Last Dance," which Summer performed in the endearingly naff 1978 disco film *Thank God It's Friday*. That same year he released his own record, whose track list included an eleven-minute song about Fire Island life called "Pleasure Island," which builds from tropical, languorous verses to a futuristic and ecstatic end section, complete with male moans of pleasure. Unlike Auden's poem of the same name, published exactly thirty years previously, this out-and-out ode celebrates the island's licentiousness, its status as a carnal paradise where "no one cares about your vice"; where you can "find just what you need / no matter who or what you are." Surrounding Jabara that night were thousands of people putting that principle joyfully into practice.

To imagine entry to "Beach" today is to engage some private fantasy of the best night of your life, organized around a configuration and a culture now irrecoverable. The real thing was a resounding success, a product of the hard work and diplomacy of numerous parties. On July 8, 1979, the stars aligned and the tide stayed out. There were men and women, gay and straight people, old-timers and newcomers; people from the Pines and from the Grove. If hedonism had proved a dividing line between factions and communities, it was through some perfect and miraculous iteration of the wild ways of the decade that provided some harmony, if only for one night. That the party felt era-defining is not merely an invention of the historical gaze. Its dancers knew that a special epoch of new freedoms, sparked by riots that took place just ten summers earlier, was being toasted. Such a simple fact about parties—that they are, in their excesses, a way of marking time: blowout as climax. To the people there that night, "Beach" was not the end point of a culture that had exhausted itself, like the morbid and sometimes surreal climactic parties we find in fiction. Holleran's *Dancer*, for example, ends with a climactic pink-and-green-themed party at a Pines beach house, a lavish and literary signal of an era coming to end. Characters skulk at the fringes of this glamorous spectacle with an "odd sensation of death" as they look at all the old faces, struck by the realization that they "had all been new faces once." At the end of this party, both of the novel's main characters will be dead or missing. Like Fitzgerald's Gatsby, their demises also signal to those around them the end of an era.

The larger atmosphere of "Beach" in 1979 was not one of morbidity, like the party in *Dancer*, but unprecedented festivity. False utopias are all too easily made out of the calm that precedes a storm, and although the world that hung gloriously in the balance that night was not a perfect communal dream, there were still many aspects worth celebrating. For one, the party offered an implicit reprieve from the Anita Bryants of the world, and the backlash against gay liberation that fomented throughout the country at this time. But it was also an anathema to the larger cultural backlash against disco that had taken hold. Debates raged among gay leftists about whether the musical form was consumerist and heteronormative. And the increasingly racist and homophobic prevalence of the slogan "Disco Sucks" was gaining momentum in the wider culture. The infamous Disco Demolition Night, a promotional theme launched at a baseball game in Chicago just four days after Beach, on July 12, 1979, saw a stunt where a crate of disco records was blown up live on the field.

In the Pines, more fun-loving fires were burning. No one at that party could have predicted what awaited them in the next decade. That many of those in attendance would be gone just ten years later would have seemed unthinkable. For that reason, it resonates today as a singular moment in time, a tipping point. "Our freewheeling lifestyles would slowly turn somber," Martin remembers, "and our hedonism on Fire Island would dissipate as we struggled valiantly but unsuccessfully to keep each other alive." But for now, or then, on that night as it turned into morning, proceedings were governed by the jubilant ethos of disco, by songs like "The Main Event," the Jabara-written Barbra Streisand hit that played as the sun came up after a night of revelry. "I gotta celebrate!" Streisand shouts, in that inimitable, theatrical voice, and "thank my lucky stars above." Love, indeed, was the main event. That summer, it was the hottest ticket in town. You had to be there.

PART FOUR:

PLAGUE

(1981–2021)

9

Until Dawn

JUNE 30, 2019, WAS NO ORDINARY SUNDAY MORNING. I STEPPED out of the apartment-share I was renting near Union Square onto Sixth Avenue and joined the crowd moving north. The morning was warm, the scene charged and vibrant. Everywhere you looked were flags and signs about various issues: Palestine, police brutality, transphobia, ICE detention, sex workers' rights. This was a very different march from the one traveling south down Fifth, just a block away, with its corporate-sponsored floats and garish shows of rainbow capitalism. Retracing the route of the original Pride of 1970, then called the Christopher Street Liberation Day March, the 2019 Queer Liberation March was organized by the Reclaim Pride Coalition, with the aim of resisting the corporatization and depoliticization of the annual festivities and returning to Pride's more radical roots. There would be no police or corporate floats. At Twenty-Third Street, a swath of the marching crowd came to a halt and dropped to the floor, playing dead. This die-in, a peaceful but potent protest method, was a ritualized expression of solidarity with the queer fallen. As with any everyday New York spectacle, this tableau attracted a mixed crowd: confused tourists looking on with impassive faces; kids asking their solemn parents what was going on; a guy on a bike cycling past and shouting something incomprehensible. But this arrangement of fake-dead bodies was hardly everyday. I had never heard such silence in Manhattan before.

The march continued up to Central Park, where a huge crowd gathered on the Great Lawn to hear an address by a speaker whose name alone lent this honoring of the dead a particular context. Larry Kramer, an icon of AIDS activism, now age eighty-four, took to the stage in his wheelchair. It was one of his final public appearances before his death just under a year later. "What does Pride mean to you?" he asked the forty-five thousand people congregated there. "I'll tell you what it means to me." Kramer, who was HIV-positive, recalled that he "almost died, three times," and "started a couple of organizations to fight with me against this plague." In reflecting on his activism as a founding member of Gay Men's Health Crisis and, later, ACT UP (AIDS Coalition to Unleash Power), both of which were formed in the 1980s at the height of the epidemic, Kramer spoke to his 2019 audience with a clear and galvanizing message. His speech was structured around the acknowledgment that we, and he, had somehow "failed," had "lost the fight against AIDS." There was, and is, still "no cure for this plague"; PrEP, a preventative HIV medication, has made us "complacent," and treatments are still "woefully expensive."

But the real failure, Kramer said, was one of political inactivity among younger generations, who appear to be spurning their "duty of opposition." "Most gay people I see appear to have too much time on their hands," Kramer announced. "Hell, if you have time to get hooked on drugs, and do your endless rounds of sex-seeking cyber searching until dawn, you do have too much time on your hands. We are better than that. I repeat, we are better than that." This moment was met with cheers from the audience, but it will hardly have endeared everyone present to Kramer's message, least of all those who dance, take drugs and "go on apps to find more sex," who were told, "These are useful lives being wasted."

Later that day, walking back to the apartment across Fourteenth Street, I stopped at Fifth Avenue and waited to cross at the intersection, which was being patrolled by wardens. The Pride parade was still going on, though the crowds had dissipated and the residual vibe was now on the cusp of day-drunk and night-ready, geared towards the parties that were heating up downtown. As I waited to cross Fifth Avenue, the Grindr float went by. The men on board, dancing to music from a boom box, cooled themselves with paper fans that displayed the app's distinctive yellow-and-black branding. I thought again of Kramer's excoriation of dating apps and sexual "cyber searching," which seemed to him a particularly egregious aspect of contemporary gay culture. The reason I was in New York in the first place was to work on a PhD thesis about what seemed to me to be "cruising proper," in the years before Grindr's virtualized sexual life. But that didn't mean I didn't still use it myself, even if I found it easier to meet people "IRL" in New York than I had in London. Like many users of these apps, I felt peculiarly doubleminded about what it meant. Kramer's point, that our collective absorption by screens could lead us further towards disinterest and political impassivity, didn't feel like an entirely new question. His lament seemed less about the loss of cruising's democratic potential because of technology than a problem he had with the act of sexual searching itself. Hadn't there long been a tension between cruising and organizing, politics and pleasure?

Kramer's choice of words in his identification of a party and cruising culture that raged "until dawn" seemed to me telling. Fire Island's 'til sunrise lifestyle is, after all, a paradigm of that culture, and it was during one of his first trips there in the early 1970s that Kramer began planning this critique, which ultimately took the form of an infamous novel that would render him a Pines pariah. A Yale graduate and Oscar-nominated screenwriter, thirty-nine-year-old Kramer settled in New York, after almost a decade in London, and was ostensibly a card-carrying member of the city's hedonistic, middle-class gay scene. This was the world that would be his subject. In the early stages of the writing process, he wrote to a friend about the island's contradictions. This place, which should be among the freest in the world, seemed to him anything but, structured around archaic rules, restrictions and expectations.

What were the chains that shackled the gay men summering there? *Faggots*, the book that resulted from Kramer's Fire Island years, published in 1978, sought answers. This sprawling, restless satire depicts the romantic plight of Fred Lemish, Kramer's surrogate, who struggles to find love while navigating what he sees as the sex-crazed milieu of urban gay life. The novel ends with an extended sequence set on Fire Island on Memorial Day weekend, complete with a farcically framed sequence of fucking, fisting and father-son wrestling in the Meat Rack. There's a moment where Fred defecates in the back garden of a beach house, a visceral analogy for his decision to purge himself of the Fire Island lifestyle and choose love over lust. Still, even as Kramer came to the decision, through his character, to leave behind the island, and seemed to operate throughout the writing of the book as a novelist-cum-double-agent, he wasn't completely immune to the charms and chains of the place. "I was living with all the Fire Island clones and was participating in that life and struggling to stay thin and go to the gym every day and find love," he remembers. Even as he was writing, he continued to participate in its seasonal lifestyle, including a winter Caribbean cruise organized by the Islanders Club, the private members organization that ran the summer bus services between Sayville and Manhattan. In a newspaper interview he gave with playwright Robert Chesley when the book was published, Kramer conceded that "It's very, very hard to give up the life." Or, to put it another way, "It's hard to walk away from a good blow job."

Kramer had put in the hours in the gay ghetto, he had done the deeds and the drugs, and his message seemed to be that gay men ought to choose the virtuous art of abstention—which for him represented a form of self-love—over the self-destructive habits of promiscuity and drug-taking. But it was no surprise that, less than a decade after the radical loosening of the moral noose, other gay men didn't take well to being told that their bountiful expression of sexual freedom was, in fact, a manifestation of inner shame, and needed to be kept in check. Particularly those gay men who were only thinly fictionalized in the book, and evidently recognizable from what was still a small scene. When a British house floated the idea of publishing an edition of *Faggots*, its editors sought legal advice about whether the novel could make it past the UK's stringent obscenity laws. The lawyer who read the manuscript advised that it would likely be fine, for the gay sexual practices in the novel were depicted in such a damning way that there was no risk of readers being beguiled by the lifestyle—in fact, the novel would act as a deterrent.

Kramer wasn't the only one on Fire Island stirring controversy in this era. It was also a time of heightened awareness around questions of representation. When the film director William Friedkin, who previously adapted Crowley's play *The Boys in the Band* for the screen, announced in 1979 that he was making a film called *Cruising*, based on a novel about a series of real-life murders of gay men in and around bars in Greenwich Village, it caused uproar in the gay community. The journalist Arthur Bell, who had earlier covered this string of murders, wrote in the *Village Voice* that Friedkin's film, starring Al Pacino as a heterosexual detective who goes undercover in the S and M gay world to investigate, would serve only homophobic purposes, by painting gay life as dark and wanton. He encouraged gay readers to boycott the film and hassle its director if they chanced upon the production shooting in the city. Bell had seen Friedkin give a talk in which he mentioned his experience of going to the Meat Rack as research for his adaptation of *The Boys in the Band*, where "200 or 300 guys in a daisy-chain" were "balling each other in the ass," and running a mile as soon as a guy approached him. What business did a heterosexual man with this familiar, age-old homosexual dread have making a thriller about New York's gay sexual culture, other than to make money? But more than this, what effect would such a representation, which would be seen by perhaps millions of moviegoers, have on the lived experience of the demographic it depicted? On Fire Island, protesters handed out flyers that simply read, "*Cruising*—the movie that kills."

Around the same time, in 1979, Felice Picano published his novel *The Lure*, which depicts an ostensibly straight male detective who goes undercover in the gay world. The novel sold well and garnered positive reviews in the gay press, no doubt because its inversion of the trope of the closeted double life, reworked into a thriller plot, was self-conscious and deliberate; and because it was written by a member of the community it sought to depict. Referring to a scene in which the detective visits the Pines, initially horrified and overwhelmed by its drug-fueled, orgiastic economy, in which sex is the greatest currency, Picano said in an interview that he wanted to explore the perspective of a character who saw Fire Island very differently from him, who was "ignorant of the gay world" and saw the island "from one particular view…that is, as somebody who's frustrated, confused and unsure." In the same interview, he also spoke to the heightened sensitivity of the contemporary gay culture. "The gay critics are claiming everything that's being done by gay writers is now, in one way or another, sensational […] *Dancer from the Dance* is sensational because it overromanticizes everything. And *Faggots* because it overcriticizes everything."

"I hope the gay community won't lose its sense of humour about this book," wrote Edward Albee for one of the first blurb quotes for *Faggots*, though if you had looked around at the time in the pages of gay newspapers, and at dinner parties on Fire Island, you'd have seen that few in the community seemed to be laughing. Over time, it went on to become a best seller; while its critical mauling in the gay press may have turned many readers off or against it politically, the flipside of the controversy was perhaps an increased curiosity. Still, the critiques were unambiguous. Writer and historian Martin Duberman wrote in a review for the *New Republic* that Kramer's novel was "no match for the inventive flamboyance of Fire Island hedonism when viewed from an angle wider than primitive moralizing," such that it was "indistinguishable from the most rigid kind of mainstream morality." To be viewed as a kind of enemy fire, or a relic of a more repressive time, emanating from the ideology the community had worked hard to escape, was perhaps the most damning criticism a gay novel of that time could receive. And critics weren't the only people to disown Kramer on that basis.

When he went back to Fire Island after the novel's publication, as a guest rather than a renter, Kramer "kept a decidedly low profile," though he couldn't totally avoid some "nasty moments." The proprietor of the Pines Pantry "had glared at Larry when he was buying an orange juice" one morning and told him, "You're trying to ruin the island [...] I don't understand why you come here." Kramer's perspective no doubt seemed, on Fire Island, to be that of the ultimate party pooper, but this tension also ran deeper, for it seemed to lack a coherent politics. Kramer was the first to admit that he wasn't exactly espousing activism at the time. "I'm not saying be political," he stated, "and I'm not saying march in parades [...] I'm saying be yourself, be free, be homosexual, be free to love, live in a relationship, build a house, build a business, take a part in society instead of living in the ghetto." To those in the gay ghetto

of Fire Island, the proscription of monogamy over sexual freedom seemed reactionary, a political vision based on conformity
rather than pride. But if Kramer's divisive views distanced him
from the wider community, preaching into what he saw as the
hedonistic void of the late 1970s, in the years immediately following he would be playing an integral part in a much larger
project of resistance.

It is July 1981. The Pines season is in full swing. A man wakes
early in the beach house he's a guest in and goes for a morning
run along the beach. He strips and enters the ocean for a bracing
swim. Walking back along the boardwalk as he puts his clothes
back on, he passes an attractive bearded man carrying groceries
back from the store. They share a loaded glance. The bearded
man extends a backwards glance again, to offer another signal,
but it seems they have missed each other. The bearded man gets
back to his house, unpacks his groceries and prepares breakfast.
He takes his breakfast to the upper deck, looks out at the view
across the Pines, and opens the day's edition of the *New York
Times*. In the house the other man is staying in, his hosts are already reading aloud a story on page twenty of the paper. They
continue to read it aloud as they proceed onto the patio with a
jug of Bloody Marys. The bearded man, meanwhile, has found
this story, too, and is reading it to his housemates in their bed
as they rouse, sleepy and shirtless.

It's little wonder why choice phrases from the story will reso-
nate through the community, pierce the surface of this particular
morning. Its title is evidence enough that the men reading this
story, here, in this place, could be affected. "Rare Cancer Seen
in 41 Homosexuals: Outbreak Occurs Among Men in New York
and California—8 Died Inside 2 Years." Still, there is no cause
for alarm just yet—this cancer, Kaposi's sarcoma, which mani-
fests on the body in "violet-colored spots," still has the status of
a rare mystery; there "is as yet no evidence of contagion." The

couple in bed brush it off. "This is bullshit," says one of them. "I hate the *New York Times*." The men with the Bloody Marys sunbathe on the deck and muse sardonically on what the gay men afflicted by this illness might have in common. It's "probably from using poppers, I bet," one of them quips. The *Times* concurs, and reports that "most cases had involved homosexual men who have multiple and frequent sexual encounters with different partners, as many as 10 sexual encounters each night up to four times a week." Even the mere mention of the word "contagious" prompts another of the men to say, "It's like the CIA trying to scare us out of having sex." But there is little chance of such a deterrent working here. Not yet.

Among the healthy and oblivious, this is perhaps what it felt like, the summer that Fire Island first came to learn about HIV/ AIDS. The sequence is not of my own invention, but rather taken from Norman René's film *Longtime Companion*, the 1989 drama charting the development of the epidemic among gay men in New York, with several memorable scenes, such as this opening sequence, set on Fire Island. For the 2014 television adaptation of his 1984 play *The Normal Heart*, directed by Ryan Murphy, Larry Kramer added a similar opening sequence set in the Pines, which culminates in the character Ned Weeks, a version of himself, opening the *Times* to read the same article. For those completely in the dark about the novel disease, this alarmist report from the precipice of a new historical chapter was perhaps not significant enough to derail business as usual. You'd just have to look at the men having sex in the Meat Rack, or cruising at the tea dance, or ogling the beauties on the beach with a glass of cold white wine, to see the island's carnal routine in action. But some signs were already there.

It is no surprise that there are numerous scenes that imagine and visualize that summer of 1981 on Fire Island. Ever since the publication of journalist Randy Shilts's controversial history *And the Band Played On* in 1987, the island had been immortalized as a kind of Ground Zero for this new disease enmeshing sex with mortality, a place where cases were concentrated, where the devastation upon the body, however honed or perfect, was first made legible. Shilts gives an account of 6 Ocean Walk, a Pines beach house rented by island A-listers, some of them Kramer's friends, who were among the epidemic's earliest casualties. It was over a meal in that house in the summer of 1980 that Kramer first heard of the debilitating illness of his friend Nick Rock, whom he had met on the Islanders Club's gay cruise of the Caribbean. Rock lived at 6 Ocean Walk with his lover, Enno Poersch, and their friend Paul Popham, who had this season replaced previous tenant Rick Wellikoff, also ill at this time with mysterious symptoms. That summer in the Pines, "Larry thought how strange it was"; all that people "seemed to talk about were the latest intestinal parasites going around," and dinner conversation "often evolved into guys swapping stories about which medications stomped out the stubborn little creatures." Rock and Wellikoff, who were among the epidemic's earliest casualties, died just months later. By the summer season of 1981, when people were properly becoming aware of this mysterious new illness, Wellikoff's ashes had already been scattered at the Pines, as he had wished, in the idyll he remembered so fondly. He would be joined on the Atlantic breeze by many more in the years to come. Eventually, all of his former housemates from 6 Ocean Walk would meet the same fate.

The initial reaction of the Fire Island community was not uniform. Although the Pines is a small place, where it doesn't take long for news to spread, there were different levels of awareness. Some people were already mourning friends and nursing lovers. Others, having read the *Times* on the ferry over to the island that July morning, "spent the long weekend examining each other's flesh," writes historian and filmmaker David France, "finding purple lesions by the dozen." But many more still were blissfully unaware, or blissfully unfazed, and simply carried on. During

the Labor Day weekend in September 1981, Kramer and a group
of men including Paul Popham, Edmund White, and the phy-
sician and medical journalist Larry Mass, who published some
of the earliest reports on the illness, went to Fire Island to canvass. They set up tables at the Pines harbor, with a banner that
read, "Give to Gay Cancer," and went about placing a copy of
one of Mass's articles in front of every house in Pines and the
Grove. The overall reception to their efforts was frosty. The
Pavilion, the new dance club that had opened on the site of the
Sandpiper in 1980, wouldn't allow the group to canvass on its
premises. When Kramer went to the Ice Palace on the Saturday night to collect money in a cash box, the crowds of affluent gay dancers flowing in and out seemed uninterested. Only
$126 dollars had been raised that night, between midnight and
8:00 a.m., and the weekend's total haul came in at under $800.
The men left the island somewhat dejected by the apathy they
were met with, though comforted, at least, by the knowledge
that they had spread some awareness.

From the vantage of historical distance, it's easy to judge this
collective burying of heads in the sand, to write it off simply
as blitheness or irresponsibility. But if you had been told that
the sexual freedoms you newly enjoyed, hard-won and lacking
in your earlier life, had suddenly given rise to an illness whose
cause was so far unexplainable, you might not immediately take
it as gospel. The earlier controversy surrounding Kramer's novel
no doubt complicated his initial adoption of the cause in the
eyes of some in this community. *Faggots* had been a bitter pill
to swallow—what was to say that this fearmongering, in all its
vagary, was not in fact another instrument of the same kinds of
repression gay men knew all too well? The desire to ignore it
is not so mysterious, but as rates of Kaposi's sarcoma doubled,
this position became less and less tenable. Kramer reported on
the weekend's efforts in the gay newspaper *New York Native*,
where he also entered into a war of words with Robert Ches-

ley. "Kramer told us that sex is dirty and that we ought not to be doing what we're doing" and now, "with Kaposi's sarcoma attacking gay men," Chesley wrote, he "assumes he knows the cause (maybe it's on page 37 of *Faggots*? Or page 237?)." "Why is Chesley attacking me?" Kramer asked in his retort, and not the Centers for Disease Control or the mayor of New York and the various political and institutional bodies with the means to address the epidemic. Whether he was moralistic and "anti-erotic" or not, from where Kramer was standing, he and his friends seemed to be among the only people doing something.

By 1982, they realized they needed to organize, and formed Gay Men's Health Crisis. The cofounders of GMHC included Kramer and Edmund White and a number of the other men who had canvassed Fire Island the previous Labor Day weekend and had been proactive in the cause. As increasing numbers of people began to recognize the seriousness of the situation, the organization grew from a committee of six to a body of several hundred volunteers. Its primary aims were to raise money, disseminate up-to-date information about AIDS, as it had recently been named, and provide support and advice for those suffering from the illness and those worried about becoming infected. Ideological fissures soon showed. Kramer's vision of GMHC as an advocacy group, one whose primary purpose was to apply pressure to powerful institutions, who were giving the struggle against AIDS neither funds nor attention, bristled against the visions of others. "I was out to attack every perceived enemy in sight," Kramer remembered, whereas Paul Popham and the board, "which was composed of many of our mutual friends," felt "that softer tactics were required." Kramer perceived that Popham and others saw the purpose of GHMC as being related, first and foremost, to fundraising and information; it should not, in their eyes, involve telling people what to do or think, and as such should not employ disruptive methods. The idea that "You get more with honey than with vinegar," Kramer remembers, "was a modus operandi that was urged upon me regularly."

In March 1983, Kramer published a clarion call piece in the *New York Native* with the title "1,112 and Counting." The article identified the negligence of the Centers for Disease Control and the National Institutes of Health, and concluded by advocating for sexual caution and civil disobedience. It so contradicted the preferred approach of the GMHC board that they demanded Kramer include a disclaimer: his views were not to be attributed to the organization. The publication of the piece was the nail in the coffin for Kramer's tenure at GMHC. In a political tussle immortalized in *The Normal Heart*, Kramer was forced to resign his position, after his cofounders' lack of confidence in his approach was made clear. He sought a different kind of organization to achieve the aims he believed were crucial in the fight against AIDS, and before long he found it.

Ten days before "1,112 and Counting" was published, in March 1983, Kramer appeared on *Our Time*, a gay television show that aired on the public station WNYC, as part of a special episode on AIDS. Towards the end of his segment, he was characteristically emphatic about the challenges ahead. "We are dying. We are going to have to unite. We're going to have to be angry. We're going have to be perceived as being a threat." "I don't blame you for being angry," replied the interviewer. "I'd like to get a lot of people in this community angry. The rest of this show might just help you to get angry, because we're gonna be telling you some things that may scare the shit out of you." This interviewer, a slight Italian-American man with handsome, deep brown eyes and a thick moustache, understood acutely the power of images to inspire feeling and impact politics. His name was Vito Russo.

Russo was a journalist and gay rights activist who had been involved with the Gay Activists' Alliance in the 1970s and was known for screening Hollywood movies at the Firehouse, with the aim of introducing or reintroducing them to political activists in a gay space. By the early 1980s, he was best known as an independent film historian, thanks to the success of his lectures on gay representation in cinema and his 1981 book on the subject, *The Celluloid Closet: Homosexuality in the Movies*. He and Kramer had known one another for several years. Russo reviewed *Faggots* more sympathetically than most in the gay press, and he was amenable to the activist approach that Kramer, ten years his senior, was now taking in raising awareness and stirring up anger about the impending public health crisis.

Russo was on Fire Island that summer, a few months after this interview with Kramer. His relationship with his lover, Jeff Sevcik, who lived most of the time in San Francisco, was becoming strained, and *Our Time* had been unceremoniously pulled off the air after just thirteen episodes. Without a "compelling project," reports his biographer Michael Schiavi, he was beginning to feel restless. Russo hailed from a different world from Kramer's Ivy League and Pines set, and though he gave lectures about film throughout the country and eventually taught college classes, his status as an independent film historian meant that he didn't have an institutional affiliation and the stability that came with it. Born into a working-class Italian American family in the late 1940s, Russo grew up in East Harlem and New Jersey and first began sneaking away to Fire Island illicitly with friends as a teenager in the 1960s. He was a Cherry Grover more than he was a Pines-goer. The Grove spoke to his miscellaneous sensibility: movie-loving, radical-minded and a student of camp. He had lowered his flag for Judy Garland on the night of Stonewall, and later wrote how it was "significant" that Garland was buried on the night that "gave birth to the modern gay liberation movement," for it was an "ironic symbol of the old gay subculture which existed only in shadow and the beginning of a new militancy." But although the Grove had

come out of the shadows, so to speak, it remained relatively un-
touched by 1970s militancy. That this had hardly changed in
the early '80s, even with the onset of the epidemic, as swaths
of the Grove's summer population became visibly ill and ema-
ciated, was disillusioning for Russo, though he was steadfastly
attached to the place.

In the 1980s, Russo was also a bona fide gay celebrity. His
much-loved film work provided an accessible glimpse into Hollywood history. Russo had appeared in films himself, including the Fire Island orgy scene in *A Very Natural Thing*. He was
friends with a number of big names in show business, including Lily Tomlin and Bette Midler. Russo thus also knew the
power of celebrity to raise awareness. In 1985, Hollywood star
Rock Hudson went public with his AIDS diagnosis, an event
that proved decisive in bringing the epidemic into the news
agenda, much to the umbrage of activists and journalists, who
felt it wrong, as Randy Shilts puts it, that it needed "a movie
star to come down with AIDS" before newspapers "considered
the epidemic a legitimate news story deserving thorough coverage." This heightened awareness around AIDS also brought
with it a moral panic, which was capitalized on by right-wing
commentators like William F. Buckley, who disseminated the
barbaric idea that HIV-positive people be tattooed. In October 1985, the month of Hudson's death, Russo was involved in
cofounding the Gay and Lesbian Alliance Against Defamation
(GLAAD), which protested against defamatory coverage of queer
people, and in particular people with AIDS, at a time when the
need for support and acceptance was urgent.

Like many in the community, Russo had been affected personally by the epidemic for several years. He had lost numerous
Fire Island friends in the early 1980s, and his lover, Jeff, was now
sick with AIDS and deteriorating rapidly. It was around the time
of Hudson's public disclosure that Russo, who had been caring
for Jeff, discovered a Kaposi's sarcoma lesion on his own body.

By the time Jeff passed away the following year, Russo had received his own diagnosis. But he wouldn't go down without a fight or without building upon the work he had already offered to the world. He worked on a revised version of the *Celluloid Closet*. One of the films he included had just been released: Bill Sherwood's 1986 debut, *Parting Glances*, a low-budget independent film about a middle-class gay couple in New York. Russo admired how the film didn't seek to exploit the epidemic for melodrama, and addressed the different ways people dealt with the impact of the illness. Nick, the main character's ex-lover who is dying of AIDS, played by a young Steve Buscemi, features in one of the film's final scenes on the Pines beach. Calling his ex-lover there from the Pines harbor with a suicide threat, Nick waxes jokingly about Fire Island, laced with nostalgia about the past, but also with a dose of gallows humor about his own foreclosed future. This type of filmmaking suggested to Russo a way forward for gay representation.

In March 1987, Russo became involved with the newly formed ACT UP. Recalling in spirit the GAA's zaps of the '70s, sudden bursts of disruptive action, ACT UP was founded upon the principle that demonstrations and disruption were necessary to fight back against the bottlenecking of the Food and Drug Administration, whose response to AIDS was proving woefully inefficient; the pharmaceutical companies, who sold AIDS medication at obscenely high prices; and the media, who were guilty of treating queer people and people with AIDS as irresponsible, infectious, and essentially deserving of their suffering. Kramer's particular brand of fury could be felt in ACT UP's explosion onto the political scene with a demonstration on Wall Street, and he was for a time its most prominent spokesperson, but it was from the beginning a collective and cooperative organization. Russo himself gained a reputation as a charismatic, empathetic public speaker at protests. A speech he gave at a demonstration in Albany, New York, the following year, entitled "Why We Fight," is remembered as one of the great speeches from the height of the epidemic, revered for its balance of the personal and the political, the effervescent and the empathetic. Russo was considered "the kinder, gentler voice of ACT UP," the "implicit comparison" being, his biographer writes, to Kramer, whose extreme approach was powerful, but divisive. If the two men had not quite been friends before, but rather acquaintances from similar circles, it was now their shared anger that brought them together.

Russo's own anger at the epidemic—the way it was unfolding, the way people were reacting—reached a new peak that year. He spent the summer of 1987 in Cherry Grove, as a guest in a cottage rented by his friends, but it was a difficult time. He "had begun to resent" his friends' "relationship and relative affluence" and fell into a depression. He "acted out" and neglected to help around the house, on account of his illness. Most egregious seemed to be the reaction that healthy islanders had towards him. When "one beach bum directed him not to discuss disease at his house," Russo wrote a letter to the editor of the *Fire Island News* in which he raged over the "seeming indifference of the island's gay inhabitants towards AIDS," and the "smug atmosphere" in the community. Russo's accusation caused outrage in Cherry Grove, in part because he compared the community's response negatively to that of the Pines.

A key issue was that the crisis suddenly pitted the individual struggle against the communal struggle. While some Grovers were losing close friends week after week, others sought to turn away from the suffering. The curious, tacit silence about AIDS signaled a desire to preserve a place that had always been a haven from the heavy burden of reality for queer people. The deaths of many gay men in the community, and the downturn in gay male tourism to Cherry Grove, combined with the steadily increasing economic power of women at this time, meant that more and more lesbians were renting and buying houses. While this may have caused consternation among some of the gay men in the community, it was also the women and lesbians, as shown in filmmaker Parker Sargent's recent documentary *Grove Girls*, who cared for their dying friends and provided vital support. Russo's anger made total sense—given that Cherry Grove had made its name as a sanctuary for queer people marginalized by the hostility and neglect of the mainland, it was striking that the community as a whole failed to rally. As the decade wore on, more was done. An AIDS support group was formed, and annual memorial services were held at the Community House, as well as a fundraiser for the PWA (People with AIDS) Coalition.

The mourning rituals adopted by both Cherry Grove and the Pines seemed true to their respective characters. The annual Invasion, recalls Thom Hansen in the documentary *Cherry Grove Stories*, welcomed people with AIDS, many of whom were frail and sick and did not feel so welcome in public life back in the city. Among the queens at the Invasion, there was also a contingent of men mourning their dead, who, David Halperin observes, in response to anthropological research by Esther Newton, donned the "black frocks and veils" worn by "Italian peasant women upon the death of their husbands," a spectacle of grief that was simultaneously parodic and real. Such acts were a reminder that camp, as Newton writes, could offer a vital way of processing grief and "life's misfortunes," despite its "apparent frivolity." In the Pines, one of the most focal fundraising events was the "Morning Party" organized by GMHC. This morning dance party was first held in the summer of 1983, on the decks of private Pines houses. Eventually, as it grew in scale and fundraising potential, it was relocated to the beach. The dress code on circulated flyers read, "Swimwear or Morning Attire." Of course, it could hardly have been lost on the party's dancers that the event's name worked doubly: that this morning ritual was also an act of mourning for those already lost.

The Morning Party continued to grow bigger each year.

There, people partied until dawn, chased the sunrise, did exactly what Larry Kramer had chided them for ten years earlier. Except now the partying had an explicit purpose, offering a moment of escape from impossible and terrifying circumstances. Save for outreach efforts and occasional retreats in the Pines organized by members of ACT UP, these parties were among the island's most visible responses to the ongoing struggle of the epidemic. As symbols of togetherness and perseverance, they fulfilled a community need like never before. But it was small wonder that those like Russo, who had very limited time left to live, but an outsize fire in the belly, felt that the island didn't do enough. How could a place devoted, constitutionally, to pleasure, now properly address the pain, both individual and collective, of the current moment? That Fire Island was badly hit by the epidemic seems a simple statistical fact. But it was also the identity of the place that took a blow, as it tried to confront the question of what it could represent in this new and seemingly insoluble reality.

One constant remained, however: the inarguable fact of its landscape. The island itself seemed ready-made for funereal ritual. In writer Christopher Davis's 1986 novel *Joseph and the Old Man*, about a famous writer living in Cherry Grove and his much younger boyfriend, who is killed in a car accident, the shifting sands of the island's shore, carried by the current from other parts of the Long Island coast, demonstrate its ecological precarity. The morbid thought that "[s]omeday there may be nothing left" is inflected by the old man's grief for his lover, the razing of everyday life as he knows it. Although Davis's novel is not explicitly about AIDS, it's hard not to see how its narrative set pieces—the death of a young gay man before his time, the support of other gay men and lesbians in the community—are touched by the ravages of the epidemic in that era in Cherry Grove. Many members of the Grove's older generation were also dying in the 1980s, from cancer or illness or other non-AIDS-related causes, and their losses were coincident with a time when death in the community was highly politicized. It was no surprise that they too wanted Fire Island to figure in their wake. As somewhere to die, or to be scattered into the atmosphere, there were few places quite as beautiful, nor one where the good times had been quite as meaningful, in all their fragility.

Russo made his final few trips to Fire Island in the summer of 1990. His friend, the British activist Simon Watney, remembers what fine form Russo was in when he went to visit him in Cherry Grove, even while "convalescing after massive chemotherapy." Russo insisted they watch Cher in *Moonstruck*, a movie released just three years earlier but already, for Russo, an important entry in the Italian American canon. His brother, Charles, recalls going to the island with him for the very last time, two months before his death. He "walked the entire island and was given a superstar welcome when recognized." Vito Russo died on November 7, 1990. Among the last films he ever saw or reviewed was *Longtime Companion*, which made use of the Fire Island shore to illustrate not only the beginning of the epidemic, but its imagined ending. In the film's final scene, which takes place in July 1989, the three surviving central characters take a walk along the beach. Processing the loss of their friends and discussing the ACT UP demonstration they are about to attend, the trio imagine other times, what things were like "before all this," and what they might be like at an abstract point in an uncertain future, "if they ever do find a cure." "Can you imagine what it'd be like?" one of them asks. "Like the end of World War II," another responds. As they look ahead to the boardwalk, the waves breaking behind them, hordes of gay men suddenly appear. They are making their way down to the shore, loud and ebullient and alive, beach-ready in short shorts. All around, old friends and lovers are embracing after years apart. What we are witnessing is not a world after AIDS, but perhaps a world before, or parallel to it; as if it had never happened; as if all of these lives, joyous and present, had never been lost.

The reverie that concludes *Longtime Companion* is, like any utopia, an impossibility. This fact doesn't make it any less potent, or the camera's return to the beach's emptiness, populated once more by the central three characters, any less crushing. As in another fiction work by Christopher Davis, the short story "History," from the 1989 collection *The Boys in the Bars*, which is written from the future perspective of a gay man in his sixties after a cure for AIDS has been found, Fire Island acts a repository for the good times that might yet be found again. The film's quasi-happy ending was, at the time, one of the numerous aspects of the film that was criticized, along with its focus on white gay men. Russo, for his part, admired it.

Happy endings are relative, a question of scale: personal and political. The fictionalized longing for an ending in the final years of the 1980s can tell us something about that time, but it is also in another sense timeless. What else can we do, under siege, in those moments when things are too much to bear, but imagine that they are otherwise? That Fire Island became the venue of imaginative acts should come as no great surprise. "Last night I danced as we did two years ago," wrote the poet Michael Lynch in his 1989 Fire Island beach poem "Sand," "alive with love, with Larry, Vito" and "unnamed others / the virus thinks it has taken from the floor." The clinging to the departed met with imaginings of the future.

When Kramer gave his speech at the Queer Liberation March in 2019, and when he passed away a year later, any such illusory end to HIV/AIDS remained far from view. Although medication for those who can afford it enables people with HIV to lead long and healthy lives, there has been no mythical cure, universally available, that brings the epidemic to a sudden or triumphant end. In his 1987 collection of essays about the epidemic, *Ground Zero*, there is a phrase that Andrew Holleran repeatedly refers to. It is something uttered by a friend about the crisis at hand: "There must be a beach at the end of this." Like the end of *Longtime Companion*, the utopian wish underlying such a statement imagines a site of pleasure as the payoff following years of adversity. But as activists past and present have understood, the idyll is not easily found for all; the promise of leisure first requires the work of resistance. *There must be a beach*. A hope and a demand. It's a nod to a paradise both abstract and extant, and to a fight that's not yet over.

10

For Life

THERE COULD HARDLY HAVE BEEN A WORSE TIME FOR
Hurricane Gloria to make her entrance. Like her great predeces-
sor of 1938, her arrival in October 1985 threatened to wipe Fire
Island off the map. In the Pines, ten houses and eight apartments
were severely damaged. "Odd the way she selected their ruin,"
reads the first line of David Groff's poem "Gloria," published in
his 2002 collection *Theory of Devolution*. It was as if this storm
showed a certain morbid discernment, "as if she herself could
name / which bodies she'd impress / into the ocean," and could
take from the lovers left behind "all they thought they owned."
Groff's earlier poem "A Scene of the Crime," from 1989, recalls
the "last great party / Of the '78 season," the "suction of two
men fucking," the "shrill, orgasmic cry." The transition from
ember to ash provided the "usual comparison to AIDS," something that sweeps the island "like fire."

Heading into the 1990s, the island's natural bounty now met
with the desecration of the life that had been made there as
citizens of the Pines and Cherry Grove continued to disappear
one by one. It had long been expected, even natural, that things
changed on Fire Island year upon year. For those who had been
away from it for some time, like Holleran when he returned to

the island in the early 1980s to write a travelogue, the changes could produce "a ghost structure" of how things used to be, one that "existed as a blueprint in my mind." Venues changed names or hands; freak natural events would burn an old favorite to the ground, only for something new to take its place. Estranging as this could be, to experience a once-familiar place differently, this ghostly quality would soon become all too real. Reflecting on his earlier travelogue in 1991, Holleran wrote that "I suspect nothing written in 1983 applies. In 1983 everyone was still alive." The change now was profound. While it was still a beautiful spot, Fire Island became too a place of lack, defined by the superimposition of the past, sensual and rich, upon a present that seemed, to many of those living it, volatile and emptied out. What could its future be?

In the summer of 2019, a few days after WorldPride, I caught the 1 train to the Upper West Side. After stopping first to take a walk by Lincoln Center and cool off from the day's brewing heat, I went to meet the poet Walter Holland, whom I'd been in touch with a couple of days previously, at his apartment. He and his partner live together in a building a few blocks west of Central Park and spent a lot of time in the Pines in the 1980s and 1990s, before opting instead for the beach resort of Asbury Park in New Jersey in the 2000s. Fire Island has featured extensively in Holland's writing, both in his poetry and in manuscripts for two works of fiction set in the Pines. Having burrowed for the better part of a year into books about the island, I would learn more acutely that day the distinctiveness of an intergenerational conversation; how talk can register the depths of feeling, the live legacies of the past, in ways that reading alone cannot. Over coffee, we began at the deep end. Empty houses. Dying men pushing their IV drips along boardwalks; covering up their lesions with makeup and long-sleeved shirts; booking out swan song stays at the Pines Botel to bid everyone their farewell. Ashes being scattered into the ocean. So ubiquitous are the pictures of dying men in the way that AIDS is remembered that I had assumed in advance some familiarity with the images he would describe to me. To hear someone paint a picture with the particulars of their own memory, punctuated by the countless names of the lost, is another thing entirely.

But for all the loss and grief, the Pines did not simply become, as the scholar James Miller points out in an essay on AIDS poetry, a "zone of apocalyptic despair, a nuked prospect of desolate dunes, windswept beachgrass, and bare ruined pines where late the sweet boys cruised." You would still go to tea on Sunday, Holland recalled, and still got to speak to the person you hooked up with the night before. House dinners of grilled protein were still taken late, around 10:00 p.m., in between High Tea and dancing at the Pavilion. You might still go to "Dick Dock" (a name borrowed from its Provincetown counterpart), between Ocean Walk and Atlantic Walk, if you hadn't gotten lucky by the end of the night. The things that made the place distinctive were sustained—the sex, the dancing, the rituals—but now the sex was safe, and the nights of dancing were laced with a sense of loss, marked by the bodies no longer gracing the dance floor.

"I couldn't stop thinking about them," writes Holland in his poem "At the Pavilion," from the 1992 collection *A Journal of the Plague Years*. They would "be here too, in the centre of it all." Observing this felt absence, he asks himself, "Who am I? Last listener to silence. The best / were taken—strange, that I should be the one / left to speak in the end." For those who remained, a summer in the Pines could produce not only a strange sense of survivor's guilt, but a nostalgia, for a time only recently lost. Sitting on the beach at the start of the season in another poem, his speaker sees himself as a "strange queen of recollections / wanting those lost / to make a come-back, sauntering / up from the celluloid surf." On the afternoon of a different weekend, when one of his housemates "looked ill," he recalls lying on the beach "reading the paper until we saw," in a tableau of quiet solidarity, "the thin boy coming from the Grove— / a friend helped him climb the dunes."

Another element of quotidian summer life in the Pines involved the Sunday edition of the *New York Times*, Holland told me, which would arrive by the stack on a Sunday morning and was sold by an old lady at the harbor. The obituaries page was a go-to—dishing took a morbid turn—as housemates pored over the paper's prim euphemisms for AIDS deaths. Natural causes. A heart attack. The same ritual is performed by the characters in Allen Barnett's blistering short story "The *Times* as It Knows Us." Barnett, a friend of Holland and his partner's, was a safe-sex instructor for GMHC, an activist, and a founding member of GLAAD. He published his first collection of fiction in 1990, just months before his death from AIDS at age thirty-six, and immortalized the messiness of house-sharing on Fire Island in this era.

Then a typical Pines refrigerator might contain not only Bloody Mary mix and gin chilled for cocktails, but AL721, an AIDS treatment drug made from egg yolks. Men with positive diagnoses procured the ingredients for their macrobiotic diets. Some also turned to crystals and amulets, the paraphernalia of faith healing. Wholly effective medical solutions continued to elude sufferers and, not coincidentally, faith healing became increasingly popular. The British writer Nick Bamforth, in his book *AIDS and the Healer Within*, argued that one way people could stave off the destructive implications of the illness was by not allowing themselves "to be infected by the hopelessness instilled by the media and the orthodox medical establishment" and instead pursuing "their own inner journey of healing." People were desperate. The adaptation of the Pines lifestyle to incorporate the material culture of what we now might term wellness, in the hope of defending the body against seeping illness, and the taking of mortality in its stride, was a sign of its perseverance. Men, sick and well, continued going to the gym to get in shape, and later to the tea dance to show off their work. But the visible ravages of the disease could hardly be hidden from view.

The response of queer writers amounted to a mode of knowing each other, and themselves, differently than their representations in the media; a reckoning with a reality that was wholly theirs. The flourishing literary scene was galvanized into action, as novelists, poets and dramatists published their accounts of living in the shadow of AIDS with a renewed sense of purpose and urgency. They offered portraits of queer lives as they were being lived, by turns extreme and banal, as in Barnett's story. Friends and lovers could be known as they were in life, not in death, in that curious shorthand of a *Times* feature, the almost brutal brevity of an obituary. Christopher Davis's 1988 novel *Valley of the Shadow* charts a love affair between two gay men who eventually die of AIDS and again makes use of Fire Island as a past paradise. But it also, like Barnett's short story, riffs upon the language of the newspaper by ending with a short obituary of one of the protagonists and asks what it means to shore up a person's story, in all its complexity, in this public and often perfunctory way.

Walter Holland's and David Groff's Fire Island poems appeared in the 1989 anthology *Poets for Life*, one of many literary responses to the epidemic, and the island has remained a site of mourning and memory for both poets in their later work. Writers came to the island to give readings, sometimes in the makeshift venue of the liquor store. Literary books by gay writers were sold in the shop at the harbor, and mass market and erotica paperbacks were for sale in the Pantry. Writing and reading fulfilled a vital community function, for it was on the page that the comeback of dear friends and life partners, who departed with little notice, could return to life.

Although the hedonistic side of Fire Island might have seemed ill-fitting in the face of death and illness, the need for escapism

among the healthy and the sick was surely at a high. And AIDS
was not only an abstract harbinger or atmosphere of feeling; it
brought a number of changes to the structure and demographic
of island life. The narrator of Barnett's story criticizes Nils, another of the houseguests, who is himself an anthropologist, for
one such commentary: "all I've heard this week is that the Pines
is going to tea later, that we're eating earlier, that there's more
drag, fewer drugs, more lesbians, and less sexual tension. For
an anthropologist, he sounds like the *New York Times*." That
these observations held or acquired some truth was not really
the issue. Did any of this, the stuff of the normal Pines lifestyle,
really matter when people were dying? Nils was not wrong that
there were more lesbians, though what you made of this surely
depended on how invested you were in the gay male monopoly
of the Pines. But the deaths of homeowners also created a more
awkward set of circumstances. Without the legal recognition of
a civil partnership, the property and assets of the gay men dying
of AIDS would be inherited not by their partners or lovers, unless specified, but their closest relatives, who were often, in the
eyes of the law, the next of kin.

What this meant in practice was the appearance of puzzled
straight family members, compelled to Fire Island to decide what
to do with the properties they had inherited from their gay relatives, at a time when the epidemic caused something of a moral
panic among even well-meaning onlookers. Terrence McNally's
play *Lips Together, Teeth Apart*, which premiered off-Broadway
in 1991, took the temperature of the times, with its depiction
of two straight couples spending the Fourth of July weekend in
a Pines beach house that one of the women has inherited from
her dead brother. McNally knew the island milieu—he had spent
time writing at Morris Golde's Water Island home in the 1960s,
alongside his onetime lover Edward Albee—but the novelty of
his stage scenario was in placing paranoid outsiders right in the
middle of a community determined to persevere in an age of

anxiety. At the beginning of the play, which takes place over one day, Sally, the inheritor of the beach house, spots a swimmer waving at her from the ocean. We later discover that the swimmer drowned, and Sally's description of him speaks of AIDS metaphorically: "He was very young. Even though his features were swollen from the water, he was very handsome. Nobody wanted to look at him like this, but I made myself."

This was no vacation, after all. To go to the Pines with any squeamish reservations about the lifestyle incubated there was to be made to face your own conviction. The environment would not bend to latent bigotries. Whether it's the opera music or show tunes or Billie Holiday torch songs blaring from the neighboring houses, or the sight of gay men touching and dancing, the intolerance displayed by the couples in McNally's play is a sure sign that they are out of their depth, away from their native New Jersey or Connecticut homes. Along with the dramas of their own lives (a pregnancy, a secret affair, a cancer diagnosis), they are forced to examine their own inability to look at or empathize with gay men both dead and alive. Sally finds in the Pines a house haunted by the memory of her dead brother, whom she never meaningfully helped in his struggle to come out to the family. Why would she want to keep such a house, one tainted with regret and surrounded by things she hardly approves of? "Hang on to it," one of the guests tells her. "Property like this is only going to go up in value. There's no shoreline left, from Maine to Florida. It's all been developed. There's no more where this came from. Ten years from now it will be worth two million."

True as this proved to be, many of the vacated Pines houses were put straight on the market. Sally also stumbles over the more fundamental question of whether the house can even meaningfully be considered hers. Shouldn't it really belong to Aaron, her brother's lover, with whom he shared many happy times in it? Her husband laughs off the idea that they would give away a million-dollar beach house, and not without drawing attention to the fact that Aaron is Black. At the end of the play, Sally finally addresses the elephant in the room—that none of them will get in the pool because they all think it's infected with AIDS. Dipping her toes in the crystal-clear water, she leans in to this shameful admission: "One drop of water in your mouth or on an open sore and we'll be infected with my brother and his black lover and God knows what else was in here. Pissing, ejaculating. I think we're very brave to dangle our feet like this. They may fall off." Whether any real-life surrogates for the mainland's moral panic stuck around in the Pines in this era, McNally's play tested levels of white heteronormative paranoia and observed how sexual anxieties were interwoven with racial ones.

After an hour or two of chatting in his apartment, Holland and I walked out into the neighborhood to grab lunch at a Japanese restaurant nearby. We took a brief tour first, as it so happened that this corner of the Upper West Side was awash with queer cultural significance. We walked by the Ansonia Hotel, where, in the 1970s, Bette Midler had made her name as a gay icon performing at the Continental Baths in the basement, and often cracked jokes in her set about performing in Cherry Grove, where "they couldn't find room for me in the bushes." We also walked to the north lawn of the Ramble, one of Central Park's forested areas, and a famous gay cruising spot since the 1920s, so much so that it gained the nickname the "Fruited Plain." This fruited and furtive wood provided the setting for a key scene in Tony Kushner's 1993 AIDS fantasia *Angels in America*. Walking with Holland and hearing about his experiences, and his perspectives on the ways gay culture had changed over the years, I reflected too on the dense map of relation between the rustic queer spaces inside and outside of the city limits, and how Fire Island has acted as a satellite of the city.

On the way to the park, Holland and I had passed another

important site on West Seventy-First Street. We paused on the opposite side of the street to get a look at what seemed like an unremarkable building, a vertical row of white bricks and black-framed windows, which had been purchased by James Baldwin in 1965. This building remained Baldwin's New York residence until his death in 1987, and he brought his mother, sister, and nieces and nephews to live in the apartments upstairs. Luminaries of the city's Black creative scene, including Amiri Baraka, Miles Davis and Toni Morrison, also lived briefly in the building at different times. Baldwin had purchased and curated a refuge in the city for his family, friends and peers, a home and a hub close to Harlem and distant, though still reachable, from the bohemian climes of the Village downtown. Baldwin knew very well the value and need for such sanctuaries. For him, Fire Island had not been one of them. After all, his trips there in the 1960s and later were not social in nature, but mostly deliberate and isolated. He went there to write.

The Black gay writers of the East Coast literary scene in the 1980s and '90s, many of them explicitly influenced by Baldwin, remained suspicious of Fire Island's claim to the status of haven. Joseph Beam, writer and editor of the anthology *In the Life*, called for representations that looked beyond the scope of the "incestuous literati of Manhattan and Fire Island," which was still mostly comprised of white gay men. Individuals, Esther Newton writes, were treated indifferently, although this did not itself exclude the possibility of micro-aggressions. Groups of Black and Latinx day-trippers, on the other hand, were treated with hostility by white members of Cherry Grove in the late 1980s, who seemed not to care that "like themselves, gay day-trippers of all races had nowhere else to go."

The Haitian American poet and performance artist Assotto Saint sometimes visited the Pines with his partner, the Swedish composer Jan Holmgren. It was during a particular Fire Island party-turned-orgy, Saint told friends, that he feared he was in-

fected with HIV. He knew all too well that this summer idyll
could offer but a momentary reprieve. This "is not the fire island
sand," he wrote in a poem about living with AIDS, but "molten
lava." Saint figures the island's sand as a ground of luxury, or at
least the luxury of turning away from the "burning" urgency
of the "homo epidemic" in motion. To look at the epidemic
squarely and without illusion was to see that it was not only
"homo"-related, but racially contingent too. It was reported in
the news that Haitians were among the first Black demographic
to be recorded as particularly vulnerable to the disease, in the
early 1980s, and by 1985, African Americans accounted for a
quarter of new AIDS diagnoses. Rates among this population
rose alarmingly throughout the 1990s. This shift in the epidemic's profile built up a picture of preexisting inequalities. Saint
died of the disease in 1994, and much of his writing, including
his experimental essay "Sacred Life: Art and AIDS," reflected
on the despair of inequality and the artist's responsibility to resist the orthodoxies of racist society.

    To the poet, novelist, and Baldwin scholar Melvin Dixon, the
particular burden the disease placed on the Black community
seemed neither new nor surprising. Perhaps now, Dixon stated,
his white gay and lesbian compatriots would better understand
the realities of racial oppression. "Some of you may have never
before been treated like a second class, disposable citizen," he
told the audience of the queer literary conference OutWrite in
1992. "We," by which Dixon meant queer people of color, must
"guard against the erasure of our experience and our lives." As
"white gays become more and more prominent—and acceptable
to mainstream society—they project a racially exclusive image of
gay reality." For Dixon, to be Black and gay in the age of AIDS
was a "double cremation," an exclusion from both the straight
Black and white gay communities. Against such erasure, he advocated taking up space, by leaving the "legacy of our writing…
Our voice is our weapon."

Dixon was born in Connecticut in 1962 and attended Wesleyan University and Brown University for his doctorate. He spent most of his academic career as a professor of English at Queen's College in New York, and was acclaimed as a poet, translator and novelist. His 1991 novel *Vanishing Rooms*, set in 1970s New York, explored the politics of gay interracial relationships. His early poetry, which examined Black migration, dovetailed with his academic work on the way that Black cultural forebears have historically sought refuge, both spiritual and actual, in natural landscapes. His later poetic work, which explicitly addresses the political context of the epidemic and was published only posthumously, brought these concerns together in examining how the surrounding environment could illuminate, as well as palliate, the individual and collective plight of living with AIDS. In his poem "Land's End," Dixon reflects on how a "fickle sandbar / where graves and gravity conspire" will eventually shore up those who have been lost, brought back by the sea in the form of ashes or other animated debris. It could easily be describing Fire Island, which Dixon was familiar with, although it was in fact written about the other gay beach community of Provincetown in Massachusetts.

Dixon had a house in Provincetown with his partner, Richard Horovitz, who died a year before his own death. "I shall return to our summer home in Provincetown without him," Dixon declared in his OutWrite speech, "but not without the rich memories of our many years there," and "he is everywhere inside me listening for his name." What the sea made vivid was this sense of return, and in turn our own accountability to the dead. "If I don't make it to Tea Dance in Provincetown or the Pines," Dixon ended his self-elegizing talk, "I'll be somewhere listening for my name." Dixon didn't make it back to Provincetown or the Pines, but died of AIDS-related complications just months later, in October 1992. These final words emphasize the melancholic tense of gay island culture, how the tea dance—

associated on Sundays with the last hurrah before the weekend hedonism draws to a close—recalled in miniature just how short life could be, and emphasized that it was incumbent on the survivors, those "charged by the possibility of your good health, by the broadness of your vision, to remember us."

The poet Reginald Shepherd, a contemporary of Dixon's, found in the Fire Island shore a vocabulary for thinking about community, risk and interracial desire. Shepherd often drew upon canonical literary traditions and languages that, "as a black gay man raised in Bronx housing projects," he did not feel were naturally his. In his 1998 poem "Icarus on Fire Island," Shepherd interpolates lines from a Shakespeare sonnet to reflect on having white lovers: "*Two loves I have*, each one / too fair for me to be completed / in his eyes." The Fire Island beach, "spangled with tan men, their perfect skin / reproach and visible reward," produces in the speaker not desire but withdrawal: "I couldn't want them less." Shepherd had written previously in the *In the Life* anthology about how desiring white men could amount to a troubling expression of hegemonic dynamics, in which "whiteness and beauty are equivalent in my society and my mind." This was nowhere more true as a visual and social principle than in the bodily pageant of the Pines. In a memoir piece for the *Sojourner* anthology, edited and published by the Black, gay writers' collective Other Countries, the ACT UP activist Allan Robinson name-checked Fire Island as a space associated with Black gay men "chasing white boys." Robinson even argued that chasing white men on Fire Island, rather than loving other Black men, could not, from a "spiritual standpoint," have helped prolong the lives of Black men dying of AIDS, insofar as "positive self-image has to be a major factor in one's health."

Although fairly few of Shepherd's poems directly address AIDS, he observed in an essay on illness in poetry that his 1994 HIV diagnosis was no doubt a "ghost presence in many poems." Shepherd had numerous health problems throughout his life—including kidney stones caused by the HIV medication that was keeping him alive—and died in 2008 of colon cancer at the age of forty-five. Unlike many of his contemporaries, he was alive long enough after his HIV diagnosis to access antiretroviral treatment, whose efficacy was discovered in 1996. This medical breakthrough, a cocktail of protease inhibitor drugs that could save the lives of AIDS patients and render their viral loads undetectable, cost a pretty sum of $8,000 to $12,000 a year. This medication remained inaccessible to HIV/AIDS patients who didn't have health insurance coverage. The wider narrative, which disentangled diagnosis from death sentence, would once again change what risk looked like in the gay community, not least on Fire Island.

To age in the Pines, where youth was prized, could be to feel the gradual drift away from social significance, although one's decline can be countered with money or status, and fashion or liposuction. But to face the island's new generation as a survivor is to feel this distance differently. As life in the Pines, or one version of it, began to renew itself, the generational split became apparent. If you were to travel back to some mid-August Saturday afternoon in the 1990s, and stumble onto the beach at the eastern end of the Pines, you might, at first, struggle to place it in time. The sight of thousands, literally thousands, of shirtless men, dancing in the sun; kissing; inhaling from vials; all of this might seem like a pre-AIDS sight, a tableau of a more innocent time, untroubled by the bad rap that hedonism would acquire.

Circuit parties, the unbridled and international gay dance parties that were all the rage in the 1990s, had their roots in the disco events of the 1970s, not least in Fire Island precursors like "Beach." But there were palpable differences. For one, the men seemed buffer, the stuff of steroids as well as toil, and their chests were hairless. Standard poppers and powders were now accompanied by a liquid option, a few drops of which were mixed into drinks on the go. GHB ("G") became a popular Pines party drug. GHB not only aids growth and athletic performance for bodybuilders, but also, in the right dosage, produces the kind of euphoric and aphrodisiac drowsiness perfect for long days and nights of dancing and fucking. In the wrong dose, however, it can fell or kill. This is the Morning Party, 1990s edition: bigger, wilder, more dangerous. And, for the men on the national and international Circuit, one of the events of the season.

A possible side effect of the antiretroviral cocktail was a mysterious weight gain known as the "protease paunch." Although a small price to pay in exchange for lifesaving treatment, it was an unfortunate situation for people who were committed to the display culture of the Pines. The trademark sensuality of a Pines summer, which had been dulled if not erased in the face of death, had returned in earnest, and the amped-up aesthetic of the hairless party queens was notable. This new look was reminiscent of a 1980s aesthetic, as if it were a physical rejection of the disease's ravages upon the gym body. "This summer everybody is putting Nair on their chests to remove all the hair," observes a character in activist and author Sarah Schulman's novel *Rat Bohemia*, during a visit to the Pines in 1984. "They want to be boys again. Thousands of hairless, gleaming, waxed, bionic men strutting around like a bunch of cars. The whole place felt like a parking lot." The party queens could no more become boys than they could machines. Whatever sensual Eden of anatomical perfection and unbridled pleasure was being sought, it was now difficult, fifteen years into an epidemic, to simply recreate it without censure or complication. The Morning Party, in other words, was becoming a problem.

It was in August 1996 that the infighting around the beach party went public. The event had become associated with drug use and a heightened sexual atmosphere that seemed out of keeping, critics argued, with safe-sex guidance and the era's continued moral panic. Larry Kramer was one of the first people to raise his voice. "We started [GMHC] to change all that, not perpetuate it," he told the *New York Times*. He had been to the party two years earlier and observed that "it was as if AIDS never happened and I was back in 1974 again. The drugs were rampant and so was the sexuality of it all, the hedonism." Wasn't this totally at odds with the aims of GHMC, claimed the critics, which by day offered substance-use and addiction services but appeared, by neglecting to enforce rules, to rubber-stamp dangerous substance use every year at its summer fundraiser? Still, the Morning Party reliably attracted more than four thousand affluent attendees every year, who paid $75 plus for a ticket, and raised hundreds of thousands of dollars. It also belonged to a longer history of gay dance events that delivered fun and pleasure in the name of a political cause. Many of the partiers, a good number of them former activists, were seeking an escape from the traumas of the past decade, whether they were still afflicted, directly or indirectly, by the epidemic. One Pines resident who had AIDS told the paper that summer that he didn't particularly approve of the party either, but: "You bite your tongue and go. It's a beautiful party. It's been out there so long it's like going to church."

Mainstream squeamishness around AIDS began to be met with an increasingly assimilationist politics among gay men themselves—shouldn't gays grow up, behave themselves and get married, just like anyone else? Just a few hours before the 1996 Morning Party, a man fell into a drug-induced coma and was helicoptered to the hospital and around twenty people at the party were caught by police with drugs. "We're talking about a benefit of a health agency," said the writer Michelangelo Signorile, a critic of the Circuit. "Would the American Cancer Society throw a drug party?" Two years later, a man overdosed on GHB and died, and although this happened several hours before the 1998 party began, it was still connected to it in accounts of the weekend.

Overdoses, obviously, are not unique to Fire Island. The problem was that the Pines wasn't just anywhere—voluntarily or not, it bore a representative function as a predominantly gay male destination. GMHC had held substance-abuse support sessions on Fire Island during the Morning Party week for several years. They had discouraged people from taking drugs and got the police involved. But although GMHC could not be held directly responsible for the GHB-related death, they couldn't contend with the intense scrutiny of a media ready to suggest otherwise. Given the organization's focus on substance abuse and its relation to HIV infection, the media attention meant that the association with the Morning Party event became untenable. Their public statement described the pain at ending this Fire Island tradition. The cancellation of the Morning Party proved that, far from being secluded, the Grove and Pines were on the mainstream cultural radar, and anything perpetuating the image of gay men behaving badly, out of line with the strictures of a world in the shadow of AIDS, would be spotted.

After so much death, the continuation of business as usual on the island, its way of life, seemed fragile and volatile. But away from the spats around the culture of the Circuit, there could still be signs of renewal. In his 1999 short story collection, *In September, the Light Changes*, Andrew Holleran frames the return to Fire Island as a cathartic process of readjustment. In one of them, Morgan, a recently sober man in his forties, comes back to the Pines for a summer to run a restaurant, after a stint in New Orleans that came to a dramatic end on account of his drinking. There he half recognizes old faces, remembers lost ones and senses his own obsolescence: "Not only was the Pines full of ghosts, he felt like one himself." "There was disagreement among the survivors of his age and older over the quality of the newest generation," but Morgan "thought they were quite handsome." After all, "nothing on the island seemed to have changed, except the fact that no one had moustaches, beards, or even body hair"; they looked in their underwear "like Hitler Youth."

Morgan falls in love with one of the waiters at the restaurant, a young Long Island man, and they have a brief rendezvous. It doesn't work out, but the connection holds some renewing power for Morgan, who consoles himself "with the idea that at this stage in life one could enjoy the young without possessing them." Still, when Morgan moves back to the city for the winter, in a subsequent story, he regales a friend about the island's shallowness, "all these forty-year-old men in the Pines with twenty-eight-inch waists" who "had liposuction." Walking through the Ramble in Central Park, he reflects that it's "all become so predictable" there, "[s]elf-conscious and bourgeois. They're so concerned with the right resume, the right dog, the right amount of body fat—it's like the whole generation is art-directed. There's no craziness anymore, no characters, no spontaneity or sense that things are being done for the first time." Instead, the contemporary Fire Island culture signaled to Holleran's character the repetition of older motivations and desires. In the title story of the collection, set on the island during the autumnal, emptied-out period after Labor Day, the season's change maps emotional landscapes: "In September, the light changes," muses the narrator, "but not the human heart."

In 1999, the Morning Party became the Pines party, a new annual beach blowout with a different theme each year, organized by the Pines Property Owners' Association. Hope was abundant but tentative. Convention was an order of the day, although, as Morgan opines to his friend in Central Park, "[a]ll this so-called assimilation is only because of AIDS. We wouldn't get any sympathy at all if we weren't dying." Gay marriage and adoption became increasingly visible prospects, as featured in Bravo's 1999 reality series *Fire Island*, which depicted two share houses in the Pines, one all-male and the other all-female. Two of the men describe themselves as married, and one of the lesbian couples has children, though this proves its own source of drama in the unfolding of a Pines summer. The show, writes Steve Weinstein, was "loathed by island hands for the way it depicts two Pines shares...as dens of backbiting and petty arguments over everything from lovers to food bills." Some things never change. The Stonewall generation, approaching the autumn of their lives, watched as the light changed; observed, paradoxically, its fundamental sameness. The survival of both the Pines and the Grove, which had by now become a resolutely mixed community in which lesbians comprised at least half of the summer population, attested to the island community's capacity for perseverance. For the men and women of different generations who found themselves here, in the Grove or the Pines, staring down the injuries and riches of the recent and historical past, there would be, to recall a line from Melvin Dixon's posthumously published poem "October Passing," "no easy fire" to raze and renew. But caught on the precipice of a new millennium, "the only thing to do," to quote a line from O'Hara, an earlier martyr of the island's shore, "is simply continue." And so they did.

CONCLUSION

A Paradise

TO PARAPHRASE A CHARACTER FROM *THE BOYS IN THE BAND*: What is Fire Island, what was it, and what does it hope to be? At what moment, in other words, does its past join with the place as it is today, or the place that it might yet become? Historical memory is understandably sacred in these multigenerational communities, but it is in the most recent decades of the island's past that its contemporary self comes into view.

A sense of fatigue marked the early years of the twenty-first century, the feeling that Cherry Grove and the Pines had, in persevering as protected communities, also dwindled into something less unique than they once were. An older generation of homeowners, traumatized by the events of the preceding two decades, stayed put in their summer enclave, although many former visitors stopped going altogether. For them, Fire Island had become a kind of graveyard. Younger generations continued to make the journey and discover this place anew, although some visitors found that the party culture of the island was increasingly homogenized, and its rich artistic history seemed like a thing of the past. Along with the many artists and writers lost to AIDS came the loss of an engaged and informed audience; the

readership that kept gay publishing afloat, and the wider sense
of a community consuming and critiquing the work of its own
luminaries and emerging voices.

But the new millennium would bring a resurgence, eventually. The blossoming of Fire Island's contemporary culture has
largely been the result of initiatives and organizations brought
to the community by newcomers and external parties, many of
whom have had to prove their worth. The Underwear Party,
which club promoter Daniel Nardicio first brought out to the
Ice Palace from the city in the late 1990s, revived the club culture of Cherry Grove. Now a central fixture on Friday nights,
the Underwear Party brought a new injection of sexuality to the
community, but this was at a time when public displays of sexuality had become somewhat taboo. Initially, there were calls to
boycott this scantily clad event, which was complete with go-go
boys, in-demand DJs, and condoms to encourage safe sex. The
fact that it became a consistent weekly staple of gay island life
speaks to the relaxing of anxieties around partying and sex that
had lingered throughout the previous decade. Nardicio's other
ventures in Cherry Grove, such as a performance by Lady Gaga
in 2008, when she was on the brink of international fame, and a
show by Alan Cumming and Liza Minnelli in 2012, which the
pair revived in the city the following year, harkened back to the
community's historical identity as a space of performance. Icon
Minnelli's arrival to the island, which was treated by many like
a papal visit, recalled Cherry Grove's long-standing tradition of
diva worship, as well as a certain duality of gay life, Nardicio
says, whereby the same space you might visit on Friday to meet
men and have sex would the next night play host to a performance by a camp legend in her late sixties.

The nightlife (and daytime) fixtures of social life in the Pines
also held strong. The Pines Party proved to be an annual success,
filling the gap left by the Morning Party, and the tea dance has
long remained a cherished summer tradition, with a changing

roster of DJs. As Edmund White had noted back in the 1970s during its heyday, the tea dance was where the "best-looking men in the city are assembled." But what had changed, perhaps, was the valence of Pines exceptionalism, which had once been a product, if not exactly a cause, of gay liberation and its fervor. The high glamour of the Pines lifestyle had never exactly endeared the entire gay community, particularly activists and radical thinkers like the editors of the '70s gay anarchist newspaper *Fag Rag*, who banned Fire Island as a subject in poems submitted to the publication on account of its commercialism. In the twenty-first century, what was now a somewhat retro fixture of gay New York life was even more open to the charge of being retrograde in its exclusivity. It was in this contemporary milieu that the trope of the "Fire Island gay" was born.

The Fire Island gay, though a character of the twenty-first century, reads as an updated version of parallel figures in history. He is, perhaps, the successor of the apolitical disco queen of the '70s and '80s, or the Circuit queen of the '90s. He exists in the Fire Island that found its mojo again in the 2000s, when it was in need of a makeover after a period of what we might think of as posttraumatic stagnation. This distinctively contemporary figure moves in a world where same-sex marriage is legal and AIDS seems a thing of the past. He is anywhere between twenty-five and fifty, on either side of a generational gap. But whatever his age, he is toned, groomed and moneyed, or at least of sufficient enough means that he can afford a summer share in a house in the Pines. (And it's worth noting that when people use "Fire Island" as a shorthand for bad gays, they're usually talking about the Pines, rather than the more mixed and relaxed Cherry Grove). Through the winter and the spring, he puts in hours at the gym for the necessary body. He probably lives in Hell's Kitchen. He likes to party. He's a top, or a bottom. A twink, or a muscle daddy. Race is one of his blind spots. He is politically liberal, on the surface, but a cursory glance at his social media profile might suggest he holds a number of problematic views when actually pushed on his beliefs. He is the White Gay par excellence.

The particular person being described doesn't exist—he's a type, a composite of numerous examples fictional and real. He can be seen on social media, reality TV, literature and pop culture. He is the target of many a hit piece and a mainstay of memes on Gay Twitter, a convenient shorthand for the least attractive aspects of contemporary gay culture. And he can be painted with various ideological stripes. When the trailer for Logo's 2017 reality television show *Fire Island* premiered, it produced a range of suspect responses. Without even having seen the show, which closely followed the spats and sex lives of six men who share a Pines house over the course of the summer, one commentator, who went to great pains to communicate that he didn't drink or approve of partying, suggested that the show contributed to "Gay America's Moral Decline." What effect could "documenting the escapades of a bunch of gay men" on Fire Island have, this writer wondered, "on gay preteens who have yet to come out," or on someone "who has yet to actually meet a gay person in real life"? This singling out of Fire Island gays as vain and irresponsible was conservatism in different clothes, wedded to a politics of respectability that is not so far away from the right-wingers who use community division to stoke the fires of their own prejudiced views.

That is not to say, however, that the most outwardly visible aspects of Fire Island's culture are not exclusionary. The Fire Island gay is someone who can make you feel bad about yourself just by the way he looks and moves. As an archetypal iteration of a norm, a conventionally desirable masculine type, this symbolic alpha of the gay male world alienates other men who don't fit this model of (mostly) white athleticism. Like Usher, the narrator of Michael R. Jackson's Pulitzer-winning 2019 meta-musical *A Strange Loop*, whose encounters with the "sexual marketplace" of Fire Island make him feel "too fat and Black to live at all." And although drag and gender nonconformity have long been celebrated on the island, and in Cherry Grove in particular, trans, nonbinary, and gender nonconforming people are also shortchanged by the relative conformity of the island's dominant sexual culture. "The Men," a poem by Ari Banias, depicts the difficulties of finding pleasure in the Meat Rack as a trans man, just as Jameson Fitzpatrick's poems about the Pines capture the oppressive quality of cis-male uniformity. For Reese, the trans protagonist of Torrey Peters's 2021 novel *Detransition, Baby*, a sometime visitor to Fire Island with her partner, the queer beach is a combination of "the worst parts of a high school lunchroom with the worst parts of a nightclub, only everyone is also nearly naked." The body has remained the battleground upon which Fire Island's status as a political space, with its historic lack of racial diversity, and lack of diversity in genders and different body types, is contested.

The establishment of artists' residencies in both Cherry Grove and the Pines in the 2010s restored some much-needed cultural energy, harking back to a time when they were fertile creative hubs for queer artists and writers from the city. The Fire Island Artist Residency (FIAR), which began in 2011, catered to emerging LGBTQ artists and later expanded to include poets, with plans to incorporate filmmakers and drag queens in the future. BOFFO (named after a slang term for "success"), an arts organization founded in 2009, first hosted an artists' residency in 2012 with the aim of making the Pines more inclusive. BOFFO artists perform their work at an annual summer festival and have access to the networking opportunities. BOFFO also rents a house for previous artists to come and stay in during subsequent summers. The two organizations are distinct and distinctive in their outlooks and programming, but both aim to establish a sense of longevity by building up the Fire Island artistic community and ensuring that their residents are more reflective of New York's LGBTQ+ landscape than the island's usual demographic. Alumni of both residencies return each summer as speakers or renters. According to painter and resident alum Nicole Eisenman, the residencies have helped to produce "a loose association of friends and friends of friends who flow through," a collective of "art queerdos" that offers an alternative to the "mainstream party scene" of the Pines.

Many of the artists and writers have engaged with the space of Fire Island itself, through its landscape, its history or its living community. Sam Ashby (FIAR 2014), a filmmaker and editor of the queer film magazine *Little Joe*, undertook research into Fire Island's cinematic history, and amassed clips from the numerous films made there. Ashby then activated this archival work through a collaboration with fellow resident artist Ginger Brooks Takahashi, who added sound to the montage of film clips, for a live collaborative performance called "Fire Island Film + Sound" that took place at the Community House in Cherry Grove. Derrick Woods Morrow (FIAR 2016) made work about his experience of Fire Island as a queer Black man by intervening in the contractual cruising culture of hookup apps such as Grindr, which have perhaps by now become predominant over the "analog" mode of cruising in the Meat Rack. Using technology that prints Polaroids from mobile phones, Morrow produced photographic "receipts" of the people he had sexual contact with, in a reflection upon trust, sex and connection. The Institute of Queer Ecology (BOFFO 2019), a collective working to address the climate crisis, engaged with Fire Island's landscape more literally through organized nature walks.

Leilah Babirye (FIAR 2015), who found refuge on Fire Island quite literally after leaving her home country of Uganda, where she had recently been publicly outed, used found objects from the surrounding landscape, such as beer cans, to create a mirror in homage to the island's drag queens. She installed the mirror in the Meat Rack, allowing the queens to stop and touch up their makeup on the walk between the two communities. Babirye subsequently found asylum in the US, stayed in New York, and has had numerous solo gallery shows. Her work to date has similarly incorporated found objects and trash from the streets of New York to produce sculptures capturing and challenging notions of queer West African identity, while her drawings have been inspired by the drag queens she met in Cherry Grove.

Although the island is, for many artists and writers, its own kind of muse, neither residency program requires that artists generate work reflective of the place itself. Having a diverse range of artists in a white and male-dominated space has been a radical act in the history of the place, even if the divisions between the alternative residency communities and the mainstream of the Grove and the Pines remain intact. What the residencies crucially provide for artists is space, time and resources to work. The artist Kia LaBeija (BOFFO 2018), whose work is informed by her experience as a queer woman of color born HIV-positive, observed in an interview for a BOFFO publication that Fire Island is an example of "how one community could come together and create a safe space for themselves," but this doesn't change "the reality of being a woman and being a person of color" and not feeling safe in that space. Instead, the island provided LaBeija with the ability to be "alone on the beach" and feel safer "with the ocean, the sand, the sky, and my thoughts." What stayed with LaBeija were the images she made during her trip, which included a pair of self-portraits captured in the surf.

Artist, musician and writer Brontez Purnell (BOFFO 2018) worked on a fictional piece about Fire Island during his residency, while also finishing the manuscript for his 2021 book *100 Boyfriends*, a collection of short stories documenting encounters in the spaces of America's diverse gay sexual subcultures, which extend far beyond the type and topography of the Pines. The

following year, in the summer of 2019, playwright and BOFFO
resident Jeremy O. Harris performed his piece *Water Sports:
Or, Insignificant White Boys*, as well as a poetic work in progress. The "Wall Street faggots" and "Saks Fifth fairies", Harris
declaimed in the latter piece, have "banded together" to build
themselves an island. This island off the coast of Manhattan is
far from the "the bright lights" and "dark dungeons" of Manhattan. Far from the city's population of queer and transgender youths of color, living on the streets, the "dolly-boys" and
"boyish dolls" who "swish their throbbing cunts" against "the
poles on Uncle ACE", the long subway tunnel of the A, C and
E trains where many homeless adolescent sex workers live. In
the full show, *Black Exhibition*, which he performed under the
name @GaryXXXFisher in Bushwick, Brooklyn, a few months
later, while his show *Slave Play* was on Broadway, Harris used
the setting of the Pines to reflect upon his own relationship to
sexuality as a queer Black man. The show's set was made up of
boardwalks representing the structure of the Pines, boardwalks
upon which Harris lay prostrate and exposed. "I went to Fire
Island to write, but all I did was fuck and cry" is a refrain in the
piece. Harris categorizes the work as a "choreopoem," a genre
pioneered by the Black feminist writer and dramatist Ntozake
Shange, who herself took a share in the Pines in the early 1980s,
but didn't stay for long.

The Fire Island "fags," Harris writes, have "colonized the
driftwood forests of Long Island and are conceiving new cultures"; a place of "germs, germinating contagions, where no one
but their ilk can contract the culture of tea!" Just a year later,
in 2020, Harris's epidemiological images describing the island's
closed-world traditions of tea would become metaphorically
apt amid the COVID-19 pandemic. P. J. McAteer, the director
of the Pines commercial district, added social distancing mea-
sures, such as a table service tea dance sitting, and the community adapted to a new normal. Daniel Nardicio, in partnership

with GHMC and the Governor's Office, set up the COVID Destroyers. Named after Rebecca More and Sophie Anderson, the porn performers who gained fame on Gay Twitter as the "Cock Destroyers," the island's COVID Destroyers were a brash and lighthearted alternative to pandemic police, made up of drag queens and nightlife performers, many of them out of work because of the pandemic, who distributed masks and hand sanitizer and encouraged social distancing in and around Cherry Grove and the Pines.

The worldwide uprising following the killing of George Floyd in Minneapolis, and of Breonna Taylor in Kentucky a few months earlier, also shook Fire Island that summer. Black Lives Matter protests were organized in both Cherry Grove and the Pines. Marchers paid to attend and helped to collect money from affluent residents for the cause. Carrying flags with slogans like "White Silence=Black Death," a clear nod to ACT UP, and "What Have You Done With Your White Privilege?", protesters paused on the beach and kneeled for eight minutes and forty-six seconds, the same amount of time that Derek Chauvin had violently kneeled on George Floyd's neck. To escape to a summer haven at a time of crisis is itself an expression of privilege, and this was a fact that could no longer be ignored. The march in the Pines raised over $32,000. Many protesters were white, a reflection of the communities' demographics, and these protests were an expression of allyship and a call to no longer treat race issues with silence, as they had been before.

A number of fallouts in Cherry Grove, which included a community member describing the spray-painted letters "BLM" on the Community House as vandalism, and the raising by another of a "Blue Lives Matter" flag, exposed the friction between the island and the national reckoning taking place beyond its shores. Tomik Dash responded instantly with a galvanizing piece in his magazine *Fag Rag* called "A Guide to Being Anti-Racist in Fire Island," in which he identified Fire Island's historic race problem and drew attention to what was going on in Cherry Grove in the light of the Black Lives Matter movement. Dash had been coming to Cherry Grove for several summers for both work and vacation, and in the previous months had been setting up his print magazine, named after the radical Boston newspaper, to be distributed in Cherry Grove and the Pines. *Fag Rag* is both an art mag and a resource guide, with fashion and photography that explicitly center people of color and diverse body types. While the magazine received a good reception, there was still resistance from some members of the community.

Building upon his work through the magazine, Dash founded the Cherry Grove Black and Brown Equality Coalition (BaBEC), which advocates for Black people and all people of color in Cherry Grove and seeks to promote a more racially diverse community by encouraging tourism, homeownership and commerce more generally. (The Fire Island Pines Property Owners' Association [FIPPOA] also established a diversity and antiracism task force.) In 2021, BaBEC organized a weekend celebration of the Juneteenth national holiday, which involved a march, a Mx. Fire Island pageant competition, and a panel discussion about inclusion.

Towards the end of that same summer, the artist Lola Flash, an active member of ACT UP in the 1980s and '90s, presented the work she had undertaken during her BOFFO residency. Flash staged an installation called "We Are HERE: The Unsung Fire Island". It featured an exhibition of her photographs of Black and Brown residents and visitors, combined with a sound installation of interviews that revealed their untold stories. The work spoke directly to the "important conversations percolating around race and racism on this tiny island, which reverberate back to communities across the globe." The artist residency programs had, over the course of the last decade, worked to embed creativity and inclusive practices in the communities. Now, steps were being taken in the Grove and the Pines at a municipal level. The dust settled after the upheaval of the 2020 season, and candid conversations would light the path, hopefully, for a more inclusive way forward.

Queer people have a particular stake in the question of paradise. Psychologists like Walt Odets tell of the "longing, loss and nostalgia" that shape our fear, the fear that life outside of heteronormative structures will never return us to the "paradise lost" of "perfect and perfectly consistently parental attention." Queer theorists like José Esteban Muñoz describe true queerness as something abstract and vivid, continually deferred or on the brink of emergence, "the warm illumination of a horizon imbued with potentiality." It is not a naive desire to chase something that, by its nature, can't exist. Instead, the fantasy of a world away from shame and silence, a place made for us, where trouble melts like lemon drops, where, as O'Hara puts it, "we shall have everything we want and there'll be no more dying," is a sustaining force.

Paradise reminds us of who we are and are not, of who we have in mind in its design. Paradise is a place that exists in the future and the past. No one's paradise will look identical, but for some it probably looks quite a lot like Fire Island, a place whose natural beauty can defy words, and whose manmade beauties are rather more constructed, though sometimes no less awe-inspiring. It fulfills that distinct American desire, found in the narratives of the frontier, to escape to the edges, to a "sandbar, as slim as a parenthesis," as the narrator of Holleran's *Dancer from the Dance* puts it, the "very last fringe of soil on which a man might put up his house, and leave behind him all—absolutely all of that huge continent to the west." But parentheses exclude as well as contain, and in other respects, Fire Island feels like a case study of utopian imperfections, of the way norms become entrenched and inequalities perpetuated in a place defined by the fact that it is not, simply, for everyone. We seek out utopias in real places, but learn, as W. H. Auden or Patricia Highsmith did on Fire Island, that this can be a dangerous or disappointing game. Sometimes oases are made through our romantic relationships, like Windham and Campbell in their Pines house, or the shared solace of friendship groups, documented in the gay literature of Holleran and White, Picano and Whitmore.

In the darker moments of my early twenties, wracked by a sense of inaction and unfulfilled desire, I felt the pull of paradise thinking. My version was always some kind of subterranean disco wonderland, conjured in reverie. In this queer, sweaty vision of spectacle and embrace, I am dancing in a focal spot on the dance floor with people I love. Lyrics from Arthur Russell's disco track "Go Bang!" echo in my head: "I wanna see all my friends at once." I'm not sure where this particular scene is set—probably in New York, probably in the 1970s—but the feeling of it is idyllic, never quite found, existing only in my head.

For a long time I had a kind of wallflower sensibility where my sexuality was concerned. I didn't actively seek out a queer community, perhaps out of fear, or see myself as a particularly committed member of it. I often felt intimidated by other gay men and mostly resisted making friends on the basis of identity or likeness. At college, the gayest my night out would really get would be an app hookup arranged in the small hours, out of sight of friends. My engagement with the "scene" in London often involved last-minute drunken decisions to go to the gay bar Heaven, alone. The way I felt then, my sexuality was more a thing I did than who I was.

I remember in the aftermath of a particularly drunken night going to a sexual health clinic and being referred to a therapist there. I had mentioned heavy drinking habits and feelings of insecurity on my processing form, and he wanted to talk about these things. It was the first time I had ever spoken to a professional about these aspects of my life, and the first time I'd been so honest about them with anyone. I wanted to cry with relief.

A gay man himself, he reminded me of the need to be kind to ourselves and to each other; that we often forget or fail to practice this. He left me with a piece of advice that has since taken on, in my mind, the aura of a proverb. "When you walk past another gay person in the street," he said, "give them a smile." It's a reminder that they have a friend in you, that you're part of the same world together. It was the wisdom of those words—the truth of feeling yourself part of a community with only a look, the knowledge that the queer community has been historically adept at sustaining itself on such passing looks—that I thought of the first time I went to Fire Island. Walking the streets back home, in everyday life, shared glances and smiles can feel, if not a novelty, then a random gift, a pick-me-up, an expression of solidarity in the crowd. In Cherry Grove, those smiles are practically the norm. Although the lofty scowl or flirtatious look-away of the Pines conjures a different atmosphere, it is a similarly shared language. It wasn't until I'd experienced the magic of that particular welcome to Fire Island, the safety and simplicity of it, I think, that I could feel what I'd been missing out on in my agnosticism about community.

Still, in reality, discovering Fire Island felt as much like an assignment as an epiphany. Its lure was its atmosphere of historicity, of a place graced, or haunted, by so many luminaries. I had to know more about them and their time here. To build this collage, I would need to talk to people, to learn from intergenerational conversations, to conceive of this place as in some sense being my own community, even if I am British, reside elsewhere, and am neither an owner nor a renter. Fire Island came into my life as an opportunity to fill in the gaps left by growing up queer in a heteronormative world, gaps in knowledge and experience. It compelled me to do what queer people, as the theorist Eve Kosofsky Sedgwick puts it, must often do "with difficulty and always belatedly": to "patch together from fragments a community, a usable heritage, a politics of survival or resistance."

Because here's the other thing about paradises. They are fragile and easily lost. Neither Cherry Grove nor the Pines sprang up organically as ready-made queer havens. They attained their status by persistence. Their integrity has been threatened by hurricanes, police raids, prejudice, attacks from the mainland, and ideological conflicts. Their populations have been decimated by disease. They find strength in community, the shared desire to create a world, even if finding a consensus about what that world looks like, and how it operates, is elusive. The work of making that world more inclusive is ongoing. In a public sphere still organized around white, heteronormative standards, meaningful and inclusive queer spaces are at a premium. The fact that vacation communities are by design exclusive does not exonerate Fire Island from the hidden assumptions made there about class and culture and bodies.

It's unsettlingly easy to imagine how Cherry Grove and the Pines could be lost or otherwise jeopardized. As persecuted groups know all too well, the illusion of progress can veer in unnerving directions; the clock can be turned back. That same-sex couples with children can happily coexist in these communities with people seeking, let's say, a less family-friendly vacation, has long been a sign of healthy miscellany, but one can imagine how an assimilationist mood might overtake the free sexual mores that have always made Fire Island distinctive. Nor is it farfetched to imagine that interested heterosexual buyers, given the right opportunity or set of circumstances, would have enough financial and social clout to overtake the market. It may feel like an unshakeable fact that the public beaches of the Grove and the Pines "belong" to queer people, culturally speaking, but that status is not codified or legally protected. Even ownership within the community is a divisive issue, linked to a feudal hierarchy of homeowners, renters and day-trippers that is alive and well today. The queerness of these communities is a matter of folklore, and gentrification cares little for such ineffable things. Still, Cherry Grove and the Pines are populated by proud documenters and organizers who give little reason for pessimism about the continued existence of these communities.

There is another threat, however, about which the human agents in this oasis by the ocean can do only so much. Fire Island has always been shaped and endangered by its environmental precarity, a low-lying sandbar whose structural integrity relies on its dunes, exposed to the brunt of winds and waters. Along with the threat to the island's natural habitat and wildlife posed by climate change, the impact of erosion and the risks of flooding are very real. A 2020 report by the National Park Service found that Fire Island "faces serious issues now" that "will likely increase in the coming decades due to climate change." By the middle of the century, in 2050, the vulnerability of many parts of the island will move from moderate to high. By 2100, the current forecast is ominous. Whether Fire Island's precarity produces a community-wide sense of solidarity and collaboration, as it did in the 1960s, when the towns rallied together against Robert Moses, remains to be seen. That will surely be the subject of future histories.

Amid the existential anxieties of the global climate crisis, the idea that the twenty-first century could be Fire Island's last, at least as we know it, is a sobering one, a cruel metaphor for the evanescence that makes it special, the sense of a halcyon summer whose pleasures defy its brevity. What would the map of Long Island or New York look like without it? What, for that matter, would the map of queer life in America look like without it? The disappearance of a space as eventful and storied as Fire Island is almost unthinkable. Where would it all go—the first kisses and house spats, the sunburn and sex, the morning parties and late-night embraces, the care given, the work created, the hands held in times of joy and crisis, the vexed patchwork of a sentimental history that takes us to the heart of queer life? We can remember Fire Island not as a false paradise, or a paradise already lost, but as an extant, changing site, alive and livable, suspended in the present of a shared moment, and still ripe for rewriting. Remembering is not only a backward glance but a thinking again, a reimagining. There will come a day when subsequent generations will have to excavate the traces, the texts and images and reminiscences from a place conceived, perhaps, as a lost Atlantis. But what an archive there will be, a heritage and a lesson. Across some distance—an ocean or a bay—a smile.

★ ★ ★ ★ ★

ACKNOWLEDGMENTS

This project has occupied me, in one way or another, since the extended trip I took to New York City in 2017. Its existence in the world now as a book is a surreal and wonderful thing. It also provides a vivid snapshot of the last four-and-a-bit years of my life: of the obsessions that led me here, from Frank O'Hara to Fire Island's queer literary history; of the climate in which it was mostly written, from home, during successive lockdowns; and of the community of interviewees, mentors, colleagues, friends, and family who have shaped and enabled this book, which is itself about community, in numerous ways. Thank you.

To my agent, Jane Finigan at Lutyens and Rubinstein, for being so generous, encouraging and such a great support during this first foray into the world of publishing. To David Forrer at Inkwell Management, for your enthusiasm for this book and for the alternate ways into Fire Island and its history that you offered me.

To my editors, John Glynn at Hanover Square Press and Anne Meadows at Granta, for your initial faith in this book, for your rigor and care in seeing it come to fruition. To the team at Hanover Square for handling the production of the manuscript. To Rowan Cope, my interim editor on the UK side, for your capacious and formative insights, and Jason Arthur.

I knew from the beginning that I was coming to Fire Island as an outsider, and I'd like to thank the people who made that journey easier. Fran Higgins and Tom Jacobs, for your warm hospitality on Fire Island and your keenness to facilitate my curiosities, whether through book recommendations or an impromptu sailing trip to the Pines. Celine Lowenthal, for bringing me there in the first place, and sharing that fateful first journey along the beach. Astrid Bulmer, for our excursion to the Invasion and back.

After several stays on Fire Island and trips to archives in the earlier stages of my research, the world shut down and the texture of daily reality changed. I was suddenly in the position of writing from afar about a place I was desperate to return to, and found myself living vicariously through the writing, summoning up an image not only of Fire Island's past, but also its unfolding present. I knew from the beginning that texts by themselves could not account for a place as dynamic and various as Fire Island, that I could not write this book alone. I am therefore hugely grateful to the people who spoke to me, before and during the pandemic, in-person, on the phone, over email, or via video chat interviews across time zones. Their insights into Fire Island's past, present and future have been invaluable. Thank you to: Faris Al-Shathir, Tom Bianchi, Chris Bogia, Kevin Cathcart, Alfred Corn, Tomik Dash, Michael Denneny, Bill Goldstein, David Groff, Walter Holland, Andrew Holleran, William Johnson, David Leeming, Matthew Leifheit, Ron Martin, Esther Newton, Daniel Nardicio, Jeffrey Peabody, Felice Picano, Brontez Purnell, Crayton Robey, Parker Sargent, Lee Sharmat, Ann Stephenson, David Velasco, Mauricio Zacharias.

Thank you to the staff at the various archives where I undertook research for this project: the Beinecke Rare Book & Manuscript Library, Yale University; the Henry W. and Albert A. Berg Collection of English and American Library, New York Public Library; the Manuscript and Archives Division, New York Public Library, and the Archive, The Lesbian, Gay, Bisexual and Transgender Community Center, New York.

This book was written during my Stevenson Junior Research

Fellowship in English at University College, Oxford. I am grateful to the College for supporting this project, and to the warmth and generosity of my colleagues: to my English colleagues Nick Halmi, Laura Varnam and Laura Wright. To Andy Bell, Robin Darwall-Smith and Peter Gilliver, Elizabeth Adams and Phil Burnett, Roxana Willis. To Joe Moshenska, for reading the first half of the manuscript and giving insightful feedback, and for our shared journeys through Joyce and Proust, which have illuminated and informed my thinking in so many ways. (Fire Island still makes me think of Balbec.) To Mirela Ivanova, for your perspectives on parts of this book; for the solidarity and so many great times.

To Daisy Leitch, for being a wonderful friend and mentor to me, both in my capacity at 5x15 and as a writer. To Robyn Massey, for your time, advice and warm hospitality when I arrived in New York. To Olivia Laing, for our conversations and shared writing mornings in the Alphabet City, and your continued support of my work. To Michael Bronski, for our weekly chats, your encouragement, and for being so generous with your encyclopedic knowledge of queer history.

To my teachers: Karen Dean, Jonathan Akin, Sarah Addison, Deborah Bowman. I continue to be grateful for the ways your teaching inspired me. To Anne Stillman, for showing me what it means to take writing seriously, and for so much more.

To my brilliant friends—it is hard to do justice here to our friendships, in all their particularities and particular joys. My love and gratitude to Charlotte, Temi, Becca, Jasmine, Katie, Mirela, Tessa, Astrid, Celine, Alex, Josie, Lauren, Steph, Mary, Josh, Emma, Ed, Toby, Adelais, Madi, Flora, Jess, Alice, Angelica, Chelsea, Cal, Sam, Jazz, Hannah, Sophie, Matt, Yass, Kitty. Alec and Jake, who kindly gave feedback on parts of the manuscript. To my friends in New York and the US: Jacqueline, Phil, Hannah, Alex. To the strangers I've met at bars and on Fire Island.

To Ola. You are everywhere in this book, from the supercut of that beautiful summer in the city, where our bond was tested and made, and where the stakes of this project first emerged, to our subsequent years together, split between London and Oxford, when I was researching and writing it. Our relationship may be in the past now, but I'm grateful for your love and for our friendship.

To my sisters Clare and Lou, to Maggie and Annie and to all our extended family, to Kay and to Gail, for your support over the years.

To my beloved parents, Linda and Martin, and sister and best friend, Hannah. I feel extremely lucky to be held in the world by you; to be heard and motivated in hard times; to be celebrated and encouraged in good ones. Your love and your confidence in me have been more important than I can say.

To write a book about an important queer space is a privilege, and I dedicate this work to the memory of those who came before us. To the queer people who have been lost, and are still being lost, all over the world, far away from Fire Island's shores, to the intersecting and insidious forces of heteropatriarchy, white supremacy and capitalism; to illness, violence, and intolerance. We will not be free until all of us are.

APPENDIX:

A *Fire Island* Reading List

This book began life as a literary history, though as the richness and expansiveness of Fire Island's cultural canon emerged, the project incorporated examples from multiple creative forms. During my research, I have put together a list, comprehensive but not exhaustive, of texts, plays and film works in which Cherry Grove and the Pines feature prominently. I share it here, arranged chronologically and by category, as a resource for casual readers, interested scholars and fellow island enthusiasts.

A real highlight, and a book to which I and any Fire Island scholar must be indebted, is Esther Newton's majestic anthropological study, *Cherry Grove, Fire Island: Sixty Years in America's First Gay and Lesbian Town* (Durham, N.C.: Duke University Press, 1993). Along with her essay "Dick(less) Tracy and the Homecoming Queen: Lesbian Power and Representation in Gay Male Cherry Grove" (collected in *Margaret Mead Made Me Gay: Essays*, Duke, 2000), Newton's book is essential reading for anyone interested in the formation of the Grove and the nature of community-building in twentieth-century queer America.

Online, fascinating and engaging work is being done by members of the island's communities. Both the *Cherry Grove Archives*

Collection, chaired by Troy Files, and the *Pines Historical Preservation Society*, created and maintained by Robert Bonnano, hold a wealth of photographs, articles and stories that are shared regularly on their websites and social media pages. Columns about the island by community historians such as Carl Luss and John Bogack can be read in the online editions of the *Fire Island News* and the *Fire Island Star*, respectively.

A *FIRE ISLAND* READING LIST

NONFICTION

Alexander Goodman, *A Summer on Fire Island* (Washington, D.C.: Guild Press, 1966)

Jack Nichols, *Welcome to Fire Island: Visions of Cherry Grove and the Pines* (New York: St. Martin's Press, 1976)

Edmund White, *States of Desire: Travels in Gay America* (New York: E.P. Dutton, 1980)

Randy Shilts, *And the Band Played On* (New York: St. Martin's Press, 1987)

John Jiler, *Dark Wind: A True Account of Hurricane Gloria's Assault on Fire Island* (New York: St. Martin's Press, 1993)

Michelangelo Signorile, *Life Outside: The Signorile Report on Gay Men: Sex, Drugs, Muscles and the Passages of Life* (New York: HarperCollins, 1998)

Steve Weinstein, *The Q Guide to Fire Island* (Boston: Alyson Books, 2007)

Kent Johnson, *A Question Mark Above the Sun: Documents on the Mystery Surrounding a Famous Poem "By" Frank O'Hara* (Buffalo, NY: Starcherone Books, 2012)

MEMOIR AND ESSAYS

Andrew Holleran, *Ground Zero* (New York: William Morrow & Co., 1988)

Alan Helms, *Young Man from the Provinces: A Gay Life Before Stonewall* (London: Faber & Faber, 1995)

Felice Picano, *A House on the Ocean, A House on the Bay* (London: Faber & Faber, 1997)

Andrew Tobias, *The Best Little Boy in the World* (New York: Random House, 1998)

William Murray, *Janet, My Mother, and Me* (New York: Simon & Schuster, 2000)

Marijane Meaker, *Highsmith: A Romance of the 1950's* (San Francisco: Cleis Press, 2003)

Greg Scarnici, *Dungeons & Drag Queens: Fire Island Through the Eyes of Its Worst Drag Queen* (Independently published, 2019)

FICTION

John Mosher, *Celibate at Twilight* (New York: Random House, 1940)

Donald Windham, "An Island of Fire," *The Warm Country* (New York: Charles Scribner's Son, 1962)

Becky Crocker, *Mr. Ladybug* (Los Angeles: Sherbourne Press, 1968)

Marijane Meaker, *Shockproof Sydney Skate* (Boston: Little, Brown, 1972)

Edmund White, *Forgetting Elena* (New York: Random House, 1973)

Patricia Nell Warren, *The Front Runner* (New York: William Morrow & Co., 1974)

William Delligan, *Cherry Grove* (New York: Popular Library, 1976)

   Fire Island Pines (New York: Popular Library, 1977)

Larry Kramer, *Faggots* (New York: Random House, 1978)

Andrew Holleran, *Dancer from the Dance* (New York: William Morrow & Co., 1978)

   "Nipples," *Christopher Street* 4.4 (December 1979)

Felice Picano, *The Lure* (New York: Delacorte, 1979)

   Late in the Season (New York: Delacorte, 1981)

George Whitmore, *The Confessions of Danny Slocum* (New York: St. Martin's Press, 1980)

   Out Here: Fire Island Tales (unpublished, Beinecke Library, Yale University)

Ethan Mordden, *I've A Feeling We're Not in Kansas Anymore* (New York: St. Martin's Press, 1985)

Buddies (New York: St. Martin's Press, 1987)

Everybody Loves You (St. Martin's Press, 1988)

Christopher Davis, *Joseph and the Old Man* (New York: St. Martin's Press, 1986)

The Valley of the Shadow (New York: St. Martin's Press, 1988)

The Boys in the Bars (Stamford, CT: Knights Press, 1989)

Walter Holland, *Fire Island Story* (1988, unpublished, LGBT Community Center Archive, New York)

Summer of Love (unpublished, LGBT Community Center Archive, New York)

Allen Barnett, *The Body and Its Dangers* (New York: St. Martin's Press, 1991)

Felice Picano, *Like People in History* (New York: Viking, 1995)

Peg Kerr, *The Wild Swans* (New York: Grand Central, 1995)

Andrew Holleran, *In September, the Light Changes* (New York: Hyperion, 1999)

Mario López-Cordero, *Monarch Season* (New York: Riverdale Avenue Books, 2013)

Edmund White, *Our Young Man* (New York: Bloomsbury, 2016)

Andrew Durbin, *MacArthur Park* (New York: Nightboat Books, 2017)

Larry Kramer, *The Brutality of Fact (The American People: Volume 2)* (New York: Macmillan, 2020)

POETRY

W. H. Auden, "Pleasure Island" (1948), *Collected Poems*, ed. Edward Mendelson (New York: Random House, 1976)

Frank O'Hara, "For James Dean," "Thinking of James Dean," "Four Little Elegies" (1955), "Ode: Salute to the French Negro Poets," "A True Account of Talking to the Sun at Fire Island" (1958), *Collected Poems*, ed. Donald Allen (New York: Alfred A. Knopf, 1971)

May Swenson, "Fire Island" (1969), *Iconographs* (New York: Charles Scribner's Sons, 1970)

Michael Lynch, *These Waves of Dying Friends: Poems* (New York: Contact II, 1989)

Walter Holland, *A Journal of the Plague Years: Poems 1979–1992* (New York: Magic City Press, 1992)

   Translatlantic (New York: Painted Leaf Press, 2001)

   Circuit (New York: Chelsea Station Editions, 2010)

David Groff, *Theory of Devolution* (Urbana and Chicago: University of Illinois Press, 2002)

Clay (Florida: Trio House Press, 2013)

Michael Klein, *The Talking Day* (Little Rock, AR: Sibling Rivalry Press, 2013)

Mark Doty, "King of Fire Island," *Deep Lane* (New York: W.W. Norton & Co., 2015)

Ari Banias, "The Men," *Anybody* (New York: W.W. Norton & Co., 2016)

Sophie Robinson, "fucking up on the rocks," *Rabbit* (Norwich: Boiler House Press, 2019)

Jameson Fitzpatrick, "A True Account of Overhearing Andy Cohen at Fire Island," "Roughly," "White Gays," "The Pines," *Birds in the Tapestry* (New York: Birds, LLC, 2020)

PLAYS

George Whitmore, *The Rights*, Network Theatre, New York, January 1980

Terry Miller, *Pines '79: A Romantic Comedy in Two Acts*, Shandol Theatre, New York, October 1981 (play text published by JH Press, 1982)

John Glines, *On Tina Tuna Walk*, Courtyard Playhouse, New York, December 1988

Terrence McNally, *Lips Together, Teeth Apart*, Manhattan Theatre Club, New York, May 1991 (play text published by The Fireside Theatre, 1992)

Charles Mee, *Fire Island*, 3LD Art & Technology Center, New York, April 2008

Matthew Lopez, *The Inheritance*, Young Vic, London, May 2018 (play text published by Faber & Faber, 2018)

Michael R. Jackson, *A Strange Loop*, Playwrights Horizons, New York, June 2019 (play text published by Theatre Communications Group, 2021)

Jeremy O. Harris [@GaryXXXFisher], *Black Exhibition*, Bushwick Starr, Brooklyn, November 2019

FILMS AND TELEVISION SERIES

Camille (dir. Jerett Robert Austin, 1950)

My Hustler (dir. Andy Warhol, 1965)

Last Summer (dir. Frank Perry, 1969)

Double Exposure (dir. Peter de Rome, 1969)

The Fire Island Kids (dir. Peter de Rome, 1970)

Sticks and Stones (dir. Stan Lopresto, 1970)

Boys in the Sand (dir. Wakefield Poole, 1971)

Fire Island (dir. Derek Jarman, 1974)

A Very Natural Thing (dir. Christopher Larkin, 1974)

Boys in the Sand II (dir. Wakefield Poole, 1984)

Parting Glances (dir. Bill Sherwood, 1986)

Longtime Companion (dir. Norman Rene, 1989)

Fire Island (Bravo TV, 1999)

When Ocean Meets Sky (dir. Crayton Robey, 2003)

The Normal Heart (HBO, dir. Ryan Murphy, 2014)

Cherry Grove Stories (dir. Michael Fisher, 2018)

Fire Island (Logo TV, 2017)

Last Ferry (dir. Jaki Bradley, 2019)

Fire Island (dir. Andrew Ahn, 2022)

American Horror Story: NYC (Ryan Murphy, 2022)

A fuller list of films, including adult and pornographic works, can be found in Sam Ashby's "List of Films Shot on Fire Island, New York," *Failed States*, 1 (September 2017)

DOCUMENTARY FILMS

When Ocean Meets Sky (dir. Crayton Robey, 2003)

The Panzi Invasion (dir. Parker Sargent, 2016)

SNAP—Year of a Queen (dir. Parker Sargent, 2018)

Cherry Grove Stories (dir. Michael Fisher, 2018)

Grove Girls (dir. Parker Sargent, 2019)

VISUAL ART AND ARCHITECTURE

David Morgan, *Beach* (New York: St. Martin's Press, 2000)

Christopher Bascom Rawlins, *Fire Island Modernist: Horace Gifford and the Architecture of Seduction* (New York: Metropolis Books, 2013)

Tom Bianchi, *Fire Island Pines: Polaroids: 1975–1983* (Bologna: Damiani, 2013)

Lorraine H. Michels, *The Invasion of the Pines: 40 Years of Fun, Frolic and Fantasy*, 1976–2015 (independently published, 2015)

Susan Kravitz, *Mascara, Mirth & Mayhem: Independence Day on Fire Island* (New York: KMW Studio, 2016)

Alex Geana, *Fire Island* (New York: Glitterati, 2019)

Jarett Earnest, ed., *The Young and the Evil: Queer Modernism in New York 1930–1955* (New York: David Zwirner, 2020)

Talking to the Sun at Fire Island (New York: BOFFO, 2019)

koitz, *Gay Fire Island: It's Good to Be Us* (koitz, 2020)

Matthew Leifheit, *To Die Alive* (Bologna: Damiani, 2022)

LOCAL/COMMUNITY HISTORIES

Charles Dickerson, *A History of the Sayville Community, Including Bayport, Bohemia, West Sayville, Oakdale, and Fire Island* (Sayville Rotary Club, 1975)

Madeleine C. Johnson, *Fire Island: 1650s–1980s* (Point O'Woods Historical Society, 1983)

Lee E. Koppelman and Seth Forman, *The Fire Island National Seashore: A History* (Albany, NY: SUNY Press, 2008)

Shoshanna McCollum, *Fire Island: Beach Resort and National Seashore* (Mount Pleasant, SC: Arcadia Publishing, 2012)

Lorraine H. Michels, *Celebrating the Heart of Cherry Grove: The Community House 1948–2013* (Independently published, 2013)

Christopher Verga, *Saving Fire Island from Robert Moses: The Fight for a National Seashore* (Mount Pleasant, SC: History Press, 2019)

Robert Bonnano, *Beach: Fire Island 79* (Fire Island Pines Historical Preservation Society, 2019)

ACADEMIC CHAPTERS AND ARTICLES

James Miller, "Dante on Fire Island: Reinventing Heaven in the AIDS Elegy," in *Writing AIDS: Gay Literature, Language and Analysis*, ed. Timothy F. Murphy and Suzanne Poirier (New York: Columbia University Press, 1993)

David Bergman, "Beauty and the Beach: Representing Fire Island," in *Public Sex/Gay Space*, ed. William Leap (New York: Columbia University Press, 1999)

Jerry Yung-Ching Chang, "The Pornethnography of 'Boys in the Sand': Fetishisms of Race and Class in the 1970s Gay Fire Island Pines," *Women's Studies Quarterly*, 43.3/4 (Fall/Winter 2015)

Jack Parlett, "The Boys on the Beach: Andrew Holleran's Fire Island," in *Narrating and Constructing the Beach: An Interdisciplinary Approach*, ed. Carina Breidenbach et al. (De Gruyter, 2020)

NOTES

INTRODUCTION: WRITTEN IN THE SAND

16 "We shall have everything…": Frank O'Hara, "Ode to Joy," *The Collected Poems of Frank O'Hara*, ed. Donald Allen, p. 281.

17 "took half…": Jameson Fitzpatrick, "A True Account of Overhearing Andy Cohen at Fire Island," *Pricks in the Tapestry* (New York: Birds, LLC, 2020), p. 17.

17 "my favourite…": Sophie Robinson, "fucking up on the rocks", *Rabbit* (Norwich: Boiler House Press, 2018), p. 75.

17 "gay life is stories…in the telling": Ethan Mordden, *I've a Feeling We're Not in Kansas Anymore* (New York: St. Martin's Press, 1985), n.p.

20 "madness, for hot nights…": Holleran, *Dancer from the Dance* (London: Penguin, 1990 [1978]), pp. 206–7

23 a "stock theme…": Henning Bech, *When Men Meet: Homosexuality and Modernity*, trans. Teresa Mesquit and Tim Davies (Cambridge: Polity Press, 1997), p. 37.

"All paradises…": Toni Morrison, conversation with Elizabeth Farnsworth, *PBS NewsHour*, March 9, 1998.

24 "too white…": Esther Newton, "Dick(less) Tracy and the Homecoming Queen: Lesbian Power and Representation in Gay Male Cherry Grove", in *Margaret Mead Made Me Gay: Essays* (Durham, N.C.: Duke University Press, 2000), p. 85.

PART ONE: ORIGIN (1882–1938)

CHAPTER 1: A SPIT OF LAND

29 "wampum…": Madeleine C. Johnson, *Fire Island: 1650s–1980s* (Point O'Woods: Point O'Woods Historical Society, 1983), p. 14.

30 "seemed to be providing…": Cindy S. Aron, *Working at Play: A History of Vacations in the United States* (Oxford: Oxford University Press, 1999), p. 79.

30 "Long Island is destined…": *The Brooklyn Daily Eagle*, August 29, 1880, p. 4.

31 "black cherry trees…": Esther Newton, *Cherry Grove, Fire Island: Sixty Years in America's First Gay and Lesbian Town* (Durham: Duke University Press, 2014 [1993]), p. 16.

"a brief flash… Fire Island": Walt Whitman, *Complete Prose Works* (Philadelphia: David Mackay, 1892), p. 160.

31 "thirty or forty…": Whitman, "A Week at West Hills," *New York Tribune*, August 4, 1881.

"south side—the Great South Bay…": Whitman, "Long Island Is a Great Place!", Brooklyn Daily Times, July 30, 1857, p. 2.

32 "adhesiveness…": Whitman, *Leaves of Grass*, ed. Michael Moon (New York: Norton Critical Editions, 2002), p. 657.

32 "proto-cruising moments…encounters…": Michael D. Snediker, "Whitman on the Verge: Or the Desires of Solitude," *Arizona Quarterly* 61.3 (Autumn 2005), p. 28.

33 "little black-eyed…": Whitman, *Daybooks and Notebooks*, ed. William White, 3 vols. (New York: New York University Press, 1977), vol. 1, pp. 229–30.

34 "I have nothing…": See Michele Mendelssohn, *Making Oscar Wilde* (Oxford: Oxford University Press, 2018), p. 65.

"I took him up...": "The Aesthetic Singer Visits the Good Gray Poet," *The Philadelphia Press*, January 19, 1882, p. 8.

35 "The kiss...": Wilde quoted in *Oscar Wilde* (London: Penguin Books, 1988), pp.163–4.

36 "first-class Summer...": "The Charms of Long Beach," *Frank Leslie's Illustrated Newspaper*, August 12, 1882, p. 6.

"surprising number of ladies...": *The New Brunswick Daily Times*, 21 July, 1882, p. 2.

"one of the most beautiful...": Charles Dickerson, "A Century at the Grove," *Fire Island News*, July 19, 1969, p. 8.

37 "A map of the world...": Oscar Wilde, "The Soul of Man Under Socialism", in *The Soul of Man Under Socialism and Other Essays* (New York: Harper & Row, 1970) p. 246.

"the first homosexual...": Rodwell quoted in "Oscar Wilde Memorial Bookshop," *NYC LGBT Historic Sites Project*, online.

"incanting lines": Jack Nichols, *Welcome to Fire Island* (New York: St. Martin's Press, 1976), p. 42.

38 "Declaration...": Newton, *Cherry Grove*, p. 239.

CHAPTER 2: CHOSEN FAMILIES

39 "rollicking hilarity...": Charles M. Bayer, "Fire Island Is Sad Over Jail Delay", *New York Times*, July 28, 1935, Section 2, p. 1.

40 "welcome deficits...": Newton, *Cherry Grove*, p. 22.

41 "relatively innocent time...": William Murray, *Janet, My Mother & Me: A Memoir of Growing Up with Janet Flanner and Natalia Danesi Murray* (New York: Simon & Schuster, 2000), pp. 31–2.

42 "so-called meat rack...": ibid., p. 33.

42 "a Kodak picture…": Janet Flanner, *Darlinghissima: Letters to a Friend*, ed. Natalia Danesi Murray (New York: Random House, 1985), p. 486.

"demolished…": Murray, *Janet, My Mother & Me*, p. 97.

43 "keeps house…": John Mosher, "Beachcombers," *The New Yorker*, May 27, 1939, p. 20.

44 "those everlasting cocktails…": ibid., p. 21

45 "sweet, vain, pouting…": Midge Decter, "The Boys on the Beach," *Commentary*, September 1980.

"Militant homosexuality…": "To the Editor," *Commentary*, December 1980.

"became the most…": George Chauncey, *Gay New York: The Making of the Gay Male World, 1890–1940* (London: Flamingo, 1995), p. 229.

46 "existence of these early…": Brian Stack and Peter Boag, "George Chauncey's *Gay New York*: A View from 25 Years Later," *The Journal of the Gilded Age and Progressive Era* 18 (2019), p. 122.

47 "larger lexicon…": See Chauncey, *Gay New York*.

"is one of the clearest…": Newton, *Cherry Grove*, p. 21.

48 "present apathy…": J. Edgar Hoover quoted in Michael Bronski, *A Queer History of the United States* (Boston: Beacon Press, 2011), p. 124.

"so that it could…": ibid.

"long-standing public image…": Chauncey, *Gay New York*, pp. 359–60.

"the 'family'…": Newton, *Cherry Grove*, p. 19.

49 "She was not…": *Suffolk County News*, September 23, 1938, p. 3.

50 "The hurricane…":, Newton, *Cherry Grove*, p. 26.

"frightened straights...": John Jiler, *Dark Wind: A True Account of Hurricane Gloria's Assault on Fire Island* (St. Martin's Press, 1993), p. 138.

51 "Fire Island School...": Oral history interview with Paul Cadmus, March 22–May 5, 1988. Archives of American Art, Smithsonian Institution.

"just to check...": ibid.

52 "manic merriment...": Murray, *Janet, My Mother & Me*, pp. 27–8.

"might have been invented...": Claude Lévi-Strauss, *Tristes Tropiques*, trans. John Weightman and Doreen Weightman (London: Penguin, 2011 [1976]), p. 163.

PART TWO: ENCLAVE (1939–1969)

CHAPTER 3: TWO PEOPLE

58 "In the summer...": For an account of these years, see Donald Windham, "St. Luke's Place," Box 23, p. 6, MSS 424, Donald Windham and Sandy Campbell Papers. Yale Collection of American Literature, Beinecke Rare Book and Manuscript Library, Yale University.

59 "Born in 1920...": This account of Windham's early life is drawn from Bruce Kellner, *Donald Windham: A Bio-Bibliography* (New York: Greenwood Press, 1991), pp. xix–xi.

60 "during a cruise...": Donald Windham, "St. Luke's Place," p. 15.

61 "I meant to get...": Quoted in Tennessee Williams, *Notebooks*, ed. Margaret Bradham Thornton (New Haven: Yale University Press, 2006), p. 414.

"When one of these...": Windham (ed.), *Tennessee Williams' Letters to Donald Windham 1940–1965* (New York: Holt, Rinehart and Winston, 1977), p. 139.

"the atmosphere...": Tennessee Williams to James Laughlin, June 9, 1944, *The Luck of Friendship: The Letters of Tennessee Williams and James Laughlin*, ed. Peggy L. Fox and Thomas Keith (New York: W.W. Norton, 2018), p. 42.

"Audrey Hartman…": *Cherry Grove Stories*.

"an entire section…": These events are detailed in Windham, "Fire Island," Box 25, MSS 424.

63 "She is such…": *Tennessee Williams' Letters to Donald Windham*, p. 233.

"are simply written…they will decay": E. M. Forster, "Introduction," in ibid., n.p.

64 "servants are…entirely left out": Windham, "An Island of Fire," in *The Warm Country* (New York: Charles Scribner's Sons, 1962), pp. 147–9.

65 "The Carrington House…": National Register of Historic Places Registration Form, "Carrington House," United States Department of the National Interior, National Park Service, online.

66 "cute little…": Laura Durkin, "A Special Home Restored," *Newsday*, August 25, 1982, n.p.

"heated phone call…": Donald Windham, *Lost Friendships: A Memoir of Truman Capote, Tennessee Williams, and Others* (New York: William Morrow, 1987), p. 157.

67 "Stories about…": ibid., pp. 38–9.

68 "People disappearing…": Windham, June 26, 1988: *The First Pages of a Memoir* (Verona: Officina Bodoni, 1992), p. 19.

"beige…": Windham, "Work in Progress," Box 23, MSS 244, n.p. Quotation with permission of © Yale University. All rights reserved.

"What happened…": ibid.

CHAPTER 4: BODY FASCISM

72 "The 'body fascist'…": Mickey Weems, *The Fierce Tribe: Masculine Identity and Performance in the Circuit* (Logan: Utah State University Press, 2008), p. 37.

73 "each spring contemplated suicide…": Andrew Holleran, *Dancer from the Dance* (London: Penguin, 1990 [1978]), p. 31.

74 "He bought a house…": Newton, *Cherry Grove*, p. 47.

"had no use…": Christopher Isherwood, *Christopher and His Kind* (New York: Farrar, Straus & Giroux, 1976), p. 81.

75 "the most famous…": Quoted in ibid.

"doing exercises…": Stephen Spender, *Journals 1939–1983* (London: Faber & Faber, 1985), p. 28.

"manhood and the strong, athletic…": Bronski, *A Queer History of the United States*, p. 132.

76 "Cadmus said…": Oral history interview with Paul Cadmus, 1988.

"manly mesomorph…": Auden, "Behold the Manly Mesomorph," *Collected Poems*, ed. Edward Mendelson (New York: Random House, 1976), p. 436.

"aged very quickly…": Richard R. Bozorth, *Auden's Games of Knowledge: Poetry and the Meanings of Homosexuality* (New York: Columbia University Press, 2001), p. 240.

"I am really too…": W. H. Auden to James and Tania Stern, May 27, 1947, MSS Auden, W. H. Auden Papers, Henry W. and Albert A. Berg Collection of English and American Literature, New York Public Library. W. H Auden's letters are quoted here with the permission of the Estate of W. H. Auden.

77 "Bassett's Roost…": Nicholas Jenkins, "Some Letters from Auden to the Sterns," in *"In Solitude for Company": W.H. Auden After 1940*, ed. Katherine Bucknell and Nicholas Jenkins, p. 57.

"served by sluts…": ibid., p. 87.

"tar-paper-covered…": Newton, *Cherry Grove*, p. 47.

"Paula Schmuck...": W. H. Auden to James and Tania Stern, July 8, 1946, MSS Auden, New York Public Library.

78 "Richard Avedon...": For an account of Avedon's time in Cherry Grove, see Philip Gefter, *What Becomes a Legend Most: A Biography of Richard Avedon* (New York: Harper Collins, 2020), pp. 106–15.

79 "I grow old...": T.S. Eliot, "The Love Song of J. Alfred Prufrock," *The Waste Land and Other Poems* (London: Faber & Faber, 1999 [1940]), p. 7.

"I arrived...": W. H. Auden to Rhoda Jaffe, August 3, 1946, MSS Auden, New York Public Library.

"unwashed dishes...": Christopher Isherwood, *Lost Years* (New York: Harper Collins, 2000), p. 129.

80 "It's the wrong blond...": Dorothy J. Farnan, *Auden in Love* (New York: New American Library, 1985), p. 21.

81 "Neither of them...": Isherwood, *Lost Years*, p. 129.

"At night...", ibid.

"very flattered...": W. H. Auden to Rhoda Jaffe, 1947, MSS Auden, New York Public Library.

82 "earthy...analysing herself": Farnan, *Auden in Love*, pp. 119–20.

"I'm so looking...": Auden to Rhoda Jaffe, 1946, MSS Auden, New York Public Library.

"real man in bed...": Farnan, *Auden in Love*, p. 120.

"affair with a woman...": Auden quoted in ibid., pp. 123–4.

83 "ash-blonde vegetable rinse...": ibid., p. 123.

"I am at a loss...": Quoted in Jenkins, "Some Letters," p. 99.

"dykes have…": Auden to James and Tania Stern, August 9, 1947, MSS Auden, New York Public Library.

"Grove founders…": Newton, *Cherry Grove*, p. 205.

"pet hate…": Auden to James and Tania Stern, August 9, 1947, MSS Auden, New York Public Library.

84 "I wish my…": Auden to James and Tania Stern, July 16, 1947, MSS Auden, New York Public Library.

"loafs through…": *LIFE*, May 17, 1948, p. 52.

85 "Mediterranean version…": Truman Capote, *Too Brief a Treat: The Letters of Truman Capote*, ed. Gerald Clarke (New York: Knopf Doubleday Publishing Group, 2005), p. 81.

"People don't understand that it's possible…": "Eclogue, 1947," *TIME*, July 21, 1947, p. 100.

"accomplishing immortal…": Auden, "Pleasure Island," *Collected Poems*, p. 266.

"if the intellectual life…": Maurice Cranston, "Poet's Retreat," *John O'London's Weekly*, February 6, 1948, p. 50.

"bosom, backside…": Auden, "Pleasure Island," p. 266.

86 "A body…": Auden to James and Tania Stern, August 9, 1947, MSS Auden, New York Public Library.

"undesirables…": "2 'Nudists' Given 90-Day Sentences in Clean-Up Drives," *The Patchogue Advance*, Thursday, July 14, 1949, p. 1.

CHAPTER 5: LIKE WATER

88 "life of a resort…": Marcel Proust, *Sodom and Gomorrah*, trans. John Sturrock (New York: Penguin Classic Deluxe, 2002), p. 256.

"Mother thinks...": Marijane Meaker, *Highsmith: A Romance of the 1950s* (San Francisco: Cleis Press, 2003), p. 45.

89 "had something else...": Newton, *Cherry Grove*, p. 83.

"Like so many lesbians...": Jenn Shapland, *My Autobiography of Carson McCullers* (Portland: Tin House Press, 2020), p. 153.

"To Fire Island...": Patricia Highsmith, "Friday 18 August, 1950", journal entry, Diary 10, C-01/10, Patricia Highsmith Life Papers and Documents, Swiss Literary Archives, Berne.

90 "reeking of liquor...": Joan Schenkar, *The Talented Miss Highsmith: The Secret Life and Serious Art of Patricia Highsmith* (London: Picador, 2011), p. 275.

"worse and worse...": Highsmith, "Sunday 20 August, 1950", journal entry, Diary 10, Patricia Highsmith Life Papers and Documents.

"notorious lesbian...": Patricia Schartle quoted in Schenkar, p. 223.

91 "gay bars...": Highsmith, *Carol* (London: Bloomsbury, 2010 [1952]), p. 311.

"If I were...": ibid., p. 311.

92 "waves of shame...": Schenkar, p. 275.

"I shall try...": Highsmith quoted in ibid.

93 "erupted...": Sally Brown and David R. Brown, *A Biography of Mrs. Marty Mann: The First Lady of Alcoholics Anonymous* (Center City: Hazelden, 2001), p. 226.

"pleasures of intoxication...": Newton, *Cherry Grove*, p. 79.

"persecutions...": "Newton, *Cherry Grove*, p. 101.

94 "insisted on having...": Highsmith, "July 1, 1953", *Her Diaries and Notebooks*, ed. Anna Von Planta (London: Weidenfeld & Nicholson), p. 606.

"Ideal weather…": "July 3, 1953", ibid., p. 607.

95 "Much drinking…": "July 4, 1953", ibid., p.607

"most physicians…": Audrey Borden, *The History of Gay People in Alcoholics Anonymous from the Beginning* (New York: Routledge, 2013), p. 60.

"beneficent results…": D'Emilio, *Sexual Politics, Sexual Communities: The Making of a Homosexual Minority in the United States, 1940–1970* (Chicago: University of Chicago Press, 1983), p. 18.

96 "most available milieu…": Thomas O. Ziebold and John E. Mongeon, *Alcoholism and Homosexuality* (New York: Haworth, 1982), p. 5.

97 "blissful days…": Meaker, *Highsmith*, p. 43.

98 "never developed…": Newton, *Cherry Grove*, p. 107.

99 "simple modernist…": Douglas Crimp, *Before Pictures* (Chicago: University of Chicago Press, 2016), p. 112.

100 "This summer…": Carson McCullers, "The Dark Brilliance of Edward Albee," *Harper's Bazaar*, January 1963, p. 98–9.

101 "numerous film adaptations…": Rex Reed, "'Frankie Addams' at 50," *New York Times*, April 16, 1967, p. D15.

102 "empathetic…": Shapland, *My Autobiography*, p. 143.

CHAPTER 6: OVER THE RAINBOW

104 "overt homosexuality…": Robert C. Doty, "Growth of Overt Homosexuality Provoking Rising Concern," *New York Times*, December 17, 1963, p. 33.

106 "I immediately phoned…": Joe LeSueur, *Digressions on Some Poems by Frank O'Hara* (New York: Farrar, Straus & Giroux, 2003), p. 66.

"jackets and…": Paul Goodman, Growing Up Absurd: Problems of

Youth in the Organized System (New York: Random House, 1960), p. 163.

"good haberdashers…": ibid.

107 "as a 'professional'…": American Legends interview with James Bellah, quoted in *The Real James Dean: Intimate Memories from Those Who Knew Him Best*, ed. Peter Winkler (Chicago: Chicago Review Press, 2016), p. 117.

"a nickelodeon…": O'Hara, "Thinking of James Dean," *Collected Poems*, p. 230.

"cold last swim…": ibid., p. 231.

108 "I seem to…": LeSueur, *Digressions*, p. 68.

"as LeSueur remembers…": ibid., p. 181.

109 "proffered the theory…": see Kent Johnson, *A Question Mark Above the Sun: Documents on the Mystery Surrounding a Famous Poem "By" Frank O'Hara* (Buffalo, NY: Starcherone Books, 2012).

"easier for me…": O'Hara, "A True Account of Talking to the Sun at Fire Island," *Collected Poems*, p. 307.

"adamantly opposed…": LeSueur, *Digressions*, p. 227.

"I have been…": O'Hara, "Poem (Lana Turner Has Collapsed!)," *Collected Poems*, p. 449.

110 "grim, inland…": Baldwin, quoted in Magdalena Zaborowska, *James Baldwin's Turkish Decade: Erotics of Exile* (Durham: Duke University Press, 2009), p. 42.

"pushing itself…": Baldwin quoted in ibid., p. 91.

"I do not…": Baldwin, "Autobiographical Notes," in *Collected Essays*, ed. Toni Morrison (New York: Library of America, 1998), p. 9.

111 "are few things…": Baldwin, "The Male Prison," ibid., p. 234.

"walking phallic…": Baldwin, "The Black Boy Looks at the White Boy," ibid., pp. 269–70.

"gay world…": Baldwin, "Freaks and the American Ideal of Manhood," ibid., p. 824.

"near the sea…": O'Hara, "Ode: Salute to the French Negro Poets," *Collected Poems*, p. 305.

112 "the increasing appearance…": see Newton, *Cherry Grove*, p. 142.

"record of white…": ibid., p. 150.

"Grove African-Americans…": ibid., p. 154.

113 "Brando…": David Leeming, *James Baldwin: A Biography* (New York: Arcade Publishing, 2015 [1994]), p. 46.

"not the black…": Baldwin, "Mass Culture and the Creative Artist: Some Personal Notes," *Daedalus* 89.2 (Spring 1960), p. 376.

114 "Lee Strasberg's": reported in Fern Marja Eckman, *The Furious Passage of James Baldwin* (New York: M. Evans, 1966), p. 214.

115 "He is not…": "The Nation," *TIME*, May 17, 1963, p. 26.

116 "I don't really…": *The Noel Coward Diaries*, ed. Graham Payn (London: Phoenix, 2000), p. 542.

"more than unattractive…": ibid., p. 543.

"household electricity…": Newton, *Cherry Grove*, p. 114.

117 "I think white gay…": "'Go the Way Your Blood Beats': An Interview with James Baldwin," *James Baldwin: The Last Interview and Other Conversations* (New York: Melville House, 2014), p. 67.

"grassroots efforts…": see Christopher Verga, *Saving Fire Island from Robert Moses: The Fight for a National Seashore* (History Press, 2019).

118 "antipolitical…": Newton, *Cherry Grove*, p. 200.

"affirmed the uniqueness…": John D'Emilio, *Sexual Politics*, p. 58.

119 "In May 1965…": Author's correspondence with David Leeming.

120 "Mr. Ladybug…": Becky Crocker, *Mr. Ladybug* (Los Angeles: Sherbourne Press, 1968).

"were wary…": Leeming, *James Baldwin*, p. 228.

121 "are outraged…": Eldridge Cleaver, *Soul on Ice* (New York: Dell, 1968), p. 102.

"racial death-wish…": ibid., p. 103.

"the various liberation…": Huey P. Newton, "The Women's Liberation and Gay Liberation Movements: August 15, 1970," in *The Huey P. Newton Reader*, ed. David Hilliard and Donald Weise (New York: Seven Stories, 2002), p. 157.

"'sortie' into…look at…": J. J. Mitchell, "The Death of Frank O'Hara," in *Homage to Frank O'Hara* (Bolinas: Big Sky, 1978).

122 "it is time…": Marjorie Perloff, *Frank O'Hara: Poet Among Painters* (Chicago: University of Chicago Press, 1998), p. 5.

"No matter…": Peter Schjeldahl, "Frank O'Hara: He Made Things and People Sacred," *Village Voice*, August 11, 1966, p. 12.

123 "blue mimeograph…": Eric Cervini, *The Deviant's War: The Homosexual vs. the United States of America* (New York: Farrar, Straus & Giroux, 2020), p. 234.

"there had been plans…": reported in Scott Schechter, *Judy Garland: The Day-by-Day Chronicle of a Legend* (Lanham: Taylor Trade Publishing), p. 381.

123 "When I die...": Quoted in Barry Conley, "The Garland Legend: The Stars Have Lost Their Glitter," *Gay News* 13 (1972), p. 11.

"She was right... One of...": Vito Russo, "Rebellion Over the Rainbow: Did Judy Cause Stonewall?," *Out Week* 1 (June 26, 1989), p. 43.

PART THREE: HALCYON (1969–1979)

CHAPTER 7: HOMECOMING

127 "butch clone...": *The Alyson Almanac* (Boston: Alyson, 1989), p. 90.

129 "The story begins...": This account draws upon the oral history accounts in Parker Sargent's film *The Panzi Invasion*.

130 "at least nine...": Susan Kravitz, *Mascara, Mirth and Mayhem: Independence Day on Fire Island* (KMW Studio, 2016), p. 21.

131 "Rose Levine named...": ibid.

"metaphorical conflict...": Newton, *Cherry Grove*, p. 282.

"dowdy immigrant...": ibid., p. 270.

"it was a problem..." This account draws upon Newton's retelling in ibid., pp. 254–65.

132 "high camp...": Andrew Belonsky, "Shel Silverstein Covered Fire Island for 'Playboy,'" *Out*, May 22, 2013.

133 "Silverstein spoke...": Golan Y. Moskowitz, *Wild Visionary: Maurice Sendak in Queer Jewish Context* (Stanford: Stanford University Press, 2020), p. 137.

"the famous...": ibid., p. 136.

"whitehaired...": Leo MacAlbert [Leo Skir], "Four Trips to Cherry Grove", Tangents 1.5 (February 1966), p. 5.

134 "$2.65...": Leo MacAlbert [Leo Skir], "Four Trips to Cherry Grove", Tangents 1.6 (March 1966), p. 11.

135 "wooden, quaint...": Nichols, Welcome to Fire Island, p. 47.

"anarchist-inspired...": J. Louis Campbell, Jack Nichols, Gay Pioneer: Have You Heard My Message? (New York: Harrington Park Press, 2007), p. 149.

"To appreciate Cherry...": Nichols, Welcome to Fire Island, p. 46.

136 "group which calls...": "Five Notes on Collective Living," Come Out! 1.7, p. 7.

"free nature...": Jack Nichols and Lige Clarke, "Fire Island Fairy," Screw, July 31, 1969, p. 17.

137 "more and more...": Tom Bianchi, Fire Island Pines: Polaroids: 1975–1983 (Bologna: Damiani, 2013), p. 16.

138 "liberation porn...": Ryan Powell, Coming Together: The Cinematic Elaboration of Gay Male Life, 1945–1979 (Chicago: Chicago University Press, 2019), p. 176.

139 "you get out...": Albert Goldman, "I Have Seen the Future—and It's Fire Island," New York, July 24, 1972, p. 30.

"People were free...": Quoted in Rosemary Feitelberg, "Freedom and Summer Fun in the Seventies," Women's Wear Daily, July 2, 2020, p. 28.

"Fag Futuristic...": Goldman, "I Have Seen the Future," p. 30.

"Edmund White first went...": Stephen Barber, Edmund White: The Burning World (New York: St. Martin's Press, 1999), p. 53.

140 "rituals of gay men...": Edmund White, City Boy: My Life in New York During the 1960s and 1970s (London: Bloomsbury, 2009), p. 57.

"thé dansant...": Newton, Cherry Grove, p. 217.

141 "aficionado Michael Fesco...": this account draws upon Michael Fes-

co's retelling in Tim Lawrence, *Love Saves the Day: A History of American Dance Music Culture, 1970–1979* (Durham: Duke University Press, 2003), pp. 39–42.

"up on the idea...": ibid., p. 69.

142 "Those who rent...": Mordden, I've a Feeling We're Not in Kansas Anymore, p. 105.

"best-looking men...": White, *States of Desire: Travels in Gay America* (London: Picador, 1986 [1980]), p. 293.

"as a person...": ibid., p. 294.

143 "stay-at-homes...": Feitelberg, "Freedom and Summer Fun", p. 30.

"lives on the island...": White, *States of Desire*, p. 292.

"dressed in white...": Peter Adam, *David Hockney* (Bath: Absolute Press, 1997), p. 102.

"a deadly, well-heeled...": Derek Jarman, *Dancing Ledge* (Minneapolis: University of Minnesota Press, 2010), p. 128.

144 "every night...": Derek Jarman, *Kicking the Pricks* (Woodstock: Overlook Press, 1997), pp. 63–5.

"If I'm not there...": Elsa Bulgari, "Interview with Robert Mapplethorpe," *Fire Island Tide*, July 3, 1979, p. 13.

146 "not of boredom...": Quoted in Adam, *David Hockney*, p. 102.

147 "nationalism...": Newton, *Cherry Grove*, p. 10.

CHAPTER 8: LOVING THE DANCES

149 "Oh, he would...": Quoted in Stuart Byron, "Frank O'Hara's Poetic 'Queertalk,'" in *Frank O'Hara: To Be True to a City*, ed. Jim Elledge (Ann Arbor: University of Michigan, 1990), p. 69.

"cross between…": Arthur Bell, "The Year 2: Toward a Gay Community", *Village Voice*, July 1, 1971, online.

150 "disco culture were arguably…": Lawrence, *Love Saves the Day*, pp. 70–2.

"all these white…": Quoted in ibid., p. 71.

151 "body […] the thing…": Andrew Holleran, "My Harvard," in *Gay American Autobiography: Writings from Whitman to Sedaris*, ed. David Bergman (Madison: University of Wisconsin Press, 2009), p. 298.

"around 1972…": Author's correspondence with Andrew Holleran.

"bronzed…": Raymond Jean Frontain, "James Purdy's Provocative Ambiguities", *The Gay and Lesbian Review Worldwide*, online.

152 "beguiling…": Mordden, *I've a Feeling We're Not in Kansas Anymore*, p.105.

"four or five…": Holleran, *Dancer from the Dance*, p. 249.

154 "Holleran left New York…": "Interview: *Dancer from the Dance* Author Andrew Holleran," *Red Bull Music Academy*, November 9, 2015.

155 "songs that went…": Holleran, "Dark Disco: A Lament," in *The Violet Quill: The Emergence of Gay Writing After Stonewall*, ed. David Bergman (1994), pp. 191–2.

156 "summer some nameless…": Holleran, *Dancer from the Dance*, p. 32.

"a bathing suit…": Eric Laurence and Richard Danvers, "The Summer When Love Was the Boss," *Christopher Street* (November 1979), p. 21.

"blue denim…": ibid., p.22.

"six muscular men…": Ron Martin, "More than a New Fire Truck: A Personal Remembrance of *Beach*," 2018.

158 "people can't dance…": Fire Island Pines Businessmen's Association poster, 1977, Fire Island Pines Historical Preservation Society website.

"One thing leads…": ibid.

159 "political friend…": George Whitmore, *The Confessions of Danny Slocum* (New York: St. Martin's Press, 1979), pp. 25–6.

160 "seminar…": Terry Miller, *Pines 79* (New York: The JH Press, 1980), p. 95.

"No matter how…": Felice Picano, *A House on the Ocean, A House on the Bay* (London: Faber and Faber, 1997), p. 185.

"began to feel…": Lawrence, *Love Saves the Day*, p. 68.

161 "Picture a beach…": This illustration of *Beach* draws upon Martin, "More than a New Fire Truck." See also Robert Bonnano, *Beach: Fire Island '79* (Fire Island Pines Historical Preservation Society, 2019).

163 "odd sensation…": Holleran, *Dancer from the Dance*, p. 226.

164 "Our freewheeling…": Martin, "More than a New Fire Truck".

PART FOUR: PLAGUE (1981–2021)

CHAPTER 9: UNTIL DAWN

168 "What does Pride…": Larry Kramer, "What Pride Means to Me," *Salon*, June 30, 2019.

170 "I was living…": Quoted in Eric Marcus, *Making Gay History: The Half-Century Fight for Lesbian and Gay Equality* (New York: Perennial, 2002), p. 163.

"It's very, very…": "It's Hard to Walk Away from a Good Blow Job," *Gaysweek*, January 1, 1979, p. 13.

172 "200 or 300…": Quoted in Edward Guthmann, "The Cruising Controversy: William Friedkin vs. the Gay Community," *Cineaste* 10.3 (Summer 1980), p. 2.

"ignorant of…": Michael Denneny, "Interview with Felice Picano," *The Christopher Street Reader* (New York: Coward, McCann & Geoghegan, 1983), p. 34.

"The gay critics…": ibid., p. 37.

173 "no match…": Martin Duberman, *Midlife Queer: Autobiography of a Decade 1971–1981* (New York: Scribner, 1996), p. 21.

"kept a decidedly…": Randy Shilts, *And the Band Played On: Politics, People and the AIDS Epidemic* (London: Souvenir Press, 2011 [1987]), p. 26.

"I'm not saying…": "It's Hard to Walk Away from a Good Blow Job," p. 12.

174 "violet-colored…": Lawrence K. Altman, "Rare Cancer Seen in 41 Homosexuals," *New York Times*, July 3, 1981, p. 20.

176 "Larry thought…": Shilts, *And the Band Played On*, p. 25.

"spent the long…": David France, *How to Survive a Plague* (London: Picador, 2016), p. 14.

"During the Labor…": For Kramer's full account, see *Reports from the Holocaust: The Making of an AIDS Activist* (New York: St. Martin's Press, 1994), pp. 14–15.

178 "Kramer told us…": Quoted in ibid., p. 16.

"I was out…": ibid., p. 32.

180 "compelling project": Michael Schiavi, *Celluloid Activist: The Life and Times of Vito Russo* (Madison: University of Wisconsin Press, 2011), p. 223.

"significant...": Vito Russo, "Rebellion over the Rainbow: Did Judy Cause Stonewall?," *Out Week* 1 (June 26, 1989), p. 43.

181 "a movie star...": Shilts, p. xi.

183 "had begun to...": Schiavi, p. 248.

"smug atmosphere...": Martin Duberman, *Hold Tight Gently: Michael Callen, Essex Hemphill, and the Battlefield of AIDS* (New York: The New Press, 2014), p. 156.

184 "black frocks...": David Halperin, *How to Be Gay* (Cambridge: Harvard University Press, 2012), p. 179.

185 "someday there...": Christopher Davis, *Joseph and the Old Man* (New York: St. Martin's Press, 1986), p. 136.

186 "convalescing...": Simon Watney, "Vito Russo 1946–90," *Imagine Hope: AIDS and Gay Identity* (London: Taylor & Francis, 2002), p. 35.

"walked the entire...": Quoted in Will Kohler, "The Untold Story of How Lily Tomlin Helped Vito Russo Before He Passed Away from AIDS," *Back2Stonewall*, September 3, 2019.

187 "Last night...": Michael Lynch, *These Waves of Dying Friends*, p. 6.

188 "There must be...": Andrew Holleran, *Ground Zero* (New York: William Morrow, 1988), p. 219.

CHAPTER 10: FOR LIFE

189 "Odd the way...": David Groff, "Gloria," *Theory of Devolution* (Urbana and Chicago: University of Illinois Press, 2002), p. 16.

"last great party...": Groff, "A Scene of the Crime," ibid., p. 13.

190 "a ghost structure...": Andrew Holleran, "Fire Island, New York," *Hometowns: Gay Men Write About Where They Belong*, ed. John Preston (New York: Dutton, 1991), p. 304.

"I suspect nothing…": Holleran, "Ectoplasm," *Christopher Street* 163 (October 14, 1991), p. 4.

191 "zone of…": James Miller, "Dante on Fire Island: Reinventing Heaven in the AIDS Elegy," in *Writing AIDS: Gay Literature, Language and Analysis*, ed. Timothy F. Murphy and Suzanne Poirier (Columbia University Press, 1993), p. 269.

191 "I couldn't stop…": Walter Holland, "At the Pavilion," *A Journal of the Plague Years: Poems 1979–1992* (New York: Magic City Press, 1992), p. 52.

"strange queen…": Holland, "Season Opener, Fire Island," ibid., p. 45.

"looked ill…": "Death in Venice (Fire Island 1988)," ibid., p. 48.

192 "to be infected…": Nick Bamforth, *AIDS and the Healer Within* (New York: Amethyst Books, 1993), p. 6.

194 "all I've heard…": Allen Barnett, "The *Times* As It Knows Us," *The Body and Its Dangers* (New York: St. Martin's Press, 1991), p. 83.

195 "He was very…": Terrence McNally, *Lips Together, Teeth Apart* (New York: The Fireside Theatre, 1992), p. 109.

"Hang on…": ibid., p. 68.

196 "One drop…": ibid., p. 118.

197 "incestuous literati…": Joseph Beam (ed.), *In the Life: A Black Gay Anthology* (Boston: Alyson Publication, 1986), p. 13.

198 "not the fire…": Assotto Saint, "The Quilt," *Spells of a Voodoo Doll*, p. 69.

"Some of you…": Melvin Dixon, "I'll Be Somewhere Listening for My Name," *Callaloo* 23.1 (Winter 2000), p. 80.

"We […] guard…": ibid., p. 82.

199 "fickle sandbar…": Dixon, "Land's End," *Love's Instruments*.

"I shall return…": Dixon, "I'll Be Somewhere," p. 81.

"If I don't…": ibid., p. 83.

200 "as a black gay…": Quoted in "Reginald Shepherd 1963–2008," *Poetry Foundation*, online.

"*Two loves…*": Reginald Shepherd, "Icarus on Fire Island," *Callaloo* 21.2 (Spring 1998), p. 284.

"whiteness…": Shepherd, "On Not Being White," in *In the Life: A Black Gay Anthology*, p. 53.

"chasing white…": "Allan Robinson, AIDS Activist," in *Sojourner: Black Gay Voices in the Age of AIDS* (New York: Other Countries Press, 1993), p. 59.

"ghost presence…": Shepherd, "Illness and Poetry," *Poetry Foundation*, March 8, 2008.

202 "This summer…": Sarah Schulman, *Rat Bohemia* (New York: Dutton, 1995), p. 60.

203 "We started…": Quoted in David W. Dunlap, "Fire Island Fund-Raiser Is Criticized over Drug Use Linked to Unsafe Sex," *New York Times*, August 17, 1996, p. 22.

"You bite…": ibid.

"We're talking…": Quoted in Anthony Ramirez, "Fire Island Party's Morning After," *New York Times*, August 24, 1997, Section 13, p. 6.

204 "Not only was…": Holleran, "Petunias," *In September, the Light Changes* (New York: Plume, 2000), p. 121.

"There was…": ibid., p. 122.

205 "with the idea…": ibid., p. 131.

"all these forty...": Holleran, "The Housesitter," ibid., p. 256.

"all become...": ibid., p. 263.

"In September...": Holleran, "In September, the Light Changes," ibid., p. 306.

"all this so-called...": Holleran, "The Housesitter," p. 256.

206 "loathed...": Steve Weinstein, *The Q Guide to Fire Island* (Boston: Alyson Books, 2007), p. 190.

"no easy...": Dixon, "October Passing," *Love's Instruments* (Chicago: Tia Chucha Press, 1995), p. 54.

"the only thing...": O'Hara, "Adieu to Norman, Bonjour to Joan and Jean-Paul," Collected Poems, p. 329.

CONCLUSION: A PARADISE

208 "certain duality...": Author's interview with Daniel Nardicio.

209 "best-looking men...": White, *States of Desire*, p. 293.

"banned Fire Island...": Author's correspondence with Michael Bronski.

210 "Gay America's Moral Decline...": Jason Wimberly, "Logo's Fire Island Contributes to Gay America's Moral Decline", *The Advocate*, March 9, 2017, online.

"sexual marketplace...": Michael R. Jackson, *A Strange Loop* (New York: Theatre Communications Group, 2020), p. 34.

211 "The Men": Ari Banias, "The Men", *Anybody* (W.W. Norton: New York, 2016), p. 31.

"the worst parts...": Torrey Peters, *Detransition, Baby* (Serpent's Tail: London, 2020), p. 321.

212 "a loose association…": "Like Many Before Them, a Band of Friends Find Respite on Fire Island," *New York Times Style Magazine*, April 12, 2021, p. 62.

"Ashby then activated…": Author's interview with Sam Ashby.

"intervening in…":"Derrick Woods Morrow", Fire Island Artist Residency Vimeo page, Februrary 2017, online.

212 "found objects…": "Babiyre Leilah", Fire Island Artist Residency Vimeo page, September 2015, online.

213 "drawings have been inspired…": "Yinka Shonibare CBE RA and Leilah Babiyre in conversation with Alexandria Smith", YouTube, June 5, 2021, online.

"how one community…": Vivian Crockett, "Interview with Kia LaBeija", *Talking to the Sun At Fire Island* (New York: BOFFO, 2018), n.p.

214 "Wall Street… Uncle ACE": "Untitled Work in Progress by Jeremy O. Harris for BOFFO Residency Fire Island on Saturday, 22 June 2019", Instagram video, June 25, 2019, @boffo_ny, online.

"I went to Fire Island…": quoted in Dan O'Neil, "Inciting Conversation: @GaryXXXFisher's Black Exhibition", *CultureBot*, November 18, 2019, online.

215 "Black Lives Matter protests…": see Tim Murphy, "The #BlackLivesMatter Movement Has Finally Gripped Fire Island, New York's Gay Elite", *The Body*, June 22, 2020, online.

216 "Dash had been…": Author's interview with Tomik Dash.

"important conversations…": "We Are Here: The Unsung Fire Island", event description, BOFFO website, https://boffo.art/event/we-are-here-the-unsung-fire-island/

217 "longing, loss…": Walt Odets, *Out of the Shadows: Reimagining Gay Men's Lives* (London: Allen Lane, 2019), p. 129.

"warm illumination…": José Esteban Muñoz, *Cruising Utopia: The Then and There of Queer Futurity* (New York: New York University Press, 2009), p. 1.

"we shall have…": O'Hara, *Collected Poems*, p. 281.

"sandbar, as slim as…": Holleran, *Dancer from the Dance*, p. 23.

219 "with difficulty…": Eve Kosofsky Sedgwick, *The Epistemology of the Closet* (Berkeley: University of California Press), p. 81.

221 "faces serious issues…2100…": "Fire Island: Integrated Vulnerability Assessment", National Park Service, U.S. Department of the Interior, August 2020, online.

INDEX